THE OTHER WAR

THE OTHER WAR

ISRAELIS, PALESTINIANS AND THE STRUGGLE FOR MEDIA SUPREMACY

STEPHANIE GUTMANN

ENCOUNTER BOOKS
SAN FRANCISCO

Published by Encounter Books, an activity of Encounter for Culture and Education, Inc., a nonprofit, tax exempt corporation.

Encounter Books website address: www.encounterbooks.com

Manufactured in the United States and printed on acid-free paper.
The paper used in this publication meets the minimum requirements of ANSI/NISO Z39.48-1992 (R 1997)(*Permanence of Paper*).

FIRST EDITION

Library of Congress Cataloging-in-Publication Data
Gutmann, Stephanie.
    The other war : Israelis, Palestinians, and the struggle for media supremacy / Stephanie Gutmann.
        p.   cm.
    Includes bibliographical references and index.
    ISBN 1-893554-94-5 (alk. paper)
    1. Arab-Israeli conflict—Mass media and the conflict.   2. Arab-Israeli conflict—Press coverage.   I. Title.
DS119.7.G88 2005
070.4'4995605—dc22   2005015740

10   9   8   7   6   5   4   3   2   1

CONTENTS

Introduction		1
ONE	War: The Reality Show	9
TWO	"Dura"—A Case Study	39
THREE	The Lynching—Another Case Study	85
FOUR	If It Bleeds, It Leads	95
FIVE	Jenin	145
SIX	Jerusalem the Battered	179
SEVEN	Behind the Veil	199
EIGHT	Fixing the News	207
NINE	Outside the Press Van: Travels with Faraj	215
TEN	His Own Private Jihad	243
ELEVEN	From Observers to Participants	259
Acknowledgments		273
Index		275

INTRODUCTION

*It's no accident that the great age of terror coincides pre-
cisely with the expansion and globalization of the broadcast
media.*
   —Ralph Peters, Lt. Col. (retired), U.S. Army, 2004

*In the last few years, cable [news executives have] gotten to
like the idea of creating continuing characters—as in a soap
opera—because [they] feel it might be easier for the audience to understand than if they did different stories all the
time.*
   —Eric Burns, media analyst, Fox News, 2004

J EWS (LATER KNOWN AS ISRAELIS) AND ARABS (later known as
Palestinians) have been waging war for about a century over a
sliver of sandy, rocky land between the Jordan River and the
Mediterranean Sea. The battles—involving many other issues
besides land, of course—have been fought with fists, sticks, knives,
slingshots, arrows, rocks, grenades, Kalashnikovs, M-16s, Uzis, MiG
and Mirage jets, Apache helicopters and Kassam rockets. In these
concrete, verifiable ground battles between what we traditionally
think of as armies, the Israelis have won—or could have won if they
had decided to.

But then the first Gulf War happened and television producers discovered world conflict as a riveting form of "reality program-
ming." Meanwhile, 24/7 news channels bloomed, and newly
expanded news holes cried out for a steady feed of "content." Satel-
lites, digital cameras and the internet made transmission of text and
visual content nearly instantaneous. Photos, which can communicate across national borders, became a very valuable global com-

1

modity (easily surpassing text), and news outlets around the world grew increasingly dependent on three massive image merchants: the Associated Press, Reuters and Agence France-Presse news services, which collectively supply 80 percent of the world news media's still and television images. Increasingly, wherever we live in the world, we are "informed" by the same pictures, tied together by the real-time transmission of the same images, and part of the global village that Marshall McLuhan foresaw in the 1960s.

This globalization and unification of communication have had a big impact on war. For those not involved in some material way, war has become mostly global spectacle. In practical terms, for combatants there is a new front that is almost as important as the old one on the ground. If you can dominate world media and enlist world opinion, you can defeat your enemy by letting global levers like trade sanctions, decreased tourism, and United Nations troops constrain him. This second front did not emerge overnight. The United States has fought what writer Michael Ignatieff calls "virtual wars" for short periods, although we have not realized it. In his book *Virtual War: Kosovo and Beyond*, for instance, Ignatieff says that in the Kosovo air war, the West

> did not appreciate that Milosevic could afford to lose military assets because he was not fighting with conventional military means. Instead of fighting NATO in the air, he fought NATO on the air waves. By allowing CNN and the BBC to continue broadcasting from inside Serbia, he hoped to destabilize and unsettle Western opinion with nightly stories of civilians carbonized in bombed trains and media workers incinerated by strikes on television stations. . . . Propaganda has been central to war since the dawn of democracy, but it took an authoritarian populist for the Balkans to understood the awesome potential for influencing the opinion-base of an enemy, by manipulating modern real-time news to his own advantage.

The United States has fought media-savvy opponents since then— Saddam Hussein and the young Shiite cleric Moqtada al-Sadr, for instance. But for a case study of a country fighting long-term media war with a brilliant opponent, one should look at the government of Israel and its battle with Yasser Arafat's Palestinian Authority during the period that has come to be known as "the second intifada"—which began during the summer of 2000 and ran till the death of Arafat in November 2004, when a tenuous peace took hold.

Yasser Arafat was a masterful media manipulator who very effectively used the combat theatre (the West Bank, Gaza, and inside Israel) as a kind of soundstage. With the knowing and unknowing collusion of a codependent mass media, he reduced a highly complex conflict, as the columnist Douglas Davis put it, "to a monochromatic, single-dimensional comic cutout, whose well-worn script feature[d] a relentlessly brutal, demonically evil Ariel Sharon and a plucky, bumbling, misunderstood Yasser Arafat, the benign father of Palestine, in need of a little TLC (plus $50 million a month) from the West."

Sweeping instances of media distortion—times when the majority of big media, in concert, got an important subject wrong—fascinate me. In 1989, for instance, I wrote about a "crisis" dubbed "date rape" that the news media said was "sweeping campuses." In 1999 I wrote about the "Witchhook" phenomenon, the media coverage of the rather frat-party-like 1991 Tailhook Convention for U.S. Navy and Marine aviators, which was so overblown that it prompted congressional hearings, firings, demotions, and calls for a "reform of military culture." I got interested in the coverage of Israel during the second intifada for the same reason: because there was such a wide schism between reality (and I do believe there is something called "reality," not just "versions of reality") and the media creation seen on the world stage.

Look, for example, at the way this tiny country began to seem to loom over the globe. As the Israeli columnist Amnon Lord put it in 2002, "Anyone following the world press, especially the British and European, would reach the inevitable conclusion that the Israelis are the enemies of humanity." I do not agree with Amnon Lord about a lot of things, but here he was not exaggerating. A survey of the British public commissioned by the *Daily Telegraph* in 2002 put Israel in the top five "least democratic countries in the world," alongside Russia, China, Dubai and Egypt. It was also judged one of the five "least friendly," "least beautiful" and "least deserving of international respect" (although, if it is any consolation, the United States was one of the five "least friendly" countries too). Jewish leaders in Britain were not surprised. A spokesman for an organization of

British Jews said, "The results reflect the way the media has covered the Israeli-Palestinian conflict."

A poll conducted by Germany's University of Bielefeld in 2004
found that 68 percent of Germans believe that Israel is waging a
"war of extermination" against the Palestinians, while 45 percent
said "it was no surprise" that people were against Israel, considering its policies. An Israeli scholar asked to comment on these findings said, "When you see an image in the newspaper, a caricature,
repeated day in and day out, that Sharon is equal to Hitler, then the
image catches in your head."

In 2005, Ken Livingstone, mayor of London, wrote in a newspaper opinion piece that the state of Israel is "a threat to all of us
... [because] in its abuse of the human rights of the Palestinians,
typified by the shocking image of the wall being built around them,
[it] raises the temperature of the Middle East to a boiling point...."
He also called Ariel Sharon—who had spent that year risking his
political career and his life to get Israeli settlements out of the Gaza
Strip—a "war criminal," guilty of "organizing terrorism ... and
ethnic cleansing."

Neil MacDonald of Canada's ubiquitous, state-funded CBC
(Canadian Broadcasting Corporation) network also saw Israel as a
"threat to all of us." One day in 2004, this veteran reporter and
broadcast host was talking about prisoner abuse by U.S. soldiers at
Iraq's Abu Gharib prison when he suddenly seemed to veer off topic.
The "occupation of Iraq and George Bush's unprecedented alliance
with the right-wing government of Israel has placed Americans
overseas in danger," MacDonald said. Then he cut to a video clip of
Eugene Bird, a former ambassador to Saudi Arabia, in a Capitol Hill
press conference declaring, "We know that the Israeli intelligence
was operating in Baghdad after the war was over. The question
should be: Were there any foreign interrogators among those that
were recommending very, very bad treatment for the prisoners?"

From all the possible press conferences about Abu Gharib that
MacDonald could have selected to work into his own broadcast, he
chose to amplify the charges of retired diplomat Bird, president of
an organization named the Council for the National Interest, which
states on its website that it is attempting to "repair the damage being

done to our political institutions by the over-zealous tactics of Israel's lobby."

That Israel got us into the war in Iraq and secretly pulled the strings once we were there is a popular view. Filmmaker Michael Moore, giving a lecture in Liverpool, England, in 2004, asked the audience, "Who's the beneficiary of this war?" Hearing cries of "Halliburton," he said, "Halliburton. . . . Has anyone else benefited?"

"Israel!" yelled several people in the crowd.

"The oil companies, Israel, Halliburton," Moore said, "it's all part of the same ball of wax, right?"*

Throughout the second intifada, Americans who support Israel recognized that the country, to put it mildly, was not winning the media battle, and they also often asked each other why it was that Israel, a country so full of competent, energetic people, had "let itself" become such a target and had allowed so much misinformation to fill the airwaves. I wondered that myself. After working on this book for nearly four years—about the length of the second intifada itself—I can only say that there are many reasons. Some are particular to Israel as a relatively young country that hasn't had much time to think about media strategies. Some are particular to Israel as the "Jewish state." Some are particular to all countries engaged in "asymmetric" warfare—as the United States is in Iraq. Sometimes the conventions and logistics of modern journalism are to blame. In other words, given the distorting effects of journalism in general, any country that finds itself as continually in the spotlight and under the microscope as Israel does will find itself distorted.

There are at least 350 permanently based foreign news bureaus in the city of Jerusalem covering the Israeli/Palestinian conflict— easily as many as in New York, London or Moscow. Adding to this relatively huge body of permanently assigned journalists, there are, at any given time, a hundred or so freelance journalists, authors, photographers and documentarians all sifting this ancient, overworked soil looking for scoops. About 900 articles about events in Israel, the West Bank and Gaza are published each day in the English-

---

Larissa Macfarquhar, "The Populist: Michael Moore Can Make You Cry," *New Yorker*, February 16, 2004.

language media alone—75 times more than about any other area
of comparable population.

A British editor explained in 2000 that all these reporters are
deployed with journalistic seismographs to Israel and the Palestinian territories because "if huge numbers of people die in Africa it is
a tragedy but little will change in the world. It does not affect us as
the Middle East does where the fate of the world hangs in the balance." But does the news bring the news media or do the news media
by their mere presence create the news—providing a stage on which
various actors air their grievances and threaten "the fate of the
world"? Does this kind of micro-focus just tend to make people *feel*
that the "fate of the world" must be at stake?

In any case, can the fate of the planet *really* depend on the res-
olution of the Israeli/Palestinian conflict over territory? It's more
likely that the fate of the world hangs in the balance in Iran or North
Korea, which have nuclear weapons, or in Saudi Arabia, which has
oil. As for the much-reviled security wall, there are separation barriers—walls and fences—between countries all over the world. There
is a mined fence nearly five hundred miles long between Turkey
and Syria. A fence runs through disputed Kashmir to separate Pakistan and India. There are miles of fencing and a huge checkpoint
erected by the United States to keep out Mexicans. There is a fence
between Botswana and Zimbabwe and one between Uzbekistan and
Kyrgyzstan. A fence is currently being constructed between Thai-
land and Malaysia. Even the European Union, which voted at The
Hague to chastise Israel for its separation barrier, has announced
plans to erect a fence to protect EU members Poland and Hungary
from "the free movement of migrants" from Russia, Belarus and
Ukraine. So why do editors think "our fates hang in the balance"
every time people demonstrate outside Israel's separation barrier
or there is an exchange of fire in a West Bank town?

Aside from the fundamental misconception that "the conflict"
is somehow crucial to our lives, I also aim, in this book, to address
the misconception that the daily sluice of news—whether it's from
NPR, the BBC, the *New York Times* or Fox—can tell you what you
need to know about this conflict, or indeed about any serious, complex event. Much of the information we absorb daily—often sub-
liminally, as we glance at a television in a bank lobby, for instance—is

in photographs. Sometimes pictures can give us a fair approximation of reality, mostly at times of high crisis, like 9/11, when cameras are basically just turned on and allowed to run, without editing, without manipulation and in real time. Most of the time, however, the great paradox is that all our new communication technology has given us only a better facsimile of the truth. The new technologies (digital cameras, satellite transmission, the internet) allow journalists to say more things, with an appearance of credibility, about more formerly remote places, while the things they say may be as preconceived, false or one-sided as in lower-tech days gone by. As journalist James Fallows put it, "with the internet and TV, each culture now has a more elaborate apparatus for 'proving,' dramatizing, and disseminating its particular truth." This doesn't mean that there isn't a real truth under all these competing versions (we are not living in "the Matrix" yet), but that truth is as hard to determine as it has always been.

The best summary I have seen of what new technologies (like the Web, the digital camera and the satellite camera) have done to news gathering came from a recently retired CBS News producer named Phil Scheffler. In a winter 2004 issue of the Columbia University journalism school alumni newsletter he wrote:

> When I was coming up, reporting meant a reporter and a camera crew going to where news was happening, asking questions, taking notes, shooting pictures, and than coming back or sending back a "report." Now a lot of coverage is a construction. An editor in New York decides what the story is, sends the word out to bureaus that we need a sound bite from this or that type of person saying this or that, gathers up picture coverage supplied by freelancers or agencies and writes a script that is narrated by a "reporter" who hasn't been within 500 miles of the story.

The problem is that, increasingly, producers sitting in carpeted, climate-controlled studios in New York and London are making war their subject. It is inherently exciting and inserting reporters into war has become easier. The problem is that producers and journalists, dumped on the ground with little prior knowledge, are forced to condense and "package" terribly complex and crucial events. Looking for hot pictures, they are wed—whether they like it or not, or will admit it or not—to the people who can promise hot pictures, which increasingly means they become facilitators for terrorists, whose bombings and such derive most of their power from the amplification of mass media.

In a world in which journalists have been turned, willingly or otherwise, into combatants in the most crucial events of our time, it is more important than ever that news consumers become expert at inspecting, analyzing and demystifying the news product. We need to know who is at the newsroom controls. We need to know who is doing the constructing and what their motives are, and we need to understand the (sometimes very petty) exigencies that influence their work. It is too easy to be goaded into action by images.

Millions of people became convinced that they understand the complex and tragic Israeli/Palestinian conflict because they trust the *Times* or the BBC or because, as one New Yorker I met during the second intifada put it, the pictures she saw on CNN "don't lie." I wrote this book because apparently people need to be reminded that pictures do lie. Behind every picture there is a long story and a regiment of people who brought that particular picture, of all possible pictures, to you. The second intifada was explained to the public through a series of images—images that didn't bring us the truth.

ONE

WAR: THE REALITY SHOW

I T'S HARD TO FIND A DATE for the beginning of any war, especially one like the second intifada, which existed on two planes. There was an actual ground war in which people died, and there was a war of competing narratives played out in the mass media. According to the narrative of the mainstream media, the new round of overt hostilities (or the "second intifada," a term I do not like, but will use simply because it is shorter) was started on September 28, 2000, by the "provocative and irresponsible visit by the Likud leader, Ariel Sharon" (as the *New York Times* described it) to the plaza in East Jerusalem that surrounds the Al-Aqsa Mosque. The real shooting war actually started several months earlier, but this date is important nonetheless because that is when the region was taken up as a subject, a drama, an issue in a newly wired world.

Would the second intifada have begun if cameras were not already arrayed all over the region to follow peace negotiations led by President Bill Clinton? In other words, were residents of the West Bank and Gaza stimulated to violence in part by the presence of cameras? Maybe. Was there a reality on the ground—people killing and being killed—that merited coverage? Of course. But did the coverage begin to influence events on the ground? Certainly. It is impossible to separate the second intifada from its coverage. Throughout the second intifada, the-coverage-of-the-second-intifada propelled events, was used to justify events, and amplified events. The second intifada was intended for and could not have happened without an international audience.

I know I would never have become interested in the issue if it had not been presented to me, as the subject *du jour*, by the 24/7 cable news shows to which I was addicted. I had no special interest

9

in the conflict; if anything I had rather phobically avoided thinking about it. This sort of reaction is not uncommon among American Jews. At the very least, I felt there was something vaguely geeky about being interested in Israel. At worst, I never really shook the teachings of the left-wingers who dominated my hometown (a university town), the people who said that Zionism was racism, even fascism.

I also had DNA that practically guaranteed ambivalence. I am half Jewish. On one side of my family, my mother's side, there is a bunch of New-Englandy WASPs led by a matriarch grandmother who literally used to wince if she had to say the word "Jew." Meanwhile, on my father's side there was ... Fiddler on the freaking Roof, Russian villages, tattered immigrants in leaky boats, the birth of the Zionist dream, you name it. But it was this side of the family that eventually brought me (at first before I was old enough to choose) to Israel again and again.

I do have ties to the place, in other words, and in the interest of full disclosure—and because my editor told me to—I suppose I should herewith disclose them. You could say my ties to Israel started around 1905 when my great-grandfather and his family emigrated from gray, cramped Bessarabia to a new land, Palestine, a place of light and sand and water. The golden light seems to have infused them with energy because they flourished in the tiny gathering of buildings among the sand dunes that would soon become Tel Aviv. My great-grandfather, a writer, began work expanding ancient Hebrew so it could be used as the official language of the new Jewish homeland planned by Zionists. One of his sons, Nahum, made pen-and-ink sketches of the growing city of Tel Aviv and eventually became one of Israel's most beloved artists. The oldest son, however, heard the siren call of America and took his wife to New York City.

Here they did not flourish. After settling in the Bronx, the oldest son's wife (my grandmother) died within a year of giving birth to my father. My grandfather had been trained as an engineer in Israel, but was unable to find steady work in his field in the United States and died at the age of fifty-two after a sudden bout of pneumonia.

Rootless and poor, my father—then just seventeen—joined the Merchant Marine. World War II was under way and he became an oiler in the engine rooms of the ships that carried supplies to troops overseas.

He had been in the Merchant Marine for about three years when he heard that "the Jews of Palestine" were seeking experienced seamen to crew patched-together ships that would carry Holocaust survivors from Eastern Europe to Palestine, which was then rather tenuously under British control. The British had recently imposed stringent immigration quotas and thrown a blockade along the coastline to enforce it. Each time the ships of the "illegal immigration movement," as it was called, neared the port city of Haifa, these rust-buckets were easily outrun by the British navy. The refugees—many of them Eastern European orphans who traveled in herds managed by the oldest child in the bunch—were sent to vast detention camps on the island of Cyprus, where they were held, often for several years, until the British permitted their immigration into Palestine. If the British sailors were able to sort the ship's crewmen from the passengers, they sent the crewmen to a prison in Palestine, in the town of Acre. While making the Europe-to-Palestine run, my father was captured a number of times (only one or two of the immigrant ships were able to complete their mission and deposit refugees on the shores of Palestine), and he spent time in both the Acre prison and the internment camps on Cyprus.

A British newspaper, noting the proximity of the internees to the Mediterranean Sea, had run an article about the "Holiday Camp for Jewish Queue-Jumpers." So when my father and other crewmen were shipped to Cyprus and loaded into an army truck for the trip to the camps, none of them knew what to expect. After riding for a while, they saw that they were approaching what appeared to be a neat village of barracks-like buildings, crisscrossed with well-groomed roads and strung with electric lighting. The men nudged each other as if to say, "not so bad, eh?" But the truck kept going. As it rolled past, men poured out of the barracks shouting "Heil Hitler!" This, the captured sailors realized, was a camp for German prisoners-of-war, whose living conditions were guaranteed by the Geneva Conventions. Their own camp, it turned out, was a vast expanse of muddy ground where thousands of refugees of all ages lived in army tents and tin huts. Electricity and water were intermittent at best; daily rations were kept to 1,800 calories per person;

and flies crawled over the open troughs in the ground that passed for latrines, spreading dysentery and other diseases.

■ ■ ■

I DON'T KNOW WHY MY FATHER did not settle in Israel after the war of independence was over and his job in the illegal immigration movement was done. He has never been sure either. But later, after he got a Ph.D. and became a psychologist studying cross-cultural features of aging, he managed to find excuses to return again and again, and now there was a new generation of native-born Israelis—the sons and daughters of the founding generation—to visit.

When my brother and I were old enough, he began to take us and our mother with him on his research trips to Israel and the West Bank. Our stints in Israel followed a pattern. My father would settle the family in a congenial place (a kibbutz in the Galilee, or a house in a suburb of Tel Aviv, or an apartment building in Jerusalem) while he would travel "in the field" with his trusty interpreter, a Druse Arab named Kassem Kassem. Our longest stay, for nine months, was in Jerusalem. Unbeknownst to me, my parents had been researching the prospects of making *aliyah* (immigrating). While they were wrestling with logistical questions—Could my mother, who had difficulty with languages, learn to speak Hebrew? Would the *moshav** that had expressed interest in employing my parents ever get off the ground?—I hurtled about the countryside with friends.

It was a play-sized country, the perfect size for a rebellious and hyperkinetic fifteen-year-old. Anything you'd be looking for—mountains, deserts, forests, modern cities, ancient souks full of carpets, hookahs and camels—was laid out within a relatively small space as if in a theme park. You could hitchhike (picking up hitchhikers was considered a sort of informal mass transit system, a communal project and a citizen's duty) in a day from the cool, wooded mountains of the Galilee to the broiling sand of the resort town of Eilat on the Gulf of Aqaba. If my friends and I decided that we wanted to skip school and spend a day on a Tel Aviv beach, all we had to do was jump on a bus or stick out a thumb. Young soldiers were every-

---

*A village ordered around a communal source of income—a factory, a farm, a business.

where, hitchhiking home or to base. But there was also a dependable supply of genial hippie types, expat flower children who had essentially crash-landed in the drug-saturated Old City or in one of the beach communities of Eilat and were too muddleheaded to find their way home. It was easy to crash-land in the Holy Land and never leave. The hashish—in great resin-soaked bars, like chocolate—was available for a fraction of what it cost in the corridors of my American junior high. The weather was always hospitable; not much shelter or clothing was needed. You didn't even need to master the language because, at that time, Israelis were eager to practice their English.

Occasionally one of Israel's neighbors lobbed a shell or two into the country, but things were generally peaceful during this period after 1967 and the Yom Kippur War. As for the occupied territories, they were not particularly occupied. At least there were no noticeable boundaries or barriers and little IDF presence to speak of.

My father did research in Druse villages in northern Israel and in Bedouin camps in the south. I often traveled with him and, to avoid the crowded coastal highways in Israel, we used the north/south corridor roads in the West Bank. Since we often stopped to explore, the West Bank became a real, textured place to me, not a political abstraction. In fact, it was not easy to politicize the place, to fit it into some kind of polemical slot. It was not as if there were something uniform about the people and their lifestyles. Towns of the West Bank like Nablus did not look like, say, Boston; but most of the other places I'd ever lived in as a "research brat" (a Mayan village on Mexico's Yucatan peninsula, the Navajo reservation, a mountain village in Chiapas) hadn't looked like affluent American cities either. In the Arab towns there were men who wore traditional robes and seemed to spend entire days sitting in front of stores, sucking on bubbly pipes and fingering worry beads, but there were dynamic young men in suits as well; there were factions and class divisions and movements—fundamental Islamists versus the Palestinian Liberation Organization types versus Marxist-Leninist purists. There were urban elites, an intellectual class, academics and even business people who used the West Bank as a kind of pied-à-terre, living there part of the year and part in Europe or the United States.

Attitudes toward Israel ran a wide gamut. Virulent anti-Semitism and wild conspiracy theories existed alongside pragmatism, affection, and all sorts of relationships: marriages between Palestinians and Israelis, business partnerships, enduring friendships.

My stints in Israel and the adjoining territories may have been happy, but that didn't mean I came back to my home town of Ann Arbor, Michigan, as a Zionist. Ann Arbor was a highly political university town and the standard political default was far left. My friends and I attended protest marches (chanting slogans we didn't understand) the way other kids would hang out at the beach—because marches were the cool place to be. Being cool was the goal in life, and it would have been deadly to express any positive interest in Israel. On top of Israel's "colonialism," "racism," "militarism" and everything else that made it a favorite target of the Left, there was the fact that many of my friends were Jewish, and sympathy for Israel felt like it brought us too close to our parents' world—a very stodgy place, as we saw it, where people sat around reading publications like *Commentary* and sending out pitifully small, university-professor-sized checks to the Jewish Association of this or that. In our thinking, the "good kids" embraced their Jewish roots by joining Zionist youth groups and such, while the brave, bad kids spurned all that. A few years later, Nelson Mandela endorsed our choice by informing the world that "Israel is a white country and Palestine is a black country." (Here he seemed to be referring to the fact that Israel has always been governed by fair-skinned Ashkenazi Jews, while Arabs tend to have olive skin and dark hair. The rest of the Jewish population of Israel is made up of dark-skinned Jews who were born in Palestine or immigrated from Yemen, Somalia, Egypt, Iraq, Iran, Pakistan, Morocco and so on, but his template has stuck.)

I avoided thinking about the subject much until the fall of 2000 when the klieg lights swung around and put it in front of the cable news junkies of the world. That spring, President Bill Clinton had brought Palestinian Authority leader Yasser Arafat and Israeli prime minister Ehud Barak together to try, once again, to draw up the borders of a Palestinian state next to Israel. Hope for a peaceful two-state solution was high in the Palestinian territories, some polls said. I know it was high in Israel, at least, because intermittently I would hear from relatives there who were cautiously hopeful that a solution might finally be imminent. Things abruptly came to an end in July 2000 when Arafat turned down Barak's offer of land-for-peace and simply broke off negotiations.

The next news event I was aware of was that Ariel Sharon—a person I dimly remembered from my days learning the liberal catechism as being a Very Bad Person—had apparently ignited the Arab world by leading a march on the Temple Mount, the pavilion in Jerusalem that is the site of the ruins of Judaism's most holy temple and of the Al-Aqsa Mosque, one of Islam's holiest. Now the area was in an uproar and TV news—after rather unenthusiastically following highly unvisual peace negotiations, which primarily involved shots of cabinet members getting on and off airplanes—was serving up a veritable fiesta of "good television." Riots on the Temple Mount, which went on for days after the Sharon visit, and demonstrations scattered throughout the territories were providing many shots of faceless, uniformed Israeli soldiers shooting or at least aiming guns at (the distinction is usually not treated as important) people who appeared to be unarmed civilians, usually young men and even little boys.

I found myself glued to the TV as I had been during the first Gulf War, except this time I was becoming more and more emotionally involved in what I saw. As they broadcast shots of Israeli police and soldiers chasing Palestinian rioters, the networks seemed to be aiming for a "Tiananmen Square" narrative and also trying to extend this paradigm of Large Mechanized Brutes versus Small Vulnerable Brown People to the situation as a whole.

And if I knew anything, it was that this was a huge misreading. Everyone who has had much truck with Israel has come to know the culture of the Israeli Defense Force. It is unavoidable. There are not many countries where the military and the civilian worlds are so meshed. Israel is not like the United States, where—at least in the viewpoint of society's elites—strange, barely educated people called soldiers are clumped together in distant reservations. With most of the population available for the draft at age eighteen and all men under forty-five eligible for short-term reserve duty (and long-term reactivation, if needed), the rule about life in Israel is that *there are always young and youngish people in green uniforms everywhere all the time,* waiting for buses, sitting in cafes, getting on the train to spend a weekend at home, sprawled in the living room when you go to visit a friend. (The ubiquity of reservists in society once prompted an IDF chief of staff to say that "a civilian is only a solider on 11 months leave.") All my Israeli relatives, male and female, had done military service; all my Israeli friends were about to do military service and certainly had brothers or cousins or parents who had done military service. A cousin of my father's, who went on to have a significant career as a biophysicist, had been a paratrooper and still walked around with shrapnel in his side from the Yom Kippur War. Strangely, all this military influence has never made the culture seem "militaristic" or cold. Communists probably hate this idea, but Israel's military—supported by the large majority of the population and manned by young and old, male and female, intellectuals and "workers," Israelis, Druse and recent immigrants—is the closest to a "people's military" that I have ever seen.

In watching coverage of the second intifada, I did not dispute the idea that individual IDF soldiers at some time or other could have been brutal to civilians. But the portrayal of Israel as a country that would countenance regular, systematic brutality against civilians, and produce soldiers capable of doing such a thing as a matter of course, simply went against everything I knew. It was not that the media coverage was inaccurate in the most absolute sense. But one could look at a photo in a newspaper and say, "indeed that is an Israeli soldier and indeed he is pointing a gun at that Arab woman," while still feeling that the reporter who wrote the story that went with the photo had gotten everything else about the situation wrong. Bret Stephens, editor-in-chief of the *Jerusalem Post* between 2002 and 2004, would later get at the essence of most of the news coverage of the intifada when he wrote that "the norm tends to be one of strict factual accuracy and routine contextual dishonesty":

> Little history is given. The sequence of events gets confused. Normal moral judgments are eschewed in order to ensure the supposed balance of reports. Words like "violence" are used constantly to befog distinctions between murdering civilians and killing terrorists.
>
> Most seriously, key details are routinely and inexplicably omitted from stories, to slant reports in ways that all but the best-informed readers are bound to miss.

Sometimes the news media were flat-out inaccurate as well, as an incident in those early-intifada days revealed: On September 30, 2000, in the middle of coverage of the riots that began on the Temple Mount, the Associated Press released a photo that was immediately picked up by hundreds of newspapers and given big, near-front-page play. The *New York Times* ran it on page A6 and, using information from the AP as their source, captioned it "A Palestinian and an Israeli soldier on the Temple Mount." The other papers ran essentially the same caption. The picture was indeed dramatic. A man in a uniform stood menacingly over a dark-haired man on the ground who was covered with blood. The man identified as "a Palestinian" appeared to be struggling to get up from a beating and the man identified as an Israeli soldier appeared to be ready to fell him again, for he held a nightstick in his hand and his mouth was open as if he were howling with rage.

But it turned out that there were some problems with the caption: In real life, the man with the club was not a soldier; he was an Israeli policeman (the uniforms and side arms are different). And the bloody man on the ground was not Palestinian; he was Tuvia Grossman, an American Jew studying at a yeshiva in Jerusalem. And he had not been beaten by the Israeli; in fact, the policeman had just run to his aid after he had been beaten within an inch of his life by Arabs. Grossman had been on his way to pray at the Western Wall in Jerusalem's Old City when he was dragged out of his cab by a group of Arab men while it was idling in traffic. Grossman explained later that they beat him and held him down while one of the gang kicked him in the head and stabbed him repeatedly in the back and leg. He had somehow managed to pull himself free and stumble, with the thugs still in pursuit, to the front of an Israeli police post, where he collapsed on the ground. The policeman seen in the picture rushed to Grossman's side and the gang ran away. Grossman remembers that at some point, people slung with professional-looking cameras seemed to come out of nowhere and began snapping pictures, but he was losing blood very quickly and was too badly injured to have noted much detail. The photographers did not talk to him to confirm his identity and don't appear to have spoken to the policeman either to confirm either his identity or the facts of the episode.

When he saw himself in the *New York Times*, Grossman, angry that a well-meaning policeman should be immortalized in the newspaper of record as a brutalizer of unarmed, prone civilians, called the paper to ask for a correction. It is not easy to get a newspaper of any size to print a correction—particularly one as large as the *Times*—but Grossman, who had needed stitches on his head and physical therapy for a leg lacerated with stab wounds, called again and again. On October 4, editors ran a standard small bottom-of-the-page correction box noting that the photo had actually been of "an American injured in the Old City." The Associated Press sent out a notice stating that "captions on two photos sent Sept. 29 from Jerusalem misidentified a young man injured during street battles between Israeli forces and Palestinians." This was not enough for Grossman and a growing group of sympathizers. After sustained pressure from them, the *Times* ran a short news story that went into more detail about Grossman's case. This helped clarify the historical record a bit, but Grossman continued to be troubled by the fact "that the *New York Times*, the Associated Press (and everyone else in between) had assumed that if it's a victim, it must be a Palestinian."

The error certainly suggested an unusual level of carelessness for a big, staff-heavy, reputable newspaper. Many people scrutinize a photo after a newspaper editor decides to download it from the wire and run it. Was it possible that no one had noticed the parked car, the sign in Hebrew lettering, and the circular gas station sign, which can be seen in the photo just over the left shoulder of the "soldier"? There are no gas stations or cars on the Temple Mount.

Having often freelanced for the *Times*, I remember thinking at the time that it seemed odd that at a paper where content is vetted in a process that sometimes seems as complicated as the launching of a nuclear warhead, the caption had passed through the multilayered system of controls and fail-safes. To me, the mistake felt like a Freudian slip that revealed something deeper: the prejudices and assumptions that governed most editors' thinking about the conflict. Besides, to correct a forceful image one needs a correction that makes an equal splash (the *New York Times* showed what was possible with its reaction to the Jayson Blair scandal in 2003), for even though most of the dozens of U.S. papers that carried the photo had begun to run corrections of varying size, by then it had bounced all over the world spreading its false—even libelous—message. Photos have a very long half-life on the internet. As of spring 2004, this one could still be found on an official Egyptian Ministry of Information website, as part of a horrendously gory "photo gallery" titled "This Is Israel," also featuring autopsy-like photographs of dead Arab kids under the caption, "Israel is killing Palestinian children."

■ ■ ■

Grossman may have managed to correct one picture caption, but the media's framing of the story as Brutalizer versus Passive Victim seemed to be set. On October 1, for instance, National Public Radio's Jennifer Ludden reported on a riot in Gaza with this lead:

> Today is a repeat of the last three days.... You've got this Goliath of an Israeli army with guns. In some places yesterday they used armored tanks. There were battle helicopters buzzing overhead. At one point in the Gaza strip yesterday, Israeli soldiers fired an anti-tank missile. All this directed at young kids with stones.

Of course, "all this" was not just "directed at young kids with stones"; the war (for that's what it was) between the Israeli government and the Palestinian Authority was infinitely more nuanced than that. But "boys with stones" was the image that the PA had labored hard to produce. The image was perfect for TV, as it was simple and telegenic but could be made to stand for issues of global importance. It was time, in other words, for Ted Koppel to descend and do one of his *Nightline* Special Broadcasts.

With a sick feeling, for I did not look forward to seeing the conflict Koppel-ized, I sat down on the night of October 10, approximately a week into the new fighting, to watch Ted take on the Middle East—with a hastily arranged broadcast live from an East Jerusalem YMCA.

The development of Koppel's interest in the Middle East is traced in his memoir *Nightline: History in the Making and the Making of History* when he writes with evident satisfaction about a series of shows he did in the mid-1980s about South African apartheid. The series was very successful (as serious news shows about the problems of another country go), both critically, in terms of ratings, and even, Koppel implies, as a catalyst for historical change. Koppel does not exactly say that he helped topple the de Clerk regime—he has always been "uncomfortable with the attempts to measure the series' impact," he explains modestly in his memoir — but the last pages of the South Africa chapter are filled with quotations from other people who conveniently make the point for him. A "jubilant" Archbishop Desmond Tutu is brought in to say that "those programs were an important milestone in our struggle against a vicious system," while Representative John Conyers (D-Michigan) adds that "Koppel's shows put enormous pressure on the Reagan administration" to impose sanctions.

After this triumph, naturally enough, Koppel said he began looking for "the next South Africa"—or "another conflict with international relevance, with complexities suitable for a week-long examination, with political adversaries who were ready and willing to debate." He considered "going to Northern Ireland and I suppose, theoretically, we could have done something with the Iranians and the Iraqis, but that would have been such a huge problem in terms of language and such a huge problem in terms of getting permission to travel around the country and shoot."

A few years into his search for "the next South Africa," in 1987, Koppel happened to be watching video from the Palestinian territories, where the period referred to as "the first intifada" had begun. "Children were throwing stones at men with Uzi machine guns," he writes, and the scene "suggested a replay of the biblical tale of David and Goliath . . . except that this time Israel was Goliath." Koppel had a revelation. He and his producer Rick Kaplan* decided they had found "South Africa II." As Koppel writes, "It was Israel. The equivalent of Bishop Tutu versus Foreign Minister Botha would be the Palestinians versus the Israelis."

Koppel did his first show in the region in 1988 in front of an audience composed of "Palestinians from the territories side-by-side with Jewish citizens of Israel: ancient enemies who had never congregated publicly, except to fight." The statement that Palestini-

---

*Kaplan would later become president of CNN and would greenlight a much-ballyhooed special broadcast alleging that the United States dropped deadly Sarin gas on a village in Laos during the Vietnam War. CNN was forced to retract the piece a month after the program was broadcast.

ans and Israelis had "never congregated publicly, except to fight" until Ted Koppel came along in 1988 is, of course, ridiculous; but if this is a reflection of how he saw his role there, one can see why he was eager to come back in the fall of 2000, just as this new round of violence was beginning.

Once again, as in 1988, he used a "town meeting" format in which a panel of notables ostensibly representing two sides of an argument debate each other on live television and take questions from an audience made up of people from the surrounding community. The fall 2000 show featured nearly the same cast as in 1988. Once more, the *Nightline* bookers recruited Saeb Erekat and Hanan Ashrawi, both longtime Palestinian Authority and Palestinian Liberation Organization spokespersons, and Azmi Bishara, an Israeli-Arab member of the Israeli Knesset who also rarely deviated from the Palestinian Authority's official line, to represent Palestinians. The Israeli side was somewhat symbolic of Israeli society—and accordingly, of its media problems. Ehud Olmert was then mayor of Jerusalem and a member of the Likud party. Ephraim Sneh was then Israel's deputy minister of defense and also a Likud member. Naomi Chazen, the third panelist, however, was a member of Knesset for the liberal Meretz party and usually made no attempt to hide her antipathy for Likud policies. In other words, representatives of the Palestinian Authority presented one message and a united front to the world audience, while the Israeli message seemed to be a work in progress, hammered out that day on the stage, as Meretz sniped at Likud and vice versa.

As in the 1988 show, the panelists were arrayed on a circular stage surrounded by ordinary citizens, Palestinians and Israelis— some from local political organizations—who had been invited to fill the audience.

Koppel made some chuckly opening remarks about everybody being a little older and grayer, then told the crowd they were free to ask whatever they wanted. A cherubic, black-curled, rosy-cheeked little Palestinian girl in the audience, a member of an Israeli/ Palestinian youth group named "Seeds of Peace," was the first to speak, in faltering English:

"You said that the . . . that the Israeli soldiers, they do not mean to kill these kids, or shoot them," the little girl said, apparently addressing Ephraim Sneh. "Tell me, wasn't Mohammed Al-Dura, who was shot—like they weren't even shot, they were killed like animals. Were they a threat to the Israeli government?"

Koppel interjected, "Can you—can you—explain who and what you're talking about here to—to some Americans who might not know?"

Ms. Nashashibi, as she is later identified in ABC's transcript, replied,

> I'm talking about a kid—I'm talking about the kid who was killed while he was in his father's hands, just trying not to be shooted. And—I'm saying, also that the Israel police and the Israel soldiers, they protect the settlement—the settlers who . . . attack Arab neighborhoods, and they, they, they these settlers are the ones who are the threat for the Arabs and the police—the Israeli police protect them.

In heavily accented English, Israeli deputy defense minister Sneh launched into a laborious answer:

> Well I think that everyone was shocked to see the terrible—the terrible—the terrible death of the boy that you just described. He and his father were trapped in a cross-fire between Israeli positions in Netzarim Junction and the Palestinian soldiers who attacked the place. He was caught in the middle. I saw all, all these came in the pictures, how it happened, but now to this boy the facts are no more important because he is not with us and we all mourn him. . . . But I have to ask here yourself besides the very emotional point, why, who has the interest to ignite this wave of violence. Who has the interest I tell you the political answer. Unfortunately when Chairman Arafat came to a point that he had to go the extra mile and to accomplish the agreement with us, that we were so close, which in order to evade, and to avoid the necessary last concession . . .

He was still unwinding this complex and meandering argument when PA spokesman Erekat barked: "What's simply happening outside is a massacre being committed against the Palestinian people."

"You are here by force of occupation," spokeswoman Hanan Ashrawi thundered soon after, in clear English polished by undergraduate and graduate education in U.S. universities during the

1970s. "You are the occupiers, with the army and armed soldiers. That's the only way you can win."

"You have an apartheid system. Wake up!" said Erekat.

Ashrawi chimed in, "You're an occupier and you need your army to occupy! We understand that!"

The "discussion" was barely off the ground before it had devolved into a shouting match that the patrician Ted Koppel could not control. Above the din, however, one could hear Erekat, Ashrawi and Bishara, steady and repetitive as foghorns, interjecting words and phrases like "occupation," "apartheid system," "colonialism," "Bantustans," "war criminals," "the liberation of Palestine," "killing fields," "Palestinian War of Liberation," "genocide," "ethnic cleansing" and "Jim Crow laws." The buzz phrases combined with ABC News cuts to videotape of little boys throwing stones versus faceless armed men—and especially of little Mohammed al-Dura cowering in the street before being hit by bullets—made a message that hit one's nervous system like a dose of amyl nitrate.

I remember thinking that Ashrawi and Erekat had certainly marshaled a good collection of sexy phrases ("branded" phrases, I think an advertising executive would call them, i.e. phrases that come prepackaged with a load of associations). They are the sort of words that spice up a lead paragraph, but I imagined they were especially evocative for the baby-boom-age editors and publishers who cut their editorial teeth on the Civil Rights movement, Vietnam and South Africa—and even those editors who'd had college flirtations with Marxism and Maoism, which have always favored turns of phrase like "occupation," "colonialism" and "wars of liberation."

In the weeks of early October, as I talked about the conflict to people I met, I was troubled by how thoroughly the Erekat/Ashrawi presentation (they had repeated this message on all the other major networks by now) seemed to be working on "civilians" as well as people in the news media.

"How can the Israeli people want peace?" said a *New York Times*–reading, generally pro-Israel social worker I knew. "All I see is them killing children."

She was very much like the elegant woman in the Danskin leotard I talked with as we waited to take an exercise class in a gym on New York's Upper West Side. A connoisseur of world travel, she wouldn't even consider visiting Israel. "I know what I see and what I see is Israelis brutalizing Palestinians," she snapped. "They brutalize them and take their land. Are you telling me CNN lies? Are you telling me they just make things up?"

A thirty-something bond trader I met also knew what was going on "over there." With utter confidence—though he had never visited Israel or the territories—he rolled out his own Mideast peace plan as the taxicab we were in crept down congested Park Avenue to his midtown office: The United States must send more money to the Palestinians as they are obviously rioting because they are poor, he said. "They have *nothing*. Have you seen the way they live? It is awful. They have no schools, no hospitals. . . ."

I told him that I had spent some time there and knew that, although it is too poor overall, there *are* schools and hospitals on the West Bank—even auto showrooms, universities, a stock exchange and houses with tennis courts.

"Well, I have never seen them," he said, as if that ended the argument.

The voices seemed to follow me even when I tried to get away from the city and its politics. I was reading the *Rutland Herald*, the broadsheet that covers southern Vermont, where I had gone to visit my parents, only to run across a letter from a local man who was seething about U.S. support for Israel. He seemed to know what he called "Israel's occupation of the West Bank" in an intimate, visceral way—as if he had lived through it himself. The signs of a fascist occupation are "all there," he wrote, "the helicopter gunships, the knock in the night, the theft of resources, the deliberate deep humiliation of individuals."

I was curious about how he came by his passion, so I found his number and called him. "You seem to have very strong feelings about this issue," I said. "Have you been to Israel and the territories?"

"Nope, I'm just interested," he said serenely. "Closest I ever got was Turkey in the 1970s as a Fulbright scholar." But he kept up with the news via the *Christian Science Monitor,* the Canadian

Broadcasting Corporation and "the French-language media," and he had no reason to doubt they were giving him the real dope.

My polling was unscientific but I was fascinated by the way educated people like this man and my acquaintances on the Upper West Side, and many others I would talk to before the second intifada was done, were ready to drop the skepticism they showed in most other areas of their lives and believe everything the *New York Times* and CNN told them about the conflict and then develop such great passions about this relatively small affair, in a land very far away. It was as if this image of the Boy-versus-Tank had become a projective screen for anyone and everyone's sense of personal grievance. Boy-versus-Tank could become David and Goliath, Poor versus Rich, the Third World versus Western Colonialism, Man versus Machine, even you-in-third-grade versus those-guys-who-always-beat-you-up after school.

People's deep identification with the Palestinians as victims of a rapacious Israel manifested itself in unexpected ways. That fall, my father was at a psychology conference listening to a professor delivering a rather technical paper about how language forms the brain's cortex and vice versa. "I'll give you an example," she said. "If one says 'Israeli child murderers' it sounds different than 'Israeli children murderers.'" She then began to muse about a recent *New York Times* article in which an Arab mother had told a reporter something to the effect of "I am proud that my son was a suicide bomber. I would like all my sons to be...." The professor had been bothered when she read this, she told the crowd, but on reflection she had concluded that the woman's attitude was an example of feminist empowerment.

My father was not surprised that the professor had suddenly digressed from synapses to suicide bombers; psychological association conferences were always politicized. But he did marvel at the trick of mind that could allow someone to believe simultaneously that "the Israelis are child murderers, while the Arab woman who would love to sacrifice her sons merely has different values." When he told me about the incident, I felt that a psychosis was creeping across the land.

I use the strong word "psychosis" because the schism between reality and the image being constructed on the world stage was so surreally large. In the dark fantasy of the letter-to-the-editor writer from Westport, New York, IDF soldiers resembled Nazi Stormtroopers. The comparison was so farfetched it was hard to take seriously—except that it was becoming clear to me that this was a common fantasy. More and more people were beginning to remark on the "parallels" they saw between Israel and the Nazi regime. On college campuses, for example, students at "End the Occupation" rallies were chanting, "Sharon and Hitler—just the same—the only difference is the name."

The Israelis certainly have their flaws, but it is the last society I would cast as fascistic. For one thing, Israel is simply too splintered and disorganized to run a nice, clean fascist government. After the Six Day War, for instance, the great essayist Theodore H. White had speculated about Israel's future and written, "[O]rdinary politics are even more addled here than elsewhere—too many tongues, customs, experiences, superstitions, brought from lands of exile, divide it." The *New York Times'* David Shipler once described Israel as "a nation of op ed writers"—the opposite of a nation trained to click heels and salute in unison. In the IDF, saluting a higher-ranking officer is reserved for special occasions, funerals and such. It is not a constant part of ordinary barracks life as it is in the United States. Institutions in Israel survive by scruff-of-the-neck instinct and seat-of-the-pants action—not by rigid Nazi-esque systems, codified procedures and uniformity.

The historian Martin Van Creveld has described how this independence and mistrust of "formality as well as spit and polish" has been an aspect of the national character from very early on. The general shagginess of Israeli soldiers was very annoying to the British military officers of the Mandate period. (They often found themselves working together—as when the Haganah, Israel's first attempt at an organized fighting force, helped the British fight the Germans in World War II.) Consider the way these people turned themselves out. They did wear a uniform—of sorts, Van Creveld writes, but it was made up of:

> formless home-knit headgear known as "socks," wide-open shirts, and so-called palm-length khaki shorts with the white of their pockets dangling out below. Their . . . women also wore shorts making for

an interesting anatomical display that did not escape foreign observers. Young, ingenious, and independent-minded, they were a disorderly lot and proud of it. Informality reached the point where subordinates addressed commanders by their nicknames; thus Rechabam Zeevi (who was to command the central front in 1972–1973 became "Gandhi," ... and one particularly tall officer "Gulliver."

Nicknaming and the informality it denotes are still the prevailing character of Israeli government. In the newspapers and in conversation, everyone seems to be an "Uzi," a "Mati," a "Benni," a "Yonni" ... and of course there is "Bibi." When I returned in 2002 to do research for this book, I made a call to one of the government press offices to try to set up an interview with its director and got this very Israeli response:

"A moment, ok? I look eef Dah-nee ees around," said a woman in heavily accented English. There was the clanking sound of a receiver being dropped on a desk and then her voice bawling, "Daaaaahhhhh Nneeeeeee! *Afo ata?* [Where are you?]" "*Rega!* [One minute!]," I could hear him yelling back. Soon the voice of Daniel Seaman, acting director of the Israeli government's press division, came on the line.

This was part of the press operation that the *New York Times* had recently described as "Israel's vast public relations apparatus which rolls out a press release with every tank."

■ ■ ■

One reason why the sudden turn in the U.S. press toward vilifying Israel shocked me into interest is that for a good twenty years or so, Israel was "a good guy" in the *mainstream* American press. This had a reassuring effect. Israel's friendship with the United States, blessed by the U.S. media, was solid. One didn't have to worry. The country would be okay. Daniel Seaman (per Israeli custom he was always "Danny" to every other government official), an American who immigrated to Israel and became one of its media spokesmen, observes:

If you look at the narrative, or the terminology, from 1948 to '68, the story was told from the perspective of the Jews: the restoration of the Jewish people to their ancient homeland, a young people fighting for their lives, the pioneer spirit, creating the only democracy in the Middle East. In 1967 [and during the Six Day War] there was an immediate admiration for Israel. Here we were the underdog, the weaker side outnumbered by the Arabs. Little David surrounded by this Goliath of the combined Arab states. Everybody was expecting us to lose the Six Day War and here this great miracle happened, and we succeeded.

Israel certainly seemed to have better iconography in those days: lithe young women with tanned thighs kneeling in tomato fields, and Moshe Dayan, tall, slim and handsome with that raffish eye patch. In the age of "women's lib" the Israelis had Golda, who made no concessions to patriarchal standards of female beauty. And of course there was Paul Newman as the handsome fighter in *Exodus*—even if he was just a movie star.

It certainly helped that the bad guys during this period were the Nazis, followed by strutting British military officers. Followed by the tall, coal-haired, mustachioed Egyptian president Gammal Abdel Nasser, who always dressed in expensive suits—so very different from the five-foot-four-inch Yasser Arafat, with his beard, his folksy *keffiyeh* and workmanlike olive fatigues.

American identification with Israel was heightened by the fact that the Soviet Union was supplying arms and training to Arab armies, and Cold War–era news media played up the "sinister Soviet" angle. A few days before the Six Day War started, *Life* magazine, for instance, wrote that there had been "a show of Russian naval strength" in the region: "Silently, forbiddingly, the Russian destroyer—one of 10 Soviet warships to make this passage as the crisis deepened—glided through the Bosporus past the sun-light-hazed minarets of Istanbul. It was June 3 and the ship's destination was the troubled waters of the eastern Mediterranean."

In fact, *Life* magazine was such a cheerleader for Israel during the Six Day War that it commemorated Israel's blitzlike victory with a special edition, which it got out within days after the war ended. The color photo on the cover was a close-up of a young IDF soldier, still in uniform and holding his rifle, who has just emerged dripping from a dip in the Suez Canal—which is where Israeli troops ended a ninety-hour drive across the Sinai Peninsula. It is an exhilarating picture. Seeing this battle-grimed young man shaking the water from his hair, looking gratefully at the noonday sun, one gets a kinesthetic sense of the heat and smoke and tension he has come through, of the coolness of the water and the sweetness of his relief. Any photographic close-up is an invitation to identify with the subject of a picture, and this is a picture that invites the viewer to *savor this IDF victory*.

Looking at this cover so many years later as I did research for this book was like handling a potshard from a long-dead civilization. *Life* could have used all kinds of photos—the miles of desert littered with dead Egyptian tanks, grieving widows, or somber conciliatory handshakes between combatants. But it had adopted a celebratory (or what the British newspapers now like to call "triumphalist") tone about a military victory. Even more unusual, it was celebratory about a military victory by a controversial country like Israel. One does not see news text like this, text that actually seems to be crowing with aesthetic appreciation for anyone's great soldiering (let alone Israel's), in mainstream media anymore:

> With the élan and precision of a practiced drill team, Israel's largely civilian army—71,000 regulars and 205,000 reservists—began its swift mobilization.... [I]ts air force, knowing through superb intelligence operations where to go and what to find, struck with devastating surprise at two dozen Arab airbases in Egypt, Syria, Jordan and Iraq.

About the Palestinian refugees, *Life* said:

> When terrorism and fighting mounted in 1947–48, Arab leaders urged Palestinian Arabs to flee, promising that the country would soon be liberated. Israelis tried to induce the Arabs to stay. For this reason the Israelis do not now accept responsibility for the Arab exodus. Often quoted is the statement of a Palestinian Arab writer that the Arab leaders "told us: 'Get out so that we can get in.' We got out but they did not get in."

What was also extraordinary about these paragraphs was that *Life* actually dared to say something about Arabs as *agents;* they took the risk of describing active Arab participation in shaping their own fate. Today, news media with bureaus in places like Cairo,

Baghdad and Damascus find it safest to talk only about what is done to Arabs rather than risk the ire of their hosts by saying something they don't like. And so there is always a lacuna in the text where Arab agency, Arabs-Doing-Things-Other-Than-Be-Victims, would be expected. Reporters usually accomplish this with lots of use of the passive voice.

The media watchdog group CAMERA, for instance, tracked headlines in the *Chicago Tribune* (though they could have used a run of headlines from many newspapers) to show a pattern in the coverage: On June 5, 2002, a *Tribune* headline announced that a "Car bomb near Israeli bus kills at least 14"; on June 18, 2002, a "Suicide bombing kills 14 in Jerusalem"; a month later a "Wave of attacks stuns Israel." In the same period, however, the *Tribune* headlines told us that: "Israeli tank fire kills 4 in Jenin"; "Israeli strike kills at least 12 in Gaza"; "9 Palestinians die as Israel hits Gaza" and "Israeli missile, troops kill 10 in Gaza."* In one set of headlines, "bombs" seem to explode themselves and kill Israelis, while in the second set, "Israelis" very clearly kill Palestinians.

Admittedly, headline writing is tough. You have to reduce an event to a subject and a verb—basically you have to choose "one version of reality" on very short notice. The striking thing about CAMERA's headline study is that the *Chicago Tribune* seemed comfortable making assumptions about actions of Israelis and about numbers of Palestinians killed—usually estimates offered by Palestinians with an interest in inflating death counts—but the paper got very cautious, very worried about making a false charge, when writing headlines that might cast blame on Palestinians or terrorists. (These headlines also illustrate one of the advantages of terrorist tactics in a wired-for-news world. The perpetrator of a horrendous murder may not be known for days, until a group "claims responsibility," so newspapers often have no choice but to write that "a bomb killed....")

One saw this same kind of hands-off treatment, this unwillingness to attribute characteristics or blame, this unwillingness to say anything definite really, in the coverage of Yasser Arafat, at least

---

*Israel headlines appeared on June 22, July 23, September 24, and October 7 of 2002.

in the later half of his life. News media have always seemed comfortable in characterizing Ariel Sharon. He is "a hardliner," "Israel's hawkish prime minister," "right-wing" and so on. But though Arafat had been a world player for over forty years and had become the subject of hundreds of biographies, scholarly papers and essays, reporters tended to use words like "mystery" and "enigma" when they wrote about him—as here, in a 2002 profile by the *Washington Post*'s Lee Hockstader:

> In his olive-drab fatigues and checkered headdress, he has paraded across the world stage for more than 30 years, longer than almost any world leader but Cuba's Fidel Castro. He has racked up countless air miles, chatted up dozens of kings, presidents and prime ministers and given scores of news conferences and interviews.... And still Yasser Arafat remains a mystery.

CNN correspondent Garrick Utley, in a 2002 piece, wondered, "For three decades, he's been a world figure, loved by his supporters, hated by his enemies. But who is Yasser Arafat?" Asked to talk about Yasser Arafat on National Public Radio in 2002, Serge Schmemann, who was the *New York Times'* Jerusalem-based Mideast bureau chief for three years, called him "an enigma." But if Arafat was an enigma it was because reporters let him remain an enigma, because they were reluctant to turn up—even to disturb—the ground around him to find out who he really was. There were troublesome facts surrounding Arafat and it seemed best to allow them to stay shrouded in the mists of the mysterious Middle East.

■ ■ ■

It was as if Israel were the only agent, or actor, in the area. Throughout the second intifada, Israel just kept *doing things*—firing guns, imposing checkpoints, making laws, adjudicating cases, and so on. But in response to what? Media coverage was like the scene in the movie *Fight Club* in which the Edward Norton character is seen punching and charging against the air. A map based on news coverage would have shown the state of Israel drawn in speed-addict obsessive detail sitting next to a mostly empty blob titled "Terra Incognita" or maybe "Here Be Palestinians." It was as if a vast scrim hung at the Green Line—and behind it there were only gauzy shapes.

Sometimes people were pushed close enough to the edge of the scrim to be seen, but they were always grieving women, orphans, wounded men, the wretched, the poor, the damaged. Palestinian society, which has huge class and ideological diversity, which is riven by warring clans, tribes, powerful families, militias and political groups, was invariably reduced in the news media to "the Palestinians"—who never acted but were only acted upon.

■ ■ ■

The coverage of Ariel Sharon's infamous walk on the terrace around the Al-Aqsa Mosque is a classic of the Palestinians-as-ghosts-in-the-machine genre. On October 3, 2000, several days after Tuvia Grossman was erroneously described as a beaten Palestinian, the *New York Times* editorialized that "the precipitating incident [of the second intifada] was a provocative and irresponsible visit by the Likud leader, Ariel Sharon. . . . But the fighting has now taken on a life of its own." Would a journalism professor have accepted a student's explanation that something "took on a life of its own"? In the news media, "Palestinians" seemed to move as an amoebic force—as if the Palestinian Authority, an activist, well-funded government, and the myriad political groups in the territories didn't exist.

Hidden behind the veil of the seemingly impermeable Arabic language, a very different explanation of events has always been available in the Arab media. Passivity and weakness are abhorred in Muslim and Arab culture, which is why in their most important press, the press of their peers, Palestinian Authority officials and members of militias like Hamas have always discussed the intifada in straightforward terms as *a military campaign*. In other words, running parallel to the narrative of perpetual victimization in mainstream Western media, there has always been an entirely different narrative in the newspapers, magazines, scholarly journals, television and radio of Jordan, Egypt, Iraq, Lebanon, the West Bank and Gaza. While Western media described the second intifada as a "spontaneous outbreak of rage," Yasser Arafat and other members of his government discussed the conflict in the frank, blunt, unsentimental way that military commanders discuss any war—in terms of planning, strategy, tactics, execution and results, victories and casualties.

Discussion of the Al-Aqsa riots, as a strategy in a campaign against "the Zionist enemy," were quite explicit in the Arab press. On July 25, 2000, for instance, after the Camp David negotiations for a two-state solution broke down and world leaders began to express tentative disappointment with Arafat, the PA's monthly magazine *Al-Shuhada* ("The Martyrs") published a letter from him telling "the brave Palestinian people, be prepared, The Battle for Jerusalem has begun." The word "battle" was not a metaphor. Khaled Abu Toameh, a Palestinian who covers Palestinian affairs for the *Jerusalem Post*, began, for instance, to see concrete signs of a mustering for war: Fatah called up its members for weapons training. Palestinian Authority television began to incite the population by replaying archival tape, taken during the first intifada, of Palestinians being chased and beaten by Israeli soldiers. Children and wives were sent out of the country. On August 14, a Palestinian Authority police commissioner told the PA-owned-and-operated daily newspaper *Al-Hayat al-Jadeeda* that "the Palestinian Police will lead together with the noble sons of the Palestinian people, when the hour of confrontation arrives." Ten days later, the PA justice minister told *Al-Hayat al-Jadeeda* that "violence is near and the Palestinian people are willing to sacrifice even 5,000 casualties."

In the mosques and in PA-run media, the call to war continued. According to Toameh, imams "accused Israel of distributing drugs among Palestinian youth and distributing sexually-arousing chewing gum in an attempt to turn Palestinian women into prostitutes" and began "to urge Muslims to mobilize for war against the infidels." Further: "In the words of one Gazan preacher 'all weapons must be aimed at the Jews, at the enemies of Allah, the cursed nation in the Koran, whom the Koran describes as monkeys and pigs, worshipers of the calf and idol worshipers.'"

By early September, Toameh wrote, the imams and the PA had successfully created "an eve of war climate." On September 11, for instance, one of the PA's newspapers ran an editorial saying "the time of victory and martyrdom has come. . . . The Jerusalem campaign is the Mother of all Campaigns. . . . We will move forward and proclaim a general intifada for Jerusalem. The time of the intifada has come. . . ."

Actions on the Israeli side were also far less spontaneous, far more deliberate than the news media portrayed. Though it seemed from the coverage that a belligerent Ariel Sharon had suddenly appeared at this Arab holy place, surrounded provocatively by a phalanx of guards, the reality was that both sides—the PA and the Israeli government, who jointly manage the Temple Mount site— had agreed, after some discussion, upon the details of Sharon's photo-op walk. At least four days beforehand, Sharon himself and Israeli government officials had asked that PA security officials approve the visit, and Jibril Rajoub, the head of the Palestinian Preventive Security Organization, is widely reported to have told Foreign Minister Shlomo Ben-Ami, "If Mr. Sharon refrains from entering the Mosques on Temple Mount, there will not be any problem."

Mr. Rajoub may not have known that on September 27, the day before Sharon planned to do his march, Hamas had circulated a statement to its members telling them that:

> The Jews have clearly and unequivocally declared their ambition in continuing occupation of Jerusalem and the holy Aqsa Mosque. It is quite clear that plans to demolish the Aqsa Mosque and build the so-called Jewish temple in its place were no longer the aspirations of limited or extremist groups in the Zionist society, as some believed....
>
> We call on our people to head tomorrow Thursday to the holy Aqsa Mosque to confront the terrorist Sharon and prevent him from entering the Mosque and its yards and to check his attempt to desecrate it regardless of sacrifices.

That night, colleagues from other divisions in Rajoub's own government were also at work recruiting crowds to confront Sharon on the Temple Mount. Yasser Arafat's lieutenant Marwan Barghouti, for instance, participated in a panel discussion on a local television station where, according to an interview he did with the newspaper *Al Hayat*, he "seized the opportunity to call on the public to go to al-Aqsa in the morning, for it was inconceivable for Sharon to visit al-Haram al-Sharif as a matter of course and walk away peacefully...." (In interviews since, Barghouti has explained, "I knew that the end of September was the last period before the explosion, but when Sharon reached the al-Aqsa mosque, this was the most appropriate moment for the out-break of the intifada.")

When the big day arrived, Barghouti went to the Temple Mount/al-Haram al-Sharif and "tried to create clashes, albeit without success because of the differences of opinion that emerged with others in the al-Aqsa compound at the time." Sharon walked around the structures for an hour, did not enter any buildings, and left. There were scattered scuffles in which thirty Israeli policemen and four Palestinians were injured, but it was not quite what Barghouti seems to have had in mind. Making the best of a weak turnout, Barghouti said he "remained [at the Temple Mount] for a couple of hours with some other people, and we discussed the manner of response throughout the entire country and not just in Jerusalem." He then "contacted all the factions ... [and] prepared a leaflet in the name of Fatah's higher Committee ... in which we called for a reaction." That afternoon and night, PA-run broadcast media began a new barrage of provocation. Yasser Arafat himself called upon the entire Arab and Islamic world to "move immediately to stop these aggressions and Israeli practices against holy Jerusalem." Ahmad Qurei, who was then the speaker of the Palestinian National Council (the PA's legislature), said that the visit had "defiled" the mosques and was "a clear and flagrant expression of the Israeli schemes" against Muslim holy places.

The following day, the Palestinian population was understandably more aroused. Early that morning, an Israeli and a Palestinian policeman were on joint patrol in the West Bank town of Qalqilya when the Palestinian policeman suddenly drew his gun, shouted "God is great," and shot his partner to death. Around noon, an estimated 22,000 people gathered at the Temple Mount for noon prayers. In the sermon, the imam told the crowd that "the Jews" were plotting to take down their mosque and replace it with a synagogue. "Should we respond to [Sharon's visit] only by throwing stones or by condemnation?" he asked the assembled.

When worshipers left the service, many ran to the cliff overlooking the Western Wall and began raining stones, bottles and other objects on people praying below while another group charged an Israeli police shack. In the ensuing riots, Israeli police attempted to quell the crowd using rubber bullets and tear gas. They are mandated to use live bullets only if they are in mortal danger, and there was some live fire. By day's end, fourteen Israeli police and two hundred Palestinian demonstrators were injured and four Palestinians had been killed.

That night when Tom Brokaw described the events of the day, he made no mention of the sermon, saying only that "Israeli riot police stormed the shrine, opening fire with rubber bullets and live ammunition on Palestinians who were throwing stones.... [T]he riots began after Israel's conservative Ariel Sharon went to the Temple Mount to show that Jews were in control." ABC News's Gillian Findlay did not mention the assault on Jews at the Western Wall or the day's sermon. "Israeli police and soldiers rarely come here," she said. "This is the second day in a row they have flexed their muscles here and Palestinians are furious.... Sharon said he came to insist that Israel must control the place. Palestinians again today vowed that would never happen.... Doctors who treated the wounded accused the soldiers of aiming to kill."

Deborah Sontag of the *New York Times* mentioned the sermon in the 26th paragraph of a 27-paragraph write-up. She did not quote from the sermon as she might have, writing only that "Police officials suggested that the daily sermon at the mosque had riled up the worshipers. The sermon did denounce Mr. Sharon, and raise anxieties by talking about Jewish extremists who want to destroy the mosque and rebuild the ancient temple in its place." In other words, the sermon is seen as if through the wrong end of a telescope. It exists merely as something "Israeli police officials [are] concerned about." Sontag acknowledged that the sermon had "raised anxieties" for Arab worshipers but apparently thought it was not her business to evaluate whether those "anxieties" were justified.

Meanwhile, behind the veil, a frank discussion of the Al-Aqsa riots as a tactic of war had begun in the newspapers, magazines, radio shows, and scholarly journals of the Arab world. In a summer 2001 issue of the Beirut-published journal *Majalat al-Dirasat al-Filastiniyya*, Mamduh Nofal, a political advisor to Arafat, explained that:

> the intifada was neither a mass movement detached from the PA nor an instinctive popular uprising.... Yasser Arafat viewed the visit as a flashpoint that could inflame not only the Palestinian land but also

the situation beyond Palestine's borders. Accordingly, decisions about concrete preparations were made, and the authority's various forces held meetings in which they decided to move their fighters toward al-Aqsa on Friday.... This movement was militarized from the first day.... The intifada began with blood and bullets already at the al-Aqsa compound on September 28 and 29 and continued this way to date. If we go back to the history of the movement we will discover that not a single day has passed without [Palestinian] arms or armed men playing a role in the confrontation.

In other words, after months of machinations, preparations, and telling people terrifying tales to provoke them, the PA had chosen the photogenic and symbolic Al-Aqsa Mosque as an appropriate place to launch a "popular uprising," which they thereafter referred to as the "Al-Aqsa Intifada." Thousands of Palestinian boys would be exhorted to avenge "Al-Aqsa" and many hundreds would become martyrs to this cause.

Naming the conflict was thus the first battle in this media war, and it was a battle that Israel lost. "Al-Aqsa Intifada" became the standard term used by the international press, and thereafter, as the Israeli journalist Dan Diker put it, the new war was cast "internationally in the image Arafat sought." The popularization of this name had been a "stroke of Palestinian PR genius," Diker said, and Israel's failure to "rebrand the conflict on its own terms to reflect the conflict's true nature—a pre-planned war of terror against Israeli citizens—[had] placed the Jewish state on the defensive in the international court of public opinion from the first day of the conflict."

Nevertheless, the first image in the narrative of the new war had been created. The pictures showed, as Tom Brokaw had put it, "Israeli police storming the [Muslim] shrine."

TWO

"AL-DURA"——A CASE STUDY

Interviewer: "Mr. President, what message would you like to send to the Palestinian public in general and particularly to the Palestinian children?"

Yasser Arafat: "The child who is grasping the stone, facing the tank. Is it not the greatest message to the world when that hero becomes a Shaheed?"
—Palestinian Broadcasting Corporation,

January 15, 2002 (courtesy of Palestinian Media Watch, www.pmw.org)

O N THE THIRD DAY OF RIOTING ON THE Temple Mount and in the territories, a new image—that of a "murdered" child—was added to the developing narrative. On the night of September 30, 2000, television stations around the world led broadcasts with a scrap of videotape that lasted ten to twenty seconds. It offered no orienting details and no establishing shots; there was nothing in the tape to tell the viewer how the protagonists came to be where they were. We had merely joined a situation in progress. When we think back to that event, we know what we know not so much because of what we saw in this snippet of videotape—very few people have actually seen the entire fifty-one seconds made available to news outlets—but because of the headlines that soon attached themselves to it.

Since every millisecond of the tape became extremely important in investigations done later, and because our memories are probably embellished with what we read or heard later, it's important to review exactly what the tape shows and does not show.

When the grainy, blue-tinted videotape starts, a gaunt, olive-skinned young man with a haggard, expressive face is crouching next to a small boy against a brick wall and a concrete, barrel-shaped object that protects them on one side. In one hand the man clutches something (it was a cell phone) while he loosely encircles the boy with his other arm. What are they doing there? The question is soon answered by the crackle of automatic gunfire on the audio portion of the tape. At first the man tries peering over the top of the concrete barrel and signaling in the direction of what we presume is the gunfire. He appears to be waving as if to tell shooters, "Stop, look at me! There are people here!" But suddenly he jerks around 90 degrees to his right, so he is facing the camera that has been steadily recording the two since the beginning, without moving or shifting angle. His mouth forms a large, Munch-like oval of horror and again he waves his arms as if crying "stop" to someone outside the frame of the shot. There is a break in the film, a few milliseconds of black screen (you would not know this unless you had watched the tape all the way through) and, when it resumes, man and boy are sitting against the wall, leaning into each other in a pietà-like pose. There is another burst of fire and this time large, deep bullet holes appear in the wall over their heads. A second later, the little boy goes limp in his father's lap. The film ends there and, as far as anyone who has studied the case knows, there are no filmed records showing how Jamal al-Dura and his son, Mohammed, got to Shifa Hospital in Gaza City, where Mohammed al-Dura, age twelve, was pronounced dead.

At no time in the tape do we see a shooter (the audio indicates fire coming from various directions and Jamal waves "stop" in two directions), but almost immediately the international media reported the story as if it were clear that Israeli Defense Force troops had shot the two, either deliberately or accidentally as a result of what a consortium of aid groups that called for an investigation termed "the widespread use of weapons by the security forces in Israel and the territories." Eyewitness testimony was of a "he said/she said" variety; there were no other taped records of the death, so what happened in the next weeks is a testament to how news media, without appearing to have a point of view, can "fill in the blanks" and create coherent, even fulsome, narratives out of disparate pieces of information.

The narrative was established for most of the world on the night of September 30, when France's powerful state-financed television channel, France 2, which was the exclusive owner of the videotape, reported that the twelve-year-old Palestinian had died "under a hail of Israeli bullets." The incident rapidly became "one of the most disastrous setbacks Israel has suffered in decades," in the words of Bob Simon, then bureau chief for CBS News in Jerusalem. William Orme of the *New York Times* soon wrote that the boy had become "a potent new symbol of what angry Palestinians contend is their continued victimization." The British newspaper the *Guardian* wrote, "His killing ... [was] the most damning piece of evidence for charges by international human rights organisations that Israeli soldiers have killed children and used excessive force against Palestinian protesters." Hussein Ibish, communications director of the American-Arab Anti-Discrimination Committee, called the film "one of the most damaging [images] in the history of Zionism."

A year later, a few days after September 11, 2001, Osama bin Laden would tell Westerners in a videotaped speech that President "Bush must not forget the image of Mohammed al-Dura and his fellow Muslims in Palestine and Iraq." A month after that, Pakistan's Pervez Musharraf addressed the UN General Assembly using Mohammed's death to make much the same point. Musharraf decried the attack of September 11 but continued:

> We need to ask ourselves, "What really causes these extreme acts around the world?" To my mind, it is the unresolved political disputes the world over. ... The question then is whether it is the people asking for their rights, in accordance with United Nations resolutions, who are to be called terrorists, or whether it is a country refusing to implement the United Nations resolutions who are perpetrators of state terrorism. ... Ladies and gentlemen, the media images of the Palestinian child Mohammed Aldura were etched on the hearts and minds of people all over the world. ... All forms of terrorism must be condemned but the world must not trample upon the genuine rights, aspirations and urges of the people who are fighting for their liberation and are subjected to state terrorism.

The street where the Israeli consulate stands in Cairo was renamed "the Boulevard of Mohammed al-Dura" by the Egyptian government. A park was named after the boy in Morocco. Belgium was one of several nations that issued a stamp with his picture. His face can be found on thousands of websites, on posters, and on T-shirts in the Gaza Strip next to those adorned with the face of Che Guevara. He is given a special place in textbooks and videos produced by the Palestinian Authority's Ministry of Information. In Europe, songs and performance art have been created to honor him.

Mohammed and his father, Jamal, are invoked twice in the videotape of the execution of *Wall Street Journal* reporter Daniel Pearl. The video supplied to the U.S. government by Pakistani militiamen and then leaked to news organizations around the world not only documented the killing, but also served as a political brief and was intended for use as a recruiting tool for new jihadists. Thus the videotaped record of Pearl's "confession" (a long section in which he establishes, as if in a deposition, that he is in fact a Jew by answering questions about relatives and the locations of their homes in Eastern Europe) has been intercut with file footage of bloodied, screaming Arab civilians.

Within the montage, shots of Mohammed and Jamal are given a sort of starring role: After Pearl makes his final statement in the confession portion—"my father is a Jew; my mother is a Jew; I am a Jew"—there is a cut to Mohammed and father huddling together. Seconds before Pearl is laid on the ground and hands begin to saw at his throat with long knives, a still shot of Jamal al-Dura clasping his dying son flashes on the screen. After Pearl's detached head is exhibited, hanging from something that allows it to twist slowly in the air, there is a long crawl over a black screen informing the viewer that "scenes like this will be repeated" unless the United States stops supporting Israel and its "massacres of children."

■ ■ ■

THE IMAGE OF MOHAMMED'S DEATH has been spun off in so many ways and appeared in so many places that it's natural to assume that it was widely photographed; but although there were many camera crews on the scene at the time, there is only one clip (that anyone who has studied the case knows of) showing the event.

The lone photographer is Talal Abu Rahme, a Palestinian free-lancer, one of a solid core of Palestinian stringers who supply film to foreign news bureaus based in Israel. Rahme, now in his late forties, has a hard-bitten style that suggests he's seen it all. And he's seen a lot: In 1994, for instance, the year Yasser Arafat began to establish his Palestinian Authority government in the West Bank and Gaza, he was one of several cameramen and journalists jailed briefly by the PA for attempting to film an interview with a Hamas leader—part of Yasser Arafat's blitz-like crackdown on local press shortly after taking office. On that day he was shooting for CNN, but like all freelancers he has floated around, and on September 30, 2000, he was working for France 2, also a longtime client.

Working for several different employers is easier in Jerusalem than in other major cities, simply because of Jerusalem's unusual setup. In most big cities, media outlets tend to be scattered about, but in Jerusalem, possibly because bureaus are relatively small and it is more economical to share broadcast equipment, the overwhelming majority of foreign television and radio outlets huddle together on the northern edge of the city, in warrens of offices in one tall building called Jerusalem Capital Studios. A reporter once called the JCS building "a temple of press convergence," but the outside is drab and nondescript. The only sign of the gigawatts pumped daily into the sky from the approximately fifty broadcast outlets inside is a mushroom forest of satellite dishes on the tower's flat roof, a stalagmite forest of antennae, and the directory in the lobby that lists a veritable alphabet soup of network acronyms like ABC, CBS, CNN, NBC, FOX TV, CBC (Canadian Broadcasting Corporation); TF1, DR (Denmark); SRG, DRS (Switzerland); ABC (Australia); TV Asahi (Japan); Antenna-3, TVE (Spain); RTBF, RAI-3 (Italy); ORF (Austria); NTV, ORT (Russia); RTP (Portugal); IHALS News Agency (Turkey); SVT-2 (Sweden); France 2, and so on.

On September 30, 2000, Talal Abu Rahme was working with France 2's Jerusalem bureau chief, Charles Enderlin. But Rahme, keeping his own counsel, started the day by heading north from his Gaza City office to the Netzarim Junction, which is in the northern half of the Gaza Strip. It was not unusual for a photographer in this area to sniff the wind, as it were, and dispatch himself somewhere—rather than wait for direction from a boss. Veteran newsman and

Middle East scholar Ehud Ya'ari has estimated that in the early years
of the second intifada, about 95 percent of the TV pictures going
out on satellite every evening to the various foreign and Israeli
channels were supplied by Palestinian film crews generally given a
lot of freedom to tell their bosses where news was going to break
and what or whom they would "stake out." Often, they reported
stories as well as filming them, since they were, after all, the guys
on the scene who spoke the language and had the trust of the locals.

The Netzarim Junction was not a bad call for a photographer
looking for good television. It was a desolate place where two roads,
one running due north/south, the other straight east/west, inter-
sect to make right angles, the kind of precise geometry one sees only
in the desert. The western arm of the intersection dead-ends at the
settlement of Netzarim, which then consisted of about sixty families living in trailers and small concrete bungalows. Around the
crossroads itself there were several wan, abandoned buildings. The
Israeli Defense Force had appropriated one—a small, two-story concrete box—covered the front with boards as protection from bullets, and set up an outpost to guard the entry to the Netzarim
settlement's access road. Immediately behind the IDF outpost (if we
consider the crossroads the front) and looming over it were two
abandoned, identical six-story buildings, which people in the area
called "the Twins." To fulfill one of the "joint policing" pledges of
the Oslo peace agreement, Palestinian Authority security forces had
also moved into one of the buildings at this important crossing and
established a small base, diagonally across the road from the IDF
base. There was a postapocalyptic, Mad Maxian feel about the little
square created by the group of dilapidated buildings. A little north
of the PA outpost there was a section of cinderblock wall, which held
up nothing, and a section of sidewalk leading nowhere—left over
from a building that had collapsed or been torn down. Sections of
dislocated barbed wire were scattered like tumbleweed, and the
square was strewn with other random pieces of industrial detritus—
like the large concrete barrel-shaped object, sitting in front of the
wall that may once have been part of a culvert.

At about 7 A.M., Talal Abu Rahme and his sound man arrived
and began getting ready for the day by mounting their video camera on a tripod outside the Israeli outpost. Alongside them, ten to

twenty (memories of the day vary) stringers, most of them Palestinians, representing networks from around the globe, were setting up as well.

Inside their outpost, twenty-five IDF soldiers—a few more than usual—also readied for the day, but with a feeling of foreboding. It was the second day of Roshashana, traditionally a time when attacks on Israelis intensified, and the heavy rioting around the Al-Aqsa Mosque in Jerusalem, now in its third day, was spreading to the territories. The Netzarim settlement, long a burr under the saddle of Palestinians in Gaza, had recently sustained so many attacks on its access road that its children had begun to ride to school in armored buses. Three days earlier, a nineteen-year-old medic in the IDF unit had been mortally wounded a few yards from the outpost when his vehicle was blown up by a remote-controlled roadside bomb. On the day after that, there had been the incident in Qalqilya when the Palestinian security man suddenly turned on the Israeli partner with whom he was on joint patrol and shot him point-blank.

One of the most worrying signs for the soldiers peering out from the narrow embrasures in the front of the outpost, however, was the appearance of the flock of cameramen in the otherwise deserted square. "The first people that come to the junction are the cameramen. Afterwards the other people come," one of the soldiers who was in the outpost that day later told a documentary filmmaker.*

"We know from experience, " said another soldier in the same scene, "that when cameramen turn up, then something is going to happen. That day we realised immediately that something big was going down—as there were a lot of TV crews."

The IDF soldiers had prepared for what they called "the usual—rocks and fire bombs." According to eyewitnesses and out-takes from cameramen on the scene, this is in fact how the day began. As Rahme later put it, the demonstration started "with only stones and Molotov bottles and the army answered by rubber bullets and tear gas."

At around noon, however, the action escalated. The Palestinian Authority had designated this a "Protest Day"—a day when

---

*Esther Schapira, *Three Bullets and a Dead Child: Who Shot Mohammed al-Dura?* ARD Television, Germany.

businesses and schools are encouraged to close so people can join demonstrations outside IDF outposts. As the sun climbed in the sky and children were released early from school, the crowd grew until a couple of hundred men and boys (ranging in age from about ten to fifty) milled in the square. Soon, boys in the crowd abandoned their rocks and began throwing Molotov cocktails. Some landed near the outpost; some landed on nearby abandoned buildings and started small fires. Palestinian Authority security forces were on hand but there is no evidence that they attempted to quell the demonstration as called for by the terms of agreements between the two governments.

Several teenage boys had just climbed onto the low, flat roof of the outpost and pulled down the Israeli flag when, according to the IDF soldiers, a burst of automatic rifle fire slammed through the front of their building. Seconds later, more automatic rifle fire, apparently coming from behind and above them, i.e. from one of the upper floors of "the Twins," ripped into the back of the outpost roof. The IDF soldiers say that when this burst of shooting began they were taking fire "from the junction" and "from the PA headquarters," but mostly from the Twins above. As they couldn't fire back at the Twins without stepping outside the outpost, the unit's snipers squinted into the dusty square through the embrasures in the front of their building and methodically attempted to hit gunmen across the way in the PA headquarters. It was difficult shooting through clouds of dust and tear gas, but the sights on their M-16 semi-automatic rifles were enhanced with laser. For added precision, they say, and to avoid the notorious "spray and pray" of automatic rifles, they did not switch into automatic. On the audio track of the video one hears both the methodical pot, pot, pot sound of nonautomatic and the crackling, spattering noise of automatic weapons.

Videotaped out-takes from the day show men outside the IDF building—even men wearing Palestinian Authority security force uniforms—wielding automatic rifles. On the audio track of the videotape one can hear fire from several directions and from varying distances, including very near where the audio was recorded. Eyewitnesses say that various PA policemen armed with handguns also stood around outside the PA headquarters firing the occasional shot. In fact, after the live-fire shooting started—as opposed to rubber bullets, which were used earlier in the day when the IDF attempted to control the crowd with these and other nonlethal methods—there was so much gunfire from so many sources (including shots fired into the air) that even Rahme said "the weather was raining—raining bullets."

To escape, Rahme says, he took cover with his camera and sound man behind a van parked across the street from the small section of orphaned wall next to the PA headquarters. After a minute, he says, he noticed a man and a boy, directly across from him, huddled against the wall.

Jamal al-Dura, a forty-two-year-old construction worker, had left his home in the village of El Bureish a few miles from the junction that morning and gone to an auto dealership in Gaza City to look at a used jeep for himself. Fearing that Mohammed, his oldest son, might get into trouble at the demonstration on this PA-declared school holiday, Jamal took him along. When they got to the Gaza City automart they found that it too was closed in observance of the Protest Day, so Jamal hired a taxi for a ride back to El Bureish. When they reached the outer rim of the junction, however, they were stopped by a PA policeman. It was then about 2 P.M.; rioting at the crossroads had been heavy for hours and the PA police had closed the junction to traffic so ambulances would be able to weave through the crowd to pick up casualties. Jamal and Mohammed got out of the cab and set off for home on foot. They could have circled around the roiling crossroads by walking through surrounding orange groves, but that would have made their trip longer. Jamal has said the crossroads looked quiet at that moment. The patch of shade on the aborted strip of sidewalk next to the wall may have looked inviting, so the pair started their walk across the junction there. They were at about the midpoint of the wall flanking the sidewalk when there was an explosion of gunfire. Instinctively, Jamal said, he and Mohammed went into a crouch with the concrete barrel protecting them on one side.

We do not know how long Jamal and Mohammed hovered against the wall. That time sequence, as well as exactly how and from which direction the shooting started, have become very muddy in the retellings. Rahme's various accounts have been inconsistent and Jamal has related several versions—including one in which he and Mohammed were fired on while still in the taxi and another in which a single Israeli soldier walked up to administer a coup de grâce to Mohammed. However, Rahme did sign an affidavit stating that Jamal and Mohammed had been pinned down for about forty-five minutes before they were each hit a number of times in rapid succession.

The drama did not end when Mohammed slumped to the ground. A number of news outlets (relying on the accounts of eyewitnesses, as there is no known video of this sequence) reported that the first ambulance driver that tried to get to the pair was shot dead. A number of reporters told the story in vivid terms as if they had been there themselves. Nomi Morris of the Knight-Ridder syndicate, one of the many journalists relying on secondary sources, for instance, wrote:

> For about five minutes after the boy was hit, his father yelled: "My son is dying, my son is dying." But no one could get to them because the shooting continued, according to a witness.
>
>   A Palestinian ambulanceman tried to make his way to the pair but was shot dead.

Given the drama of the story and that Mohammed was still lying in the street, many people asked Rahme later why he left with matters so unresolved. In the weeks of intense global coverage that followed the death, he told Jacki Lyden of National Public Radio:

> I was very sad. I was crying. And I was remembering my children. I was afraid to lose my life. And I was sitting on my knees and hiding my head, carrying my camera, and I was afraid from the Israeli to see this camera, maybe they will think this is a weapon, you know, or I am trying to shoot on them. But I was in the most difficult situation in my life. A boy, I cannot save his life, and I want to protect myself.

But there was another reason for a quick departure: Rahme later told the German documentary filmmaker Esther Schapira that he called his boss Charles Enderlin at the France 2 studio in Jerusalem on his mobile phone while he watched what was happening and that Enderlin urged him to get the pictures to him as soon as possible. It was now around 3 P.M. Enderlin reminded him that France 2 had a 4:30 transmission slot on a shared satellite operated out of its Gaza

City bureau and if they missed their slot, that was it for the day. When Rahme got to the Gaza City studio he was carrying about sixty minutes of footage, but he decided to "feed" only six minutes to his boss at France 2. "Just the shooting," he later told Schapira.

"Why not any more of the 60?" Schapira asks him in her film.

"I am the journalist," he bristles. "I decide what is important. All of that [other footage] was throwing stones. Why I give throwing stones, when I have shooting?"

Back in Jerusalem, Enderlin downloaded the footage from the satellite and made the requisite courtesy call to the IDF for a comment. Not having heard anything about this incident from the field (in fact, the soldiers in the outpost claimed that they did not even know about the death of an unarmed boy until as much as a day later), the spokesman offered a good generic comment. He decried the tragedy, stressed that an investigation would be done in accordance with IDF policy, but added that the death could well turn out to be another example of the "Palestinians' cynical misuse of children."

Enderlin pared Rahme's six minutes of footage down to fifty-one seconds. Then, in a move that is rare in the brutally competitive journalism world (Enderlin said later he "did not want to make money off the death of a child"), he allowed the wire services in the building—the Associated Press and Reuters, respectively the biggest and second-biggest news wires for the globe—to take "whatever they wanted . . . from the cassette."

Considering that this was a gun-saturated region and it had been a bullet-saturated afternoon, there might have been some cause to hesitate a moment before declaring who shot the boy, but Enderlin apparently did not see any reason to add qualifiers to his lead. Using the voice of omniscient narrator—as if he had seen the events himself—he opened his segment by telling France that a Palestinian child had been "cut down by Israeli fire."

Soon reporters from other outlets began to pick up on this hot story and they called well-known Palestinian talking heads for comments. Nabil Abu Rudeineh, one of Arafat's top advisors, told the New York Times, "This is a killing in cold blood, an attack on an innocent child without any excuse. This cannot be forgiven." Arafat lieutenant Nabil Sha'ath was quoted on NBC and CBS saying that

the Israelis were guilty of "premeditated murder," and Saeb Erekat
was quoted on NBC and in the *Washington Post*, saying (as he had
on *Nightline*) that a "massacre was being committed against the
Palestinian people."

Around the world, al-Dura news segments suited to diverse
formats and markets began going out. In order to convey the requisite air of authority, reporters downplayed the fact that they had
learned about the event from only one secondary source—the
France 2 video. ABC television's Gillian Findlay, for instance, declared
unambiguously that the boy had been killed "under Israeli fire."
NBC and CBS used the word "crossfire" when they showed the film,
but they cut from the France 2 clip to a shot from a different clip of
smoke curling from the slits in the front of the IDF stronghold leaving "little doubt about the causal relationship," in the words of James
Fallows, who had seen these first-night broadcasts and later wrote
about the incident in the *Atlantic*. NBC's John Siegenthaler "teased"
the story this way: "Israeli troops opened fire, killing twelve people, including a twelve-year-old boy caught in the crossfire."

The *New York Times* was cautious and exacting in its first-day
coverage. It avoided the subject of blame, merely reporting that a
little boy had been "shot in the stomach as he crouched behind his
father on the sidelines of an intensifying battle between Israeli and
Palestinian security forces" Lee Hockstader of the *Washington Post*
allowed that there was crossfire but implied blame with the sequence
of his sentences:

> In the end, the Palestinian youths were no match for the well-armed
> Israeli troops. Among the Palestinians killed was a 12-year-old boy,
> who died in his father's arms when they were caught in the cross-
> fire on a road near the Jewish settlement of Netzarim in the Gaza
> Strip.

BBC television went a step further by disposing of the crossfire factor entirely: "The footage shows the boy's father Jamal al-
Durrah, waving desperately to Israeli troops, shouting 'Don't Shoot!'
but the terrified boy is hit by four bullets and collapses in his father's
arms." One day later, the BBC allowed that "Israeli officials . . . said
he could have been hit by stray Palestinian gunfire," but in the next
paragraph the network added that "witnesses say the Palestinian

youths were armed only with stones, not guns and the shooting was all from the Israeli side."

Time.com reported that:

Talks of peace have been eclipsed by a more dramatic, reality-TV image of the state of relations between these two peoples beamed around the world Sunday: A terrified Aldura doing everything in his power to shrink his slender frame behind that of his cowering father, whose pleas for Israeli soldiers to cease fire are answered with a fusillade of bullets, leaving the boy's limp body in the lap of his badly wounded father.

Note that the writer has added a frisson of new drama with the use of *"pleas"* that *"are answered"* by IDF soldiers with *"a fusillade of bullets"*—phrases implying that the IDF soldiers saw the boy, ignored pleas for help and killed him anyway.

On October 3, *The Age* of Australia, a daily newspaper with circulation of over one million, published Nomi Morris's piece from the Knight-Ridder wire, which begins:

Like viewers around the world, Amal al-Durra, 34, watched her terrified son Mohammed die on television as his father tried to shield him from Israeli gunfire.

"I went crazy. I was screaming and crying," the mother of seven said on Sunday, as mourners filled the bare concrete house where her boy, nicknamed Rami, was born 12 years ago.

Midway through the piece, Morris added: "The Israeli Army says it is still investigating what happened. The gaping holes in the wall where Mohammed died showed clearly that bullets came from the Israeli outpost diagonally across the intersection." (She does not explain how she deduced that the holes in the wall "clearly" showed this.)

Agence France-Presse, the third-largest international wire service, which claims to serve more Arab subscribers than any other wire service in the world, tracked the al-Dura story throughout the day with bulletins noting that the child "apparently" died under Israeli fire. AFP also wrote that "the shots [in the video] seem to come from the Israeli position."

How does the footage make it "seem that the shots come from the Israeli position"? asked French journalist Clement Weill Raynal, who did a lengthy analysis of AFP's coverage. The AFP stringer does not add that information. But at around 9 P.M. that day, the AFP began running a story headlined "The Israeli Army Implicitly Admits It May Have Killed the Young Mohammed," followed by a lead paragraph stating that "the adjunct chief of staff of the Israeli Army, general Moshe Ayalon, has implicitly admitted that Mohammed al-Dura may have been mistakenly killed by Israeli soldiers." (Actually, Ayalon said it was possible that the boy had been shot by Israelis but also possible that he was shot by Palestinians and an investigation would be done. In American news reporting, people do not "implicitly" admit anything; subjects either admit or they don't; it is left to analysts and columnists to make suppositions about what a subject has implied.)

Several days later, after more days of rioting, Suzanne Goldenberg of the *Guardian* wrote:

> From their concrete fortress the Israeli gunners who inflicted the death that has become the symbol of these days of blood and rage, opened up with anti-tank missiles yesterday—blasting away hopes of an end to violence in the Middle East.
>
> By nightfall, the toll from four days of rioting across the West Bank and Gaza stood at 28 dead, and more than 700 wounded. The battle for Jerusalem—as the Palestinians call these clashes—had racked up the worst violence in four years, and made a martyr of a 12-year-old boy.

In a later wrap-up story describing the layout of the Netzarim Junction, Goldenberg called the IDF outpost "a hunkering fortress of armored steel and concrete," while describing the PA police post as "a small hut." Though these are colorful descriptions, neither is very accurate.

■ ■ ■

I HAVE READ MANY "AL-DURA" STORIES and ironically the most troubling to me is not the *Sturm und Drang* of the *Guardian* but a relatively bland one from the Associated Press. This is because of the unique role that the AP wire service plays in U.S. media. To reporters learning their craft, the AP seems to sit astride the globe like a colossus. With several hundred bureaus around the world, many staffed around the clock like hospitals, the AP wire service literally "never sleeps." In its headquarters in New York, editors work all night long, feeding dispatches from bureaus all over the world onto "the wires"— which their subscribers can access at any time like tap water. Sometimes wire stories emerge finished, in one piece, but more often breaking news emerges in "takes," a sentence or two followed a few minutes later by additional information or corrections to the first information. It's a spooky, real-time, what-hath-God-wrought experience to watch events—such as the first hour of bombing on the first night of the first Gulf War—unfold this way.

Another factor that gives "the wires" their eye-of-God quality is the diminution of the human factor. AP stories are published with a byline like an ordinary news story in a newspaper, but a subscriber newspaper is allowed to run a wire story without the reporter's byline—just the credit "from AP." Subscribers may then use the wire service writer's work as a kind of uncredited spackling material—cutting it, pasting it, interjecting their own wording. As long as there is a general credit acknowledging that "wire services" were used, this is regarded as an acceptable use of wire copy.

Wire copy is thus thought of as the purest form of news. It appears to be just the facts, pared down to their quintessence. Because of AP's deliberate purging of the quirks of individual writers, the copy seems to speak as with a wholly dispassionate, objective voice— all-seeing and all-knowing. These qualities work to enhance AP's authority. Indeed, editors consult the news wires as if consulting an oracle. If the "wires have the story," they feel assured that a tip is credible; if the wires have somehow missed it, then they reason that it's more likely a bad lead.

AP had sent their own photographer to the Netzarim crossroads but, he told me, he did not come back with film similar to Rahme's because he was in a different area at the time. Karin Laub of AP learned of the incident when she saw the France 2 video, but she, like so many others, wrote her first story using the voice of the "omniscient narrator," conveying the impression that she'd seen the event firsthand:

> [I]n Netzarim, 12-year-old Rami Aldura and his father, Jamal, were
> caught in the cross fire. The boy screamed in panic as bullets hit a

nearby wall, just inches above their heads. At one point, the father raised his head above the metal barrel that served as their cover and shook his finger, as if to admonish those firing at him. Moments later, Rami slumped to the ground, fatally hit, and the father, gravely wounded, lost consciousness.

Laub's reluctance, in that early story, to disclose that her re-creation was based on the video is perhaps understandable. A clause crediting France 2 would have slowed down the narrative, bulked up the paragraph, and in effect admitted to the world that AP was not in fact everywhere all the time. But leaving France 2 out adds another layer of supposed documentation—and implies that another highly trustworthy, disinterested source has personally watched the story unfold.

In any case, "al-Dura" was disseminated to thousands of sub-scribers as "an AP story," getting a journalistic version of a USDA stamp of approval as it passed through the great news combine. (I tried to ask Karin Laub why she did not attribute the France 2 video clip as the source of her information in that early story, but she told me that AP does not allow reporters to give interviews about their methods.)

Since AP also owns one of the "big three" photo wire services, and since it immediately put the France 2 images on its photo wire, one then began to see stills from the France 2 videotape credited as "from AP." In fact, some outlets credited the same still or stills to AP while some credited them to France 2. Since only someone who has looked at the photos carefully realizes they are identical, the impression is created that at least two powerful news organizations shot film of al-Dura's death. And thus the story continued to gain an Ethernet reality.

The next day, AP 's Jerusalem bureau dispatched a reporter named Laura King to do a more in-depth feature on little Mohammed al-Dura, whose death, she wrote, was mourned "Sun-day in the teeming refugee camp where he spent his short life."

"Teeming" is often used to describe sidewalks in Beijing or blocks in Calcutta. Many parts of the Gaza Strip can also accurately be described as "teeming," but not El Bureish. It is poor, it is run-down, but it is not especially crowded. A West Bank reporter who

heard this description chalked it up to deadlines and how easy it is
to "slip in a cliché and words like 'the teeming,' 'the sprawling'...."
On October 1, the day after this global news event, the village may
indeed have been "teeming"— with international press, international political activists, observers, Red Cross personnel, and family and friends of the al-Duras, but a good journalist should have
made clear that these were extraordinary circumstances. When I
asked the reporter later if she really found this rather sleepy village
of dilapidated buildings to be "teeming," she answered, "These people are in a camp. That would be a little crowded, don't you think?"—
which led me to wonder if, in fact, she had visited the village at all
or was still under the impression that a "refugee camp" (as El Bureish
is sometimes designated) is necessarily a place where people live in
tents and other temporary structures.

The day after the shooting, the Palestinian Authority
announced to the press that "the wall" was available for photo opportunities. When news crews showed up, a PA official was on hand to
point out bullet holes in the cinderblock wall and a stain on the
ground near the barrel, which he said was dried blood. Since the PA
would not give the Israeli government assurances that they would
attempt to control the crowds that still surged around the IDF outpost, the Israeli investigators did not attempt to enter the area, fearing that their appearance would make the unrest worse.

If anyone was going to collect forensic evidence at the site
before it degraded, therefore, it would have had to be PA police, but
they did not use the opportunity. In fact, the only people who took
photos were news photographers there for the photo op.

Apparently the PA police did not investigate because they had
no doubts about what had happened. That day the PA's Ministry of
Information put together a television segment about Mohammed
al-Dura and began to run it hourly on its own television channel.
The producers used the France 2 video as a take-off point , but apparently thinking the story could use even more pathos, they spliced
in a file clip of an Israeli soldier firing a rifle. "This," the narrator
intoned, is the "man who murdered Mohammed." (It may have
been a clip from an IDF training film. Clearly the IDF soldier has
come from "files" because he is shown outdoors, while on September 30 the IDF soldiers never, as far as anyone knows, left their

outpost and certainly would not have stood around as confidently as the soldier in the clip.) In any case, the film was soon copied onto websites under titles like "The Murder of Mohammed al-Dura." A week later the footage had been uploaded onto approximately four hundred websites.

On October 2, *Al-Hayat al-Jadeeda*, the Palestinian Authority's daily newspaper for the West Bank, explained the event with this story:

> Muhammad's mother wasn't sure that the child being shot to death in the arms of his father on the TV screen before her was her own son.... She could do nothing more than let her copious tears fall on her face while watching the execution of an entire people in the slaying of a child and his father....
>
> We [the two authors of this piece] collected hundreds of bullets from the area surrounding that cement block, behind which Muhammad and his father were hiding in an effort to avoid the Israeli soldier's bullets. This location, which bore witness to the savagery and terrorism of the Israeli Occupation, continues to echo the screams of Muhammad and his father. All who look upon the site can now only picture Muhammad hiding behind the cement block and screaming for help behind his father, who was frantically trying to protect his child from the Israeli terrorists' bullets.

■ ■ ■

ON THE OTHER SIDE OF THE GREEN LINE, Israeli government officials of every rank and department were taking calls from hundreds of reporters, and I think it's fair to say that an image consultant would have diagnosed a basic lack of "message control." In the days after September 30, everybody appeared to have offered their— usually conflicting—theories to whoever asked for them. Most of the people asked to advance opinions were military men with years of combat experience, so they expressed their views in traditional military style: bluntly, concisely, and without sentiment—a style that seems to have been unsettling to foreign press who were used to professional spinners able to produce looks of tender concern on cue.

On the evening of September 30, for instance, the commander of the southern region (i.e. Gaza, including the Netzarim Junction),

General Yom Tov Samia, who was adamant from the beginning that the shots could not have been fired by IDF soldiers, told Israel's Channel 2 radio:

> I have no doubt that the gunfire, as it appears in the television close-up, was not from IDF soldiers. We are treating this incident very seriously and are investigating it thoroughly. We are examining the photo angles and the angles of fire to understand where it came from and from whom. . . . Whoever goes to Netzarim, it's like walking into the rain. You risk getting wet, even a child.

The "rain" comment was used widely as evidence of hard-heartedness. How could you compare "getting wet" to getting killed?

A few nights later, Major General Giora Eiland, head of the Operations Directorate, was also interviewed on Israeli radio but gave a slightly different take: "This was a grave incident, an event we are all sorry about. We conducted an investigation . . . and as far as we understand, the shots were apparently fired by Israeli soldiers."

Meanwhile, Israeli cabinet secretary Yitzhak Herzog went on BBC. He also said that Israeli soldiers might have hit the pair of unarmed Palestinians, but then added the opinion that "if Palestinian policemen had wanted to save the boy, they could have walked into the square, said 'Stop the fire' . . . and rescued the kid."

Though the generals seemed to be trying to be precise—admitting that there might be a possibility, while waiting for more data—the media coverage and opinion, particularly in Europe, was becoming more and more accusatory. Robert Fisk, columnist for the *Independent*, wrote:

> When I read the word "crossfire" I reach for my pen. In the Middle East, it almost always means that the Israelis have killed an innocent person . . . so when 12-year-old Mohammed al-Durrah was killed in Gaza on Saturday and I read on the Associated Press wire that the child was "caught in the crossfire", I knew at once who had killed him.

The IDF assassination angle was developed by Suzanne Goldenberg of the *Guardian*, who wrote that there was "evidence . . . pointing to a still more chilling conclusion: that the 12-year-old boy and his father were deliberately targeted by Israeli soldiers." In other words, she opined, "For all of the claims of the prime minister, Ehud Barak, and other officials that their soldiers only fire to protect Israeli lives, Mohammed's death seems an irrefutable reply."

The Israeli government decided it was time to hold a formal press conference with General Eiland on point. If the IDF seems to have been a little slow to come together with some kind of organized response and coherent, unified explanation, it is probably because, as former IDF spokeswoman Colonel Miri Eisen explained to me, IDF officials "saw [the boy's death] as a horrible story when it broke, but [the attitude] was like 'That was yesterday, and this is today.' We took quite a while [to respond officially] because we don't understand that side of it as well as we should."

She said they didn't comprehend how quickly the other side turned the incident "into a symbol." By the time they realized how symbolic it had become, the IDF brass had begun their in-depth investigation. The bottom line, she said, was they "did not understand it as it came out . . . and then there's the next day, and the next thing, and meanwhile it's already out there."

In his press conference, General Eiland told the crowd,

[F]rom a legal point of view there is no way to prove who shot him. But from the angles from which we fired, it is most likely that he was hit from our gunfire. Soldiers inside the IDF outpost returned fire at the Palestinian position. Anyone who was close to it would likely be hit. It is very reasonable that they were hit from our gunfire. But what caused his death was his presence in a place where he shouldn't have been.

Under the headline "Israel 'Sorry' for Killing Boy," the BBC started its piece on the Eiland press conference by saying, "the Israeli army admitted that it was probably responsible for killing 12-year-old. . . ." In the weeks to come, however, qualifiers like "probably"— and the fact that a detailed investigation was still ongoing —disappeared entirely. The story had hardened into stone: Even though the IDF had not finished its investigation into the death, various generals had said "probably" or "maybe" so many times that as far as the world was concerned, the Israelis had "admitted" that they killed the boy. In an October 13 account by Deborah Sontag of the *New York Times*, for instance, Mohammed al-Dura had become "the boy shot dead by Israeli troops during a gun battle in Gaza ... caught on film by a French cameraman as he cowered behind his father. . . ." CBS's Bob Simon did a piece that referred to "12-year-old Mohammed al-Durah who had been shot and killed by Israeli soldiers as he lay cradled in his father's arms."

■ ■ ■

ALTHOUGH SOME OF ITS SPOKESMEN had perhaps prematurely offered opinions in the chaotic response to the incident, the IDF still had an investigation to complete. Straightaway, however, another public relations blunder was made: they appointed the aforementioned General Yom Tov Samia to head the investigation. The general is a steady, experienced, meticulous man who had conducted this kind of investigation before—including one carried out jointly with the Palestinian Authority. But he was also the commander of the area and was effectively investigating himself. I remember hearing about the Samia appointment at the time and thinking how typical it was of Israeli thinking—on one level utterly pragmatic, but on the other apparently oblivious to, or overly sanguine about, appearances. I could imagine the Israeli line: "Samia is a very good man, a very ethical man, he knows the area; someone else would have to reinvent the wheel; I know him (I was in training camp, a tank unit, fill-in-the-blank here) with him; he will say what has to be said."

"But how will this *look*?" I would have asked.

"Look, schmook," the Israeli would have said with finality. "Samia is a good man."

IDF spokeswoman Miri Eisen explained that to the world outside, Samia's selection "looked completely different than it looked on the inside" to Israelis. "There was never any problem within Israel [over the general's appointment]. There were no questions about this general, about his ethics, about the way he looks at things. It goes back to the IDF's own convictions about who they trust their generals to be."

When Samia was handed this new job of chief investigator, moreover, the intifada was still raging. In fact, in the first week of October, fanned by incessant repetition of the image of cowering father and son, the Netzarim Junction itself had turned into an all-out war zone. Ordinary traffic had long since stopped using the cross-roads. The IDF soldiers, who usually returned to a nearby garrison at night to sleep and eat, remained barricaded inside the outpost. The children had disappeared from the square and had been replaced with hardened pros—fedayeen and terror militia members armed with automatic weapons, who used the structures around the junction like "the Twins" as cover. Israeli Air Force (IAF) helicopters began to bring food and supplies to people in the Netzarim settlement because it was too dangerous for them to venture beyond the barbed-wire fence that encircled their homes.

In other words, Samia was wearing two hats: he had to start an investigation (for which time was critical), but he was also responsible (theoretically along with the Palestinian Authority) for keeping the peace in the Gaza Strip. Samia was first and foremost a general, accustomed to thinking about concrete, tangible outcomes, so he made a decision that was sound from a military point of view, but not so good in the more subjective world of public relations: He decided that all the structures within five hundred meters of the IDF outpost had to be razed.

The Twins were blasted to smithereens and the IDF outpost was left alone facing the crossroads, surrounded by a field of shattered stone. With no place to hide, there were no snipers, no Molotov throwers or other demonstrators. Immediately there was calm at the junction and the roads were once again useable by Palestinians and Israelis alike

Quiet in the press, however, was more difficult to achieve. "At Netzarim junction," the BBC reported, "the Israelis bulldozed everything, except their own command post, making it difficult to prove exactly where the bullets had been fired from." Anne Garrels of NPR, apparently referring to the destruction of the abandoned Twins apartment building, said that "Israeli forces reduced nearby Palestinian *dwellings* to rubble" (my emphasis), then editorialized that "Palestinian property means nothing if the security of the settlements is at stake." Jamal al-Dura told reporters from the world press who called or visited his hospital bedside that the Israelis "have covered their crime."

■ ■ ■

THOUGH THE AL-DURA STORY continued to enflame the Arab world, the attention of much of the West and Europe had been captured by the upcoming election between Ehud Barak and Ariel Sharon. The American public was focused on its own cliffhanger of a presidential election, followed by "pregnant chads" and bent ballot cards.

But somewhere out in the Negev Desert in the first weeks of November, a quiet and methodical investigation of the case was going on—all dutifully recorded on video by the IDF (which records much of what it does in the field as a matter of day-to-day policy). They had no bullets, bodies or autopsy reports. Since the "crime scene" had been razed, the Israeli investigators studied a photograph taken on September 30 by an unmanned aerial drone to ensure that distances were precise, and began to make a mock-up of the Netzarim Junction. They were able to find a double of the barrel, which was a standard piece of industrial equipment. They made a cinderblock wall of the appropriate thickness and then two cloth dummies to represent father and son, which they placed in the position of Jamal and Mohammed. They marked out distances, angles of fire and elevations; then crack IDF snipers, positioned where the soldiers in the outpost would have been, went to work trying to hit the dummies. What they found, and what is shown on tape, is that they were unable to hit the pair—the barrel and the boulder were in the way. As long as the pair stayed behind the barrel, which by all accounts they did, they had a small triangle of safety. The only way they could have been hit is if someone got quite a bit higher than the soldiers in the outpost and fired down. A shooter working from higher up—as in one of the six floors of the Twins—would have had his pick of targets, or would have been able to hit the pair if one of his bullets went astray. All eyewitnesses say the soldiers stayed inside their outpost, since gunmen stationed in the upper floors of the Twins would have been able to hit anyone who emerged from the outpost immediately.

The outpost is flanked at each corner by watchtowers, but the watchtowers are not enclosed and any soldier who climbed one of the rickety ladders would have been silhouetted against the sky, making himself a perfect target for gunmen on the ground. The only possible explanation for an IDF shooter theory is that an IDF solider had ventured into the area undercover—but then one has to ask why an undercover agent would be used to assassinate a house-painter and his twelve-year-old son, and why he would take some forty-five minutes and perhaps fifteen bullets to do the job.

The Israelis invited CBS News to view their experiments. But if they expected CBS's Bob Simon to report that the experiments appeared to absolve the IDF of the shooting of Mohammed al-Dura, they were wrong. Simon spent considerable time with the IDF filming the experiments and then delivered a scornful piece full of innuendo and even ridicule. "The Israelis," he said, "have staged a reenactment which a general thinks will exonerate his men." Simon stressed that the investigative team included "no ballistics specialists" (apparently he didn't think that snipers with over a decade of experience were qualified to talk about bullet holes) and he finished the piece with a quotation from Israeli member of Knesset Ofir Pinnes, who had told *Ha'aretz*, "It seems that instead of dealing with the incident and drawing harsh conclusions, the army preferred to conduct a fictitious reconstruction . . . with preconceived conclusions."

But there were more angles to examine and the IDF continued its investigation. By studying the France 2 video, for example, investigators knew a little about the size and appearance of the bullet holes in the barrel and in the wall and the size of the holes was important because the bullets of the IDF's standard-issue M-16 are smaller (5.56 caliber) than the 7.62 caliber bullet fired by a Kalashnikov—the weapon usually used by the Palestinian terror militias and PA security forces. When the snipers positioned themselves where the soldiers had been and attempted to reproduce the holes seen in the barrel, their 5.56 caliber bullets merely pinged off its surface. They could not replicate the bullet holes that riddle the barrel in the video—at least not from that distance with M-16s.

The depth and size of the bullet holes also offer information about the angle and location of the gun that produced them. When the investigators compared the bullet holes they had created in their reproduction of the cinderblock wall with the very deep round holes that appeared over Mohammed and Jamal's heads on the wall in the video, they found something similar to their findings about shooting the barrel. The bullet marks they created looked nothing like the holes one sees in the video. Shots fired at most angles produced an elliptically shaped hole. The bullets would skid, making a graze mark before sinking into the target's surface. But the shots seen in the last frames of video around Mohammed and Jamal are round and deep—as holes generally are when hit straight-on and from fairly nearby. This is also the direction Jamal faces when he pivots 90 degrees to his right and stares in horror. This elementary ballistic evidence stands out like a sore thumb once one thinks about it, and one of the research crew, a veteran sniper named Josef Doriel, made the mistake of saying something like this to reporters near the end of the investigation but before it was officially over. Doriel explained his thinking to *Ha'aretz:*

> In the video clip, you see four clean bullet holes to the side of them.... They are "clean" and full holes—not mere grazes that would have been formed by the 30-degree angle of the Israelis, but rather by Palestinians (stationed more directly in front of the father and son).... Suddenly, you see the boy lying down in his father's lap, with another bullet hole in the wall directly behind him—again, it could not have come from the IDF position, which was behind the barrel and to the side, but only from the Palestinian position, which was more directly in front of the father and son.... At that point in the video, you can hear the firing—but the Israeli position was far away! Rather, what happened was that a Palestinian advanced to a spot very close to the photographer, and shot the fatal shot. You can also notice that at that moment of the fatal shots, the photographer suddenly "shook" and the picture was blurred—a signal that the shots came from close to him.

Ha'aretz, which had been hostile to the IDF from the start, gave the Doriel interview big play in a news story and then ran an editorial charging that "These people, who have volunteered their services, had their own preconceived ideas about the reason why al-Durrah was killed. It is hard to describe in mild terms the stupidity of this bizarre investigation."

That seemed to be the last straw in the media case against the investigation. Perhaps because it supplies an English edition (but is not English-language only, like the conservative *Jerusalem Post*), left-leaning *Ha'aretz* is *the* paper that most U.S. TV networks and newspapers quote when they want to sample Israeli opinion. Thus *Ha'aretz*'s charge that the investigation had been biased from the start was picked up and amplified by outlets around the world.

The IDF's press conference on November 27, about a month after the shooting, was a dismal affair. General Yom Tov Samia presented his brief to a half-empty room, occupied mostly by reporters from local Israeli media who were obliged to cover this sort of thing. Follow-up investigations are usually under-reported. Done many months after "the event," they tend to be dull and replete with "unsexy" information—like Samia's presentation with all its material about angles, centimeters, and bullet trails, relying on graphs, charts and marked-up photographs to make his case.

Many of the foreign press noted the report briefly without even deigning to attend the press conference. A spokesman for Yasser Arafat said the report was merely "a desperate attempt to distort the facts. The whole world has seen the pictures and the pictures speak for themselves."

Agence France-Presse did not send a reporter. AP reported that "The Israeli army reversed itself Monday and said Palestinian gunmen, not Israeli soldiers, probably killed the 12-year-old boy whose death in a firefight was captured by a TV camera and became a symbol, for Palestinians, of Israel's heavy-handed response to their uprising." The use of the phrase "reversed itself" (even though it should have read "The IDF clarified itself . . .") made the IDF look blundering, evasive, and generally less than credible.

A story that ran on the CBS News website on November 27, attributed to CBS reporter David Hawkins, briefly mentioned the conference, then quickly went on, in effect, to contest the IDF findings by inserting a quotation from an unidentified doctor from Gaza's Shifa Hospital: "Mohammed died of stomach wounds," the CBS report stated. "According to the doctor who pronounced him dead, those wounds were caused by a large-caliber, high-velocity machine gun—a weapon only the Israelis were firing that day."

This statement is remarkably error-ridden: an M-16 does not use a "large-caliber" bullet; it is not a "machine gun"; the main point of Samia's presentation was that *both* sides were firing automatic weapons that day. So I called Hawkins to ask if he had even attended the press conference. He said that he had, but that this crucial and insinuating line must have been "an editorial interjection" since he "had not written it."

In a piece titled "Israel Washes Its Hands of Boy's Death," Suzanne Goldenberg of the *Guardian* wrote:

> A senior Israeli general waged a lonely battle yesterday to erase the stain that is the emblem of the Palestinian Intifada: the terrified 12-year-old boy shot dead in his father's arms.
>
> At a Tel Aviv press conference, Major-General Yom-Tov Samia, the commander of Israeli forces in Gaza, where Mohammed al-Durreh was killed on September 30, released the results of an investigation that purports to clear his soldiers of the boy's death.
>
> "A comprehensive investigation conducted in the last weeks casts serious doubts that the boy was hit by Israeli defense forces' fire," his report said. "It is quite plausible that the boy was hit by Palestinian bullets."

■ ■ ■

A YEAR LATER, WHEN MANY HAD STOPPED thinking about the story, a young German documentary filmmaker named Esther Schapira was just getting interested. She worked then (as she does now) for ARD (Arbeitsgemeinschaft der öffentlich-rechtlichen Rundfunkanstalten der Bundesrepublik Deutschland, or the Association of Public Broadcasting Corporations in the Federal Republic of Germany), a German public television network that is frequently compared to Britain's BBC. Schapira had done documentaries of all kinds—about the love affairs of four German women and four American GIs during World War II; about a Lebanese family attacked by German Neo-Nazis; and she had interviewed Suha Arafat, wife of Yasser Arafat. When she initially proposed a documentary involving the al-Dura case, she believed it was most likely that one of the IDF soldiers had accidentally shot the young boy while firing back at the Palestinian headquarters. Her goal in going to the Netzarim Junction with a camera crew was not to paw over evidence of who killed the boy, but to see how people were dealing with the tragedy.

After much wooing of IDF officials, who by now were quite wary of journalists dealing with the case, she was able to do on-camera interviews with the young IDF soldiers who had been in the outpost that day (though for security sake, per IDF policy, they are identified by first name only and their faces are obscured). She was not so successful with nearly all of the thirty or so press people who had been outside the outpost when the al-Duras were shot. The reaction of one AP stringer was typical. "I'm not allowed to talk to you about that," he told Schapira's assistant. "Why not?" she asked him. "You know why," he replied. Schapira's assistant said that in fact she didn't know why, but that is all he would say.

Schapira thought such reticence was unusual. These were not government officials or soldiers, after all, merely reporters and photographers. Then again, lots of things about the case began to seem strange once she really looked hard.

There was, for example, what Schapira (who knows a bit about film editing) says is a clear break, a splice, in the fifty-one seconds of France 2 videotape. The break comes in part of the tape which, as far as I know, has never aired on any of the news reports, probably because it would have distracted from the simple narrative of Boy Pleads for Life but Is Shot. At this point in the film clip, we are still looking at Jamal and Mohammed huddled together against the wall and the barrel. They are alive, but the wall around them is pocked with bullet holes. Suddenly a human hand comes in front of the lens. (There have not been any other people in the frame except for father and son, so the hand seems to come out of nowhere, though presumably it could only have come from somewhere beside and slightly behind Talal Abu Rahme.) The fingers flicker about, briefly forming a V with the index and second fingers, and then the palm of the hand descends on the viewfinder, covering it for a split second, until the film goes black. Rahme has said that he covered the lens himself by accident. But the motion of the hand looks quite deliberate—as if an on-the-spot observer had stepped in—and in any case, why would he have stopped shooting at this crucial moment if it was only his own hand waving about by accident?

Schapira was also puzzled by the "second-day" film shot by cameramen who attended the PA-sponsored "photo op." The barrel in the film shot that day does not look like the barrel from the day before, that is, the one seen in the video. The "second-day barrel" is arrayed with very large bullet holes—like a piece of Swiss cheese in a Tom-and-Jerry cartoon—and, after viewing the France 2 video dozens of times, she noticed that the boulder on top was entirely different, and smaller. But why would anyone have gone to the trouble of exchanging boulders? The only plausible reason she could think of was that the smaller one would have given Jamal less protection on the side facing the IDF outpost and weakened the IDF claims that he would have been protected from IDF bullets by the barrel/boulder combination.

Schapira began to ask questions, the sort of obvious questions reporters should have asked when the story broke. But the answers she got were so unsatisfying that when her film was ready for broadcast, it was not the human interest feature she had planned; instead it had become a mystery story, titled *Three Bullets and a Dead Child: Who Shot Mohammed al-Dura?* (The "three bullets" refer to the three shots that are said to have actually killed the boy.) Schapira's film never answers this question (although much later she would tell *Yediot Aharonot*, Israel's biggest daily, that "It is not possible to determine with absolute certainty that Palestinians shot the boy, but the extensive evidence points, with high probability, to the fact that the Israelis did not do it"). But she does something just as important: she unpacks the complex *life* around this incident. Though she continually drops what seem to be hints that she thinks there is a possibility that the boy was killed (by accident or on purpose) by Palestinians who then tried to cover this up, the scandal for which she provides the most evidence is that of the world press rushing to judgment, abandoning all journalistic principle in pursuit of an easy Bad Guy/Good Guy plot line.

Schapira's film begins by retracing September 30 in minute detail, starting with Amal al-Dura's (Mohammed's stepmother's) recollections of the day. The BBC had reported that "Twelve-year-old Mohammed al-Durrah did not go to school on Saturday 30th September. Following the rioting in Jerusalem the previous day, the Israelis had closed the border with Gaza, effectively imprisoning its inhabitants." But this is not what Amal al-Dura says in Schapira's film. Saturday is indeed a school day in the West Bank's public schools, but that Saturday had been designated a Protest Day by the Palestinian Authority, a day when children are let out early to attend demonstrations. The al-Duras didn't want Mohammed to go to the demonstration at the junction, so they endeavored to keep him with them and away from his schoolmates.

Amal was always nervous on these days, afraid, she tells Schapira's cameraman, that Mohammed would join in the demonstrations and get into mischief. After all, he had nothing to do on such days. On Protest Days, people hang around on the streets and set fire to things—which, of course, Mohammed enjoyed. But on that day I never expected that he would go there. I thought he was safe because he was with his father.

A few days before, she relates, Mohammed had asked her, "If you're killed in Netzarim, do you die as a martyr?" That question, which she didn't answer, had made her uneasy as well.

Talking about the presence of children at demonstrations without talking about the PA's campaign to instruct children in the glories of *shahada* (the act of making oneself a *shaheed*) is a little like talking about the dearth of miniskirts on the streets of Riyadh, Saudi Arabia, without talking about Islamic laws concerning female veiling. Nevertheless, in the fall of 2000, when news of *la mort du petit Mohammed* was spreading like wildfire around the globe, few reporters seemed to know about, let alone report on, the elaborate collection of incitements to suicide presented on PA-operated television channels and in the textbooks supplied to children in the PA's schools. Here, for instance, is how CBS's Bob Simon handled an interview with an Israeli general in a segment for *60 Minutes:*

> *Israeli Brig. Gen. Gantz:* Well, if the Palestinian people want to be safe regarding their kids, they must make sure their kids stay in place [*sic*] where kids should be. And when they are sending their kids forward and they are firing at us, and then the kids are in the killing zone, so unfortunately sometimes, really unfortunately, those things happen.
>
> *Simon:* Do you think that the Palestinians are actually pushing their kids to the front line?
>
> *Gantz:* Yeah.
>
> *Simon:* With the objective of creating casualties?
>
> *Gantz:* That's right, sir. I'm sure that they are trying to get the world to see that Israel is a terrible, cruel people and cruel army, and that's really what they are want—what they want to do.
>
> *Simon:* Is this something that you can really imagine, that there are people who would do that, who would get their—their kids killed or wounded to make good television?
>
> *Gantz:* Yeah.

Simon: In other words, the Palestinians are really different from Israelis in that respect?
Gantz: Unfortunately.

CBS then cuts to a taped interview that Simon did with Palestinian Authority spokeswoman Dr. Hanan Ashrawi:

Simon: You're aware that the Israeli military claims that Yasir Arafat and the Palestinian Authority pushes those children to the front so that they can become casualties, because it will be good for the image.
Ashrawi: Yes, I'm aware of that.
Simon: What do you have to say to that?
Ashrawi: To me, this is the essence, the epitome of racism.
Simon in voiceover: Hanan Ashrawi is a Palestinian legislator. She's been in the forefront of the peace movement for years.

Simon used a *60 Minutes* trademark—the openly skeptical, interrogative style—to interview Gantz, but he did not challenge Ashrawi in the same way, and she was allowed literally to have the last word:

They're telling us we are—we have no feelings for our children? We're not human beings? We're not parents? We're not mothers or fathers? . . . I don't want to sink to the level of responding, or proving I'm human. I mean, even animals have feelings for their children.

■ ■ ■

SCHAPIRA CONTINUED TO FOLLOW THE STORY by asking for answers to the questions that should have intrigued any thoughtful reporter. The lack of autopsy evidence, for example. Some reporters seem to have been content to drop the matter by stating that "autopsies are not permitted by Islam." The line appears in several articles but is not true. As in many religions, autopsies are frowned upon but permitted if a cause of death has to be established. Some reporters wrote that "no autopsies were done" and left it at that, using the passive voice to avoid any focus on the question of who should or could have done an autopsy. Others, like AP, conflated the lack of an autopsy with what they apparently perceived as general flaws in the investigation:

Samia acknowledged that the inquiry was flawed by lack of material evidence. There was no autopsy, meaning the deadly bullet could not be recovered, and the setting no longer existed a week later—Samia's forces destroyed buildings there to clear the area of cover used by Palestinian gunmen.

All the reporters seemed to have been avoiding saying anything that might sound accusatory about the Palestinian Authority, which had sole possession of Mohammed's body. It was taken first to Shifa Hospital in Gaza; from there (as seen in reports on Palestinian TV) it appears to have been put on a bier and carried through the streets. By nightfall that day, per religious law and to complete the requirements to attain the rank of *shaheed,* Mohammed was buried. In other words, the only people who could have done an autopsy were the pathologists at Shifa. Certainly they would have been racing the clock to make the "same-day funeral requirement," but even a partial autopsy could have been extremely revealing. Kalashnikovs and M-16s use different sorts of bullets. But the pathologists at Shifa say in Schapira's film that they did not open the wounds to look at bullet paths or search for bullets lodged in the body. Based on their visual inspection they were able to tell Schapira's interviewer, "The bullets had fragmented upon impact." But then they claimed to have found no bullet fragments. "It was the Israeli army because the wounds are so high," one of the pathologists said with a shrug. "Besides, the Arabs had no reason to shoot him. He was an Arab like them."

Schapira's crew then went to the office of General Saib Ajez, a high official of the PA police, to ask why they did not collect forensic evidence at the site. "When there are differences in the assessment of a specific case, when further enquiries prove necessary, then, of course, an investigation is mounted," he told them. "But where there is agreement over the identity of the culprit, then there is no need to conduct a detailed investigation."

Schapira was bulldog-like in her pursuit of forensic evidence. Photographer Talal Abu Rahme deflected her requests for an interview many times when she was in the area. (According to France 2's Charles Enderlin, with whom I spoke, Rahme had heard "what sort of film Schapira was trying to do and understandably wanted no part of it.") On the theory that he couldn't possibly turn down some-one who had come so far, she trailed Rahme to Perpignan, France, where he was collecting a "Year's Best Cameraman" award from the Sony Corporation for his video of the al-Dura incident.

Schapira includes her interview with Rahme in *Three Bullets and a Dead Child: Who Shot Mohammed al-Dura?*

Why was he so sure that Israelis had spent so much time—forty-five minutes—attempting to hit an unarmed boy and his father? she asks.

"We have evidence that the Israelis were targeting the boy," Rahme replies airily.

"What kind of evidence?" Schapira persists.

"The kind of the bullet. I filmed it, the kind of the bullet. We picked it up from the wall."

"Well," Schapira prods, "what type of bullet was it—was it a 7.62 or a 5.56 caliber?"

"I don't know," he snaps. "You interviewed one of the gener-als [of the Palestinian security forces], he could tell you."

"But the general told us they hadn't done an investigation ..." Schapira replies.

"France 2 collected," Rahme adds loftily. "We have some secrets, you know ... for ourselves. We cannot give anything. Just every-thing." With this he looks away from the camera, clamps his mouth around a smile, and seems to be suppressing a giggle.

Midway through the interview, according to Schapira, Rahme took a call on his mobile from "Charles" and told him, "Yes, every-thing's fine, everything's OK, no worries." After watching Rahme's behavior in this part of Schapira's film one begins to understand why Charles Enderlin would have been concerned about his cam-eraman giving interviews.

But Schapira's hunt was not over; there was still the frustrat-ing question of the six minutes of out-takes that were pruned away to make the fifty-one-second France 2 videotape. The six minutes actually briefly assumed a starring role in the coverage of the al-Dura investigation story because many press outlets insisted that the Israeli side had never contacted France 2 to obtain a copy of the six minutes. This failure, it is implied, is evidence that the IDF was never seriously interested in investigating the case. But this is yet another facet of the case that was forced to fit a simple Bad Guy/Good Guy template. In fact, the IDF did ask for the out-takes, Enderlin told me, just not in the way he wanted. Enderlin said that he had been waiting for a formal request but one never arrived. Instead, he said, he was contacted by the Israeli government "not in mail, not in writing. I just got all sorts of strange people calling me and asking for material."

Enderlin kept the tape.

The reasons he has given for holding the six minutes so close to his chest have varied. Immediately after the shooting he told some reporters that the tape was too gruesome for wide release. But he rebuffed Schapira a year later by saying, "it is boring, of no relevance." After yet another call, he spurned her with some ferocity, saying that her interest in the case and in his "six minutes" was amateurish and unprofessional, and that she was "stupidly obsessed with that story."

"I'll never talk to you, don't you dare come here," Schapira says he told her.

At this point, Schapira went over his head. She wrote to the chieftains at France 2 to remind them of the "good working relationship that had always existed between ARD and France 2," and expressed her dismay at Enderlin's reluctance to cooperate fully. The next time she called, Enderlin informed her that she could interview him in his office. But when Schapira met Enderlin in his control room at the Jerusalem Capital Studios tower, he was back in his belligerent mode.

"Are you police? Am I being investigated?" he asked her shortly after she entered the room.

Schapira ignored the tone and continued to pursue the issue of the video out-takes. "If there's nothing unusual on the tape," she asked him, "what's the harm?"

"I'm not taking part in any funny whitewash operation of the IDF," he stormed back.

"Is there anything that would help the IDF in this tape?" she asked.

When he replied, "No, of course there is not," she pressed him again: "So why not let the public judge for itself about what's seen on the remainder of the tape?" Enderlin then put the tape in the player and hit the fast-forward button several times, stopping for less than a second, each time before pressing it again.

"There," he told her, "now you've seen it."

"Can I run the tape myself?" Schapira asked.

"No," he snapped, and put the tape back into its wall file. From then on, Enderlin made clear that he was done cooperating. He threatened to sue her, to sue her bureau chief, and became "bullying and aggressive," as Schapira put it, until she left with her crew.

And as he went around Europe that summer, whenever the subject of Schapira's film was raised, he dismissed her as prejudiced and as having an agenda. In some articles he was quoted as saying that Schapira worked for the Mossad; in others, that she was "connected" with Likud or financed by a right-wing Israeli think tank.

Schapira's film won awards and was shown on public television in many countries in Europe, in Canada and in Australia. But it has never, as of this writing, had any commercial showing anywhere except in Germany, though a new owner who bought the rights from ARD has made many attempts to sell screenings. The film was offered to French television outlets for no fee, but they declined to run it even though it is tangentially about one of France's biggest TV networks. It has never appeared on U.S. television. Almost immediately after its first airing on ARD, Schapira says, people began writing to her network to say that her work on this subject couldn't be trusted because "she is Jewish."

But even the citizens of Israel were strangely wary of her work. The movie, shot on high-quality film with feature-film-quality cinematography, was rejected by the Haifa Film Festival in 2002. There was, at least in the IDF, fatalism about ever being able to change perceptions of the event. Speaking about Schapira's film and other reexaminations of Israel's most notorious "murder," Miri Eisen said firmly, "It doesn't matter anymore what we say. I think [the film] is something we can learn from, but [the beliefs, the narrative] are out there." The film did not even have its first Israeli screening until December 2002, in a classroom at the Hebrew University in Jerusalem, as part of a conference on anti-Semitism attended mostly by English-speaking Westerners. Though invitations to the screening were sent via email to the entire foreign press corps then in Israel, only three people who could meet the Government Press

Office's rather loose definition of working press attended: besides myself, there was the editor of an American newsletter and an editor of a small Midwestern newspaper.

■ ■ ■

I WAS NOT COMPLETELY UNSYMPATHETIC to the reporters who did not respond to the invitation. There are many reasons why a career-conscious journalist might have wanted to steer clear of the al-Dura affair. It *was* "old news." If one subscribes to the idea that journalism should be "helpful," reviving the issue could seem like picking at an old wound in a region that needed healing. And finally, there was the danger that one might be seen consorting with … how to put it … *crackpots*. Like any unsolved mystery, "al-Dura" had collected a following of dogged new investigators, and at first glance their elaborate conspiracy theories—involving a staged killing and even several little boys who switch-hit in the role of Mohammed—seemed too farfetched even to consider.

But it turned out that the conspiracy theorists were not so easy to write off. They are a respectable and apparently otherwise sane bunch. A French writer, an Israeli physicist, and a Boston university professor are a few who have taken up the cause. Their theories are not necessarily the same in all respects. Some posit that Mohammed was merely killed accidentally by trigger-happy fedayeen who then seized the opportunity to blame the death on Israelis. Others believe the boy was targeted by Palestinians expressly to create a martyr because the intifada was still in boost phase, so to speak, and needed the push that a young martyr would bring. In some versions of the theory, Mohammed was really killed. In some versions he was not killed or even wounded (they say that autopsy photos shown by Shifa Hospital are of a different boy) and instead spirited away to a city like Tunis.

Given the uses to which the al-Dura legend has been put, it's not hard to explain why a father and son could be persuaded to play-act a martyr scenario. But what if the injuries and the death were real? To explain how a father could apparently have offered his son for what amounted to close-range execution, most of the theorists posit that the last lethal shots had been a surprise ending for Jamal—which would explain his sudden pivot to his right and his horrified expression as he spots someone shooting at him straight on from close range.

Most of the al-Dura revisionists refer to scenes in the "rushes" (out-takes, film that was shot that day and not used) to make their case. The Israeli physicist Nahum Shahaf, for instance, spent months painstakingly collecting, wheedling, even buying footage from reluctant cameramen, and then spliced the pieces together in rough temporal order in an attempt to make an unbroken film of the day. And there is indeed curious stuff in these rushes. Why, for instance, when people in the crossroads appear to be running for cover (presumably at the time the crossfire began in earnest between the Israelis in the outposts and Palestinians at various spots across the road from them), does a white van meander slowly down the road toward the Israeli position (or into the firestorm) and then park directly across from the spot of wall where the pair will soon take cover? Another snippet of tape shows the pair (as photographed from another angle) sitting in their huddled position by the barrel while other people stand nearby in relaxed poses, smoking cigarettes. (Can it be "hailing bullets" around this barrel but bullet-free a mere twenty feet away?) Then there is something odd about Talal Abu Rahme's own footage. Most cameramen filming people hit by an unexpected barrage of intense fire tend to swing the camera—even briefly—toward the source of the fire, before returning to the victims. To get a shot that identifies the killer, after all, is the ultimate scoop. But the famous France 2 video—the only known piece of tape that records this death—is filmed from one fixed angle.

The sober, somber General Yom Tov Samia—not the type you would peg as a wild-eyed conspiracy buff—still asserts that "one day it will be proved that this whole thing was a Palestinian production." The idea of a "production"—a set-up of some kind—becomes plausible if only because it would not be the first time that events have been staged on the West Bank for the benefit of the omnipresent news cameras. In April of 2002, for instance, an unmanned IDF drone was making its way across the sky over the town of Jenin and captured footage of a funeral procession in the streets below. At one point the men carrying the bier take a detour into an alley and we see the "corpse" hop off the bier. It was the height of the IDF incursion into the Jenin refugee camp, when Israel was being charged by the international press with having massacred civilians. Presumably as a way to suggest that things are not always what they seem in the West Bank, the IDF distributed the film to Western news outlets, but it got very little play outside the United States.

The PA government, as a matter of habit if not official policy, consistently mixes news and fiction without distinguishing between the two. Toward the end of *Three Bullets and a Dead Child,* Schapira interviews a producer from the PA's Ministry of Information and asks why they had seen fit to enhance the already dramatic shots of al-Dura's death with cuts to a fictitious "Israeli soldier" whom they identify as "Mohammed's murderer." The official says piously that videos put out by the Palestinian Authority "are forms of artistic presentation. But all this serves to convey the truth and explain a specific event. We never forget our higher journalistic principle— to which we are committed—of relating the truth, and nothing but the truth."

As for the theory that Mohammed al-Dura was killed by Palestinians, the pathologist in Schapira's film asks, "Why would they shoot him? He was Arab like them." But of course the history of the Palestinian territories is full of Arabs shooting Arabs—especially in the anarchic Gaza Strip. Street justice is most often meted out for the offense of "collaboration" with Israel. The judges of the street do not usually bother to offer precise evidence when they execute a death sentence. "Suspicious" associations with Israelis will do. And it turns out that Jamal al-Dura had a long history of what members of Hamas, for instance, would call "collaboration."

Exhibit A in Hamas's case against Jamal would surely be the twenty years he spent working for an Israeli builder named Moshe Tamal. Many Palestinians work for Israelis (and sometimes Israelis for Palestinians), but the Jamal al-Dura/Moshe Tamal relationship went beyond mere work. In Schapira's film, Jamal says: "It was a true relationship between brothers. I was always popping in. He used to invite me to his home. I have slept there overnight and eaten there. I used to come and go like one of the family." Their sons were close in age, and Mohammed and Jamal attended Tamal's son's bar mitzvah; someone videotaped the occasion, and the section of the videotape in which Jamal can be seen dancing in a circle, arm over arm, with men in *kipot* somehow surfaced in the days after the al-Dura shooting and was played on Israeli news broadcasts.

Jamal gained and lost from this relationship with the builder. Clearly, his friendship allowed him to make a steady living in an area where this is not so easy. But according to Israeli police files that were opened after the incident, fellow Gazans suspected the closeness of the relationship and Jamal had been attacked several times for "collaboration." Yom Tov Samia mentioned these incidents in his November 27 press conference. Typically he wasn't clear enough about what he was getting at—it's no use mentioning that Jamal had been involved in incidents in which police were called without explaining why he had been attacked and what collaboration means in the territories—so most reporters saw this as a callous attempt to "dirty up the witness." Samia, who is now retired from the military, would not do an interview with me, but I think that by mentioning Jamal's previous problems with collaboration, he had been trying to suggest why Jamal might have been used as the fall guy in a plan to "create" a martyr. In other words, if Jamal was indeed a marked man in his Gaza neighborhood, he might have grabbed at a chance to redeem himself with the local terror militiamen by playing a starring role in a staged drama. Given the very real-looking shock we see on Jamal's face when he turns to his right to look into the face of a shooter, it's possible that the people who offered him this chance for redemption didn't tell him just how far the staging would go.

There is one faction in the territories with the ruthlessness to set up an innocent man and his son in this way: Hamas. Hamas had the means and the motivation. The group has been unapologetic and above-board about the way it recruits boys as young as nine and deliberately puts them in harm's way.* Above and beyond the public relations value of a symbol of Israeli brutality, "al-Dura" had a special meaning within the territories and thus provided Hamas with a new stream of boy soldiers. According to prominent Palestinian psychiatrist Eyad Saraf, Palestinian children "saw a father

---

*For a chilling scene of a Hamas cell flattering, hugging, and acting parental with a little boy before sending him out to act as sentry on a terror operation, see the documentary *Death in Gaza*, directed by Saira Shah.

unable to protect his son" in the al-Dura incident. So they "dropped the father figure after Dura's death." Then, seeking new, more able protectors, "they asked for arms and threw their allegiance to militant groups, particularly Hamas."

As in any good mystery story, the possible plot lines and the possible motivations of different players seem endless. Did the Israelis kill Mohammed al-Dura? Did Hamas? Did Fatah? We may never know. But there is one clear bad guy in "al-Dura" and that is the international media. It is their job to dig, to deploy skepticism, to ask difficult questions of both sides. Instead, they looked at one image, taken from one angle, by one photographer, and accepted, seemingly without skepticism, the photographer's explanation of what had happened. In contrast, two years later the IDF distributed a photograph of a baby wearing a Hamas headband and a mock suicide belt, which IDF soldiers said they found when they raided a terror militia headquarters. The BBC brought IDF spokeswoman Miri Eisen on to talk about the photo, but the show's host immediately began referring to "the *alleged* picture" of a baby bomber. His first question to Eisen: "The Mossad has the most amazing forgery capabilities in the world. Why should we believe this real?" The BBC's Orla Guerin later referred patronizingly to the "baby bomber" picture as "terror in nappies." But such has always been the case, Eisen told me. "Everything we say they have to 'check'; everything the Palestinians say they take as fact. But you have to be careful with them. If you attack them too much they kick back."

Schapira's network, ARD, eventually decided to run *Three Bullets and a Dead Child* as part of a series titled *"Das Rote Quadrat,"* which means "The Red Frame" or square. The title is intended to evoke the editor sitting at his desk, poring over a contact sheet full of thumbnail-sized images that show an event from many angles. He must look at the images—which he often knows nothing about—and select one by drawing a box around it with a red grease pencil. The picture will often go on to become the representation, the last word about the event, even though the other images on the contact sheet had added all sorts of complicating, muddying information. The people at ARD felt that too many events had been trapped and frozen within this red frame, and so the series was intended to "act as a brake ... on the flood of pictures," to revisit famous framed moments and "show what the pictures did not."

■ ■ ■

IF LITTLE MOHAMMED HAD MOVED ON to the special paradise reserved for *shaheeds*, his father had a sort of rebirth as well. Before the incident, Jamal al-Dura had labored on construction sites to support a young wife and seven children. After the incident he became, as Schapira put it, a virtual "ambassador of the Intifada."

After several days at Shifa Hospital, where he was taken after the shooting, he was moved on to the Hussein Medical Center in Amman, Jordan. By then, PA television had made him a celebrity, and King Abdullah of Jordan and Moamar Quadafi of Libya came to visit his bedside. He spent several months in the hospital in Jordan, treated free of charge, and he did a number of interviews. He had not been apolitical before losing Mohammed—one of his sons, born on the day Saddam Hussein launched his first Scud missile at Tel Aviv during the first Gulf War, was named Saddam; but, perhaps understandably, he became considerably more political afterward. In his first press conference in Amman, for instance, he said, "I appeal to the entire world, to all those who have seen this crime, to act and help me avenge my son's death and *to put Israel on trial"* (my emphasis). He also did an on-line press conference, taking questions from people who are identified, in the transcript I found, only by user names. For example:

> *Dina:* Did the Israeli army ever apologize for the killing of your son "God rest his soul"?
>
> *Jamal Al Durra:* They didn't approach in any way, I asked for an international trial, but Clinton rebuffed it. And threatened to use the right of VETO.
>
> . . . .
>
> *Samer4:* Do you think that this Intifada is going to help the Palestinian people?
>
> *Jamal Al Durra:* The continuation of the Intifada will eliminate the Zionists and retrieve Palestinian lands and rights.
>
> *Jongar:* Is it true that the Israelis were really looking to kill the young boys by shooting on their heads?

Jamal Al Durra: The Israelis intend to kill children less than 16 years
of age. So they won't grow up and build families. That is how they
will annihilate the Palestinian people.

When he was released from the hospital, Jamal accompanied
Yasser Arafat and his delegation to the United Nations Conference
on Racism held in Durban, South Africa, and gave an address of
some kind. (I have not been able to find a record of what he said.)
Outside the convention hall, demonstrators marched and carried
signs featuring a still photo of Jamal and Mohammed from the
France 2 video with the words "End Israel's Apartheid." Jamal visited Tunisia as the guest of its labor unions to see a street that had
just been named after his son. By 2002, in the role of father of the
shaheed, Jamal had made stops in Jordan, Egypt, Iraq and Libya,
where, surrounded by bodyguards and admiring and curious crowds,
he posed for photos and sold autographed photos of himself or
Mohammed. He traveled so much that in a September 2002 interview with *Newsday's* Matthew McAllister, his wife, Amal, complained that he had "been at home for only three months since the
shooting." Because she traveled with him often, she noted, her six
surviving children "sometimes feel like orphans." Accompanied by
a phalanx of aides and bodyguards, he still tours and sells photos to
this day. "When they travel—also free—even the Israeli soldiers
who control the border between Gaza and Egypt let members of the
family pass without the usual rigorous inspections that most Palestinians face when they leave Gaza," McAllister wrote.

"I have special treatment," Amal said. "I am the mother of
Mohammed al-Dura. They [even] don't stop us at airports."

After Mohammed's death, the al-Duras began to receive the
usual monthly stipend allotted to families of martyrs by the Palestinian Authority. According to *Newsweek,* they also got $5,000 from
Saudi Arabia, free medical care for Jamal wherever he went in the
Arab states, and an award from Saddam Hussein, who routinely
gave $25,000 to the families of suicide bombers. According to Ibrahim
Zanen, spokesman for the Arab Liberation Front in Gaza, Hussein
gave more than $35 million to West Bank and Gaza families because
he "consider[ed] the Palestinian people as part of his Arab nation."

■ ■ ■

PHOTOGRAPHER TALAL ABU RAHME'S LIFE was transformed as well. In addition to his "Cameraman of the Year" award from the Sony Corporation, he went on to receive at least fourteen more awards, according to National Public Radio, one of the hundreds of outlets that interviewed him. At the National Press Club in Washington, D.C., he addressed the Network of Arab-American Alumni and Professionals. Press releases announcing this talk promised that Rahme would show the now famous video clip and urged their members to come view this "brutal display of lethal force by the Israelis."

In a 2002 newspaper clip we find Rahme at a party at the French embassy in Jerusalem, where he chatted with Yitzhak Rabin, who asked him "if conditions are improving in Gaza." Though he had toiled as a worker in CNN vineyards for many years in his pre-Dura career, after 2000 Rahme began to be listed in credits as a producer, one who seems to be particularly valued for his ability to get reporters in touch with terror militia members. In 2002, for instance, we find a CNN reporter turning to "their producer in Gaza City, Talal Abu-Rahme," who "works his contacts" and arranges a meeting with members of the Al-Aqsa Martyrs Brigade. The most recent Rahme sighting I have found dates from April 2003, when Billie Moskona-Lerman, a reporter from Israel's *Ma'ariv* newspaper, hired him to take her around the city of Rafah on the Israel/Egypt border. She describes him as "a very busy man who lives in Gaza and works for foreign networks." After he consents to take her to the homes of embattled Palestinians, Rahme tells Moskona-Lerman not to utter "a word of Hebrew. If anybody asks, you are a French journalist."

Meanwhile, Mohammed al-Dura lives on. Reporters who have gone to his house in El Bureish say it's like visiting a shrine. It is said that pictures of him begin to appear on the sides of buildings blocks away and proliferate until one reaches his home, which is covered with paintings and a graffito (identical to the one seen fleetingly in the famous France 2 video on the wall behind Mohammed and Jamal) reading, "What is taken by violence can only be taken back by violence."

Though he is now found in Palestinian Authority textbooks and in paintings by children on school walls, Mohammed's greatest presence is on television and computer screens. He has become the poster boy in what Martin Fletcher of NBC called "commercials" for the recruitment of child *shaheeds*. The Palestinian Ministry of Information broadcasts many of these during the day, and they come in a range of styles, some obviously aimed at young children: "Choose Death, the Life Will Follow" is the title of one. Some are obviously targeting teens. Some—with handsome adult males as hosts and serious, well-spoken little girls espousing the importance of *shahada*—apparently target preteen girls. Some, addressed to parents, feature mothers talking about their pride at having given birth to a *shaheed*.

Some use a barrage of MTV-style effects. Some are more earnest and low-tech, in the style of public service training films. In one of these, for instance, a boy waves goodbye to his father and sets off on his bicycle. A male voice in the background tells us in song that he is off to make "the great sacrifice." Suddenly he grabs his chest, apparently "shot." There is no explosion of body tissue, no blood; he merely falls off his bike in slow motion, then lies peacefully as if he were asleep having a happy dream. The singer in the background says that the *shaheed* has "embraced the ground" in his "death for the land."

In the special video they made to commemorate the martyrdom of little Mohammed, though, the Palestinian Authority's Ministry of Education appears to have spared no expense, using every trick in the video-maker's playbook to end up with a presentation that looks like a Metallica video circa 1990 boosted with twenty-first-century digital imaging.

The production starts with an actor playing Mohammed wandering in "paradise"—a dreamy shot of a field filled with children his age. Then a barrage of images: A beautiful palace, like the Taj Mahal, surrounded by a fountain and palm trees. The sky behind the palace is purple and filled with storm clouds that race across the sky in time-lapse. A rose, filmed in extreme close-up and in time-lapse, bursts into full bloom. The camera cuts away at the apex of the explosion of its petals. Fields of wheat ripple in the wind; waves crash on a shore. "How beautiful is the breeze of the martyr, how beautiful is the scent of the land, which is fed from the waterfall of blood, springing from an angry body," intones a deep masculine voice in the background.

One of the last images in the video is a peaceful beach on a sunny day. At the water's edge, a ghostly, half-transparent young boy is running with joyful, free, loping steps that make him seem to hover above the ground. We watch him run away from us toward the horizon and then the shadowy figure turns his head and gives us a jaunty wave. It is an echo of the opening shot of the movie: a black screen with words in white Arabic calligraphy reading, "I am waving to you not in farewell, but to beckon you to follow me. Mohammed al-Dura."

THREE

THE LYNCHING—
ANOTHER CASE STUDY

O N OCTOBER 12, 2000, another image was added to the portfo-
lio of the Israeli/Palestinian media war when Sgt. Vadim
Nourezitz and Sgt. Yosef Avrahami, two reservists in the Israeli
Defense Force who had been driving back to their West Bank
base, presumably made a wrong turn and ended up in downtown
Ramallah, where a funeral procession was making its way down a
main boulevard. Once again, about two weeks after the death of little Mohammed, a flower-covered bier draped in white and bearing
the body of a beautiful little boy martyr teetered and eddied down
the street above the heads of a river of chanting men.

Apparently a rumor had been circulating that the IDF was
going to send spies to the funeral to photograph suspects or even
try to seize members of terror militias who might be attending.
When Palestinian Authority police saw men in IDF uniforms driving a civilian car (a mix they apparently considered suspicious), they
forced the reservists out of their car and took them to their headquarters for questioning. A mob split off and followed. Unhindered
by police on the street, who later said they did not believe they could
control such a mob, a group stormed up to the second floor of the
building, wrested the soldiers from officials and beat them to death,
finally tossing one of the mutilated bodies out the window to the
crowd of men who waited below.

Both men were in their early thirties. Nourezitz, a Russian émi-
gré, had been married for only one week. His widow told Israeli media
that she had called her new husband's cell phone in the afternoon.
"Where is my husband?" she asked the strange person who answered.
"We are killing your husband!" the voice shouted into the phone. He
held the phone into the room so she could hear the sounds of her

husband dying. One of the killers stepped to a window of the police headquarters and, with a broad grin, displayed his palms slick with blood to the crowd in the street. Once the body of one of the reservists was given over to the crowd, people took turns dragging it through the streets until, as one observer recalled, the face resembled a "red jelly."

The lynching happened in the morning; by afternoon (the time at which American reporters begin finalizing their stories for print) the Israeli Air Force (IAF) had surveyed possible targets with drones, warned Palestinian Authority officials to evacuate their offices, and then sent helicopters to fire on the police station where the killings had occurred and on other government buildings, including the production studios for the "Voice of Palestine" radio. As Israel's retaliation was the most recent event, most outlets led with the news that IAF "gunships" had pounded buildings in the West Bank, adding halfway down the page that this had been in response to "the seizure and killing of two Israeli soldiers."

Peter Jennings of ABC News teased the story with the statement, "Israelis and Palestinians, another day of dead and wounded, each side accuses the other of going to war." After this lead-in, he began the report:

> It has been another terrible day of fighting between Israelis and Palestinians. There was a particularly ugly incident in the Palestinian city of Ramallah. Forty-thousand people live there. This week they're all angry at the Israelis. There was about to be another funeral. Thousands of young men had congregated. At least two Israeli army reservists were clearly in the wrong place. They were stopped and taken into a police station. That was not enough for their protection.

He then cut to his correspondent in the area, Gillian Findlay, who had the habit of summarizing retaliation by the IAF on terrorist targets with the phrase, "Israel attacked from the air again today." Her report on events of October 12 once more glossed over the precipitating event (the lynching) to focus on the retaliation, and she did not tell viewers about the extraordinary attempts the IAF had made to ensure that the buildings were empty when they targeted them. "Again and again, the Israelis fired," she reported excitedly from Ramallah, "hitting not one, but two police stations, a radio and TV transmitter, and Yasser Arafat's presidential compound."

It was up to Jennings to find inclusive, summary words of wisdom to close the segment, so he said, "As everybody in the region has said today, nobody knows what will happen tomorrow. Various Palestinian factions as well as Jewish settlers in the territories are calling for another day of rage."

But the term "Day of Rage" is very specific to the PA, PLO and terror militia factions. Left over from PLO flirtation with Marxism-Leninism in the 1960s, it is part of the larger Marxist-flavored stock vocabulary favored by the PLO/PA. "Days of Rage" were routine events in the territories; in fact, Hamas had called for one on October 6, about a week before the lynching. Undoubtedly, settlers were filled with rage after the Ramallah lynching. They may even have issued calls for retaliation, but Jennings conflated organized, government-backed rioting by the PA with the threats from settlers, a faction (and not a very popular one) of Israel's population, in order to drape a soothing blanket of moral equivalence over a barbaric episode.

The BBC covered the event accurately but almost seemed to be attempting to justify the killings by implying that the two soldiers could have been spies. Its stories made repeated reference to the fact that they were driving what the BBC called "an unmarked car." What the BBC seemed to be implying was that by not driving a military vehicle, the soldiers were trying to conceal themselves or get away with something. The truth is, as usual, more mundane. The IDF is much more low-tech than the Mossad-obsessed BBC likes to believe. Israeli soldiers often drive their own cars back to base when returning from leave (if they do not hitchhike or take a bus or train), so the most reasonable explanation is that the "unmarked car" was simply the personal car of one of the reservists.

Adding fuel to the theory that the two were actually secret police come to arrest people (and therefore that the crowd's reaction was understandable), the BBC also reported that "photographs show some of the doomed men were dressed in civilian clothes and one was photographed before his death wrapped in a black-and-white Palestinian head-dress," and that:

Anger had been brewing for the last two weeks which have witnessed
the funerals of about 100 Arabs, nearly two dozen of them children,
who have been killed in the violent uprising against Israeli occupation forces.

But this outburst of fury apparently stemmed from rumours circulating through the mob that the captives belonged to the feared
and hated undercover units of the Israeli army which dress as Arabs
and strike in the heart of Palestinian towns.

In the macabre world of victimology—in which comparison
tallies of war dead, devoid of context or demographic details, are
displayed on the "ticker" during news programs and in which *Newsday*, for example, once noted sternly that since the beginning of
the new intifada, "Israel has maintained its 4 to 1 death ratio"—I
had a shameful thought. Perhaps there was a perverse kind of silver lining in this event. Perhaps the incessant playing of the "Ramallah" clip would be a sort of antidote to the "al-Dura" clip. Perhaps
this sacrifice to the gods of the victim ledger could change the tone
of the press coverage of the second intifada.

And it did slightly, though not in the way Israelis might have
hoped. In the United States, "Ramallah" was only subsumed into
a new media take on the second intifada emphasizing "the cycle of
violence"—a phrase suggesting, as David Gelernter put it, "that
Israelis and Palestinians kill each other as part of some sort of tire-
some Punch and Judy show." A flood of speeches in the "what-
fools-these-mortals-be" vein were soon delivered by just-
parachuted-in (but already weary) journalists.

On the day of the lynching, for instance, Mike Hanna of CNN
(who had just begun his stint as Jerusalem bureau chief) offered
the following:

> Throughout the past two weeks of violence, mediators have talked
> of the necessity to create a new psychology, a psychology of peace,
> rather than one of the war. Well, on this day, it was clear which psy-
> chology was dominant: a cycle of violence of gathering intensity,
> leaving a peace process already dormant in tatters.
>
> A final word perhaps from the UN secretary general Kofi Annan, who
> is still, at this time, attempting to broker an end to these hostilities: "Vio-
> lence begets violence," he says. "I plead with you to opt for restraint."

Richard Carleton of Australia's Channel 9 TV:

The television images were almost too horrible to watch. A young
Palestinian boy, cowering in fear, cut down in a hail of bullets fired
by Israeli troops. Then later, a lynch mob storms a police station and
brutally murders two Israeli soldiers.

After half a century we've almost become accustomed to the endless violence between Arabs and Jews in Israel. Each new outbreak
of fighting leads to another round of peace talks, only to fall apart
with hateful recriminations on both sides.

Ted Koppel swiftly assembled another panel and broadcast a
show the day after the lynching. The show was titled "Snapshots
from a Conflict: The Impact of Photographs on Political and Public
Opinion." Koppel brought together a journalist who had covered
the al-Dura incident and Palestinian producer Nasser Atta, who had
been in Ramallah for ABC and had seen the murders firsthand.
(Apparently, people on the street could see what was happening in
the police station because much of it happened in front of a second-
story window.) The other panelist, Dorit Long, was an American
Jew married to an Israeli and had been freelancing for ABC in Israel
when "al-Dura" occurred. "One picture," said Koppel to Long in his
most soothing tone, "must have been especially painful for Israelis
to see and that was the picture of that Palestinian child, the one with
his father trying to protect him, who ended up being shot and killed
by the Israelis." Long agreed that yes, it was nearly intolerable to
look at, but she felt it was important to show the tape because it was
important to know about such things.

Turning to Atta, Koppel seemed to have strayed from his own
point (talking about the coverage of the lynching), for he asked,
"And you, Nasser, how do you maintain any degree of objectivity
covering a story in which some of your own friends, possibly even
family members, have been hurt or injured or endangered? How
can you still stand back and say, 'Yes, I can be an objective reporter
here'?"

Atta steered the conversation back to the day of the lynchings.
Indeed they had been awful to watch, he said, but it was extremely
important to "tell the truth ... even if it is a Palestinian mob." In
fact, Atta continued, he had tried to tell the truth on film but when

he turned on his cameras "the youth tried to prevented—prevented my crew from shooting this footage. My cameraman was beaten."

This would seem to be very relevant information in a program about "the use of photographs as tools of war," but Atta's unscripted comments may have disrupted the feel-good symmetry that Koppel was apparently trying to evoke, so he ignored them and turned back immediately to Long: "Dorit, let me put the question in a slightly different way to you. You and Nasser and another Palestinian producer who is a friend of ours, Ali in the bureau, we all have differences of opinion sometimes, we have arguments sometimes, but your respect for one another, I assume, remains undiminished. But you tell me."

Richard Roth of CBS News was one of the many who began using the word "symmetry" about the two events: "These TV pictures [of Mohammed al-Dura and the Ramallah lynching] have become defining symbols of the conflict for those on each side. They are two indelible images that, in the battle for public opinion, comprise a tragic symmetry." And in this he was right. The images were frequently paired—by the news media. But it was a forced symmetry, created by the media for its convenience and because it was more soothing and less complicated to represent the situations as the same. Consider just the two pieces of videotape by themselves, which was all anyone had to work with at this time: In "Ramallah" we actually *see* perpetrators at work—men hoisting a body to a window ledge, then shoving it off the ledge to a crowd below, whom we then see all too clearly stomping and stabbing it. In "al-Dura," however, we see a boy collapsing, apparently shot. That is all. In one story, most of the who, what, where and why is answered. But in "al-Dura," virtually everything, except that two people were shot at in front of a wall, is essentially a mystery.

■ ■ ■

THERE WAS ONE SIGNIFICANT SYMMETRY about "al-Dura" and "The Lynching"—but a different kind. Although there had been dozens of cameramen at both sites, each event was hardly photographed. The television footage of the lynching that was eventually seen all over the world came from one videotape taken by one film crew, RTI of Italy; and the one still photograph, of the man displaying his bloody hands, was taken by a photographer for Agence France-Presse whose name was kept under wraps. We still do not know why "al-Dura" was captured on film by only one man. But in the case of "Ramallah," small clues—evocative of the comments by Nasser Atta about intimidation that Ted Koppel had studiously ignored— soon began to appear.

On October 22, the *Daily Telegraph* of London published a personal account by a still photographer named Mark Seager. He had

> arrived in Ramallah at about 10.30 in the morning and was getting into a taxi on the main road to go to a Nablus funeral when all of a sudden there came a big crowd of Palestinians shouting and running down the hill from the police station. I got out of the car to see what was happening and saw that they were dragging something behind them. Within moments they were in front of me and, to my horror, I saw that it was a body, a man they were dragging by the feet. The lower part of his body was on fire and the upper part had been shot at, and the head beaten so badly that it was a pulp, like red jelly. I thought he was a soldier because I could see the remains of khaki trousers and boots. My God, I thought, they've killed this guy. He was dead, he must have been dead, but they were still beating him, madly, kicking his head. They were like animals. They were just a few feet in front of me and I could see everything. Instinctively, I reached for my camera. I was composing the picture when I was punched in the face by a Palestinian. Another Palestinian pointed right at me shouting "no picture, no picture!", while another guy hit me in the face and said "give me your film!". I tried to get the film out but they were all grabbing me and one guy just pulled the camera off me and smashed it to the floor. I knew I had lost the chance to take the photograph that would have made me famous and I had lost my favourite lens that I'd used all over the world, but I didn't care. I was scared for my life.

Soon afterward, a letter appeared on page one of the PA-owned daily *Al-Hayat al-Jadeeda* and it revealed more about the media environment at the time of the lynching. The letter was written by Riccardo Cristiano, a producer in the Jerusalem bureau of the state-owned Italian TV station RAI. "My Dear Friends in Palestine," the letter began:

We congratulate you and think it is our duty to explain to you what happened on October 12 in Ramallah. One of the private Italian television stations which competes with us . . . filmed the events. . . . Afterwards Israeli television broadcast the pictures as taken from one of the Italian stations, and thus the public impression was created as if we took these pictures.

We emphasize to all of you that the events did not happen this way, because we always respect the journalistic rules of the Palestinian Authority for work in Palestine. . . .

We thank you for your trust and you can be sure that this is not our way of acting, and we would never do such a thing.

Please accept our dear blessings.

Riccardo Cristiano

Apparently what had happened was that an Italian company, RTI, filmed the body as it fell out of the window and somehow got out of Ramallah with their film intact, while other television crews were being forced to surrender their tapes. They gave their film to the Israeli embassy in Rome, which gave it to the Israeli Ministry of Foreign Affairs, which offered the tape to news outlets. Within six hours the film was shown around the world. Cristiano was therefore worried that his "dear friends in Palestine" would think his similarly named network was responsible for this bad publicity.

Usually, "understandings" between source and reporter are communicated more subtly and leave no paper trails. Even if there were no explicit "rules" promulgated by the Palestinian Authority, Cristiano was being startlingly blatant about the kind of bargains and unspoken "understandings" that reporters sometimes make with their sources and he quickly became a pariah in the journalism community. In one of the articles that followed in the *Jerusalem Post*, one of Cristiano's friends tried to defend the journalist by suggesting that his letter to the Palestinian Journalists' Union had been mistranslated. He had been "writing in his third language [English]," she argued, which had been translated into Arabic for the newspaper. Besides, she said, his perceptions might have been addled because of beatings he had sustained while attempting to cover riots in East Jerusalem in early October. "His ribs were broken; his cheek caved in, there were fears that a lung might be punctured . . . ," she told the *Jerusalem Post*. "Of all the foreign reporters, he got beaten the worst." She was a rare ally. For most, Cristiano was simply an embarrassment. There was no protest from the journalistic community when the Israeli Government Press Office suspended Cristiano's press card and when RAI pulled him off the beat and back to Italy.

Once Cristiano revealed that RTI had supplied the tape, one of that station's producers, Anna Mignotto, began to receive death threats and she too was recalled to Italy for her safety.

Apparently, other reporters had been silenced on that day and not spoken about it. Much later, in an article not directly about the lynching, BBC reporter Orla Guerin said she had been in Ramallah on October 12 and watched as "the two Israelis were hustled into the local police station." She remarked that the "media were warned not to take pictures as the crowds forced their way in"— and then resumed her piece as if this fact were of no particular significance. Her producers did not pick up on the remark, and it was swept away in the flood of words, the way Nasser Atta's comments had been allowed to slip by on Ted Koppel's show.

Her matter-of-factness and lack even of annoyance at the Palestinian Authority police (who, at the very least, had stood by allowing this blatant media censorship) was typical. When his own bureau chief was also recalled to Italy because of threats to her life, RTI editor Enrico Mentana made bitter comments to a *Jerusalem Post* reporter—but about Cristiano's error in identifying them as the creators of the surviving videotape. "As of today," he said, "our correspondents can no longer work [in Israel]. We know whom to thank [i.e. Cristiano]."

Why were they so willing to excuse the Palestinian Authority? That was a large question with many answers. A more concrete question was what had Cristiano been referring to when he apologized for breaking "the journalistic rules of the Palestinian Authority for work in Palestine"? Were there such rules? Were they *de jure* or *de facto*? And how were they enforced? Fortunately Richard Starr, an editor at the *Weekly Standard,* wanted to know too. He gave me an assignment and a few weeks later—it was then late October—I flew to Israel to look into rules of engagement for reporters working in the disputed territories and, in a more general way, at all dynamics and conditions affecting coverage of the conflict.

FOUR

IF IT BLEEDS, IT LEADS

Another day I return from a brutal day to the Reuters office and say tentatively to the photo editor, "I have pictures from Ramallah today." He says, "Ramallah? Oh, no thanks. We had a staffer today in Ramallah." "But I have a guy who was shot in the stomach," I say. His eyebrows arch. "Can you see blood?" "Yeah," I say, "there's blood." "Okay, let's see it." There is blood. He files the picture. The next day it was featured on Yahoo! [news service].

—Freelance photographer Yola Monakhov in the *Columbia Journalism Review*

J ERUSALEM IS A BIT LIKE WASHINGTON, D.C. It has the same earnest dowdiness. You get the same sense that the sidewalks roll up at 9 P.M. so everyone can get home to review briefing papers. There is a similar ratio of employees of government, think tanks, aid groups and news bureaus to normal people. Still, though it may not be as fun as hedonistic, secular Tel Aviv, where there are beaches, women in thong bikinis, and nightclubs, Jerusalem is not a bad place to be posted, as Mideast postings for journalists go. There are not many cities that compress, as if in a theme park, the always publishable subjects of Ancient History, Heads of State, Great Art and Bloody Conflict into an area this conveniently compact. Because of the relatively small size of the reporting area, it is one of few places in the world where you can zip across a fairly elastic border (reporters can usually bypass checkpoints with ease), find yourself in a region that can seem distinctly foreign (with sights of goat herds, hookah pipes and women in veils), get your quota of shots or news and then zip back to Jerusalem in time for the cocktail hour at a hotel where the desk clerks speak English, the automatic teller

machine greets you by name, and it turns out that the guy sitting
at the next table in the hotel dining room takes his kids to the same
preschool your kids go to on Manhattan's Upper West Side.

The same reporters who mutter darkly about Israel's "excessive force" or "violations of international law," or insist on strict
moral equivalency between Palestinian and Israeli conduct in the
conflict, still base themselves in Jerusalem rather than Ramallah (a
large West Bank city a twenty-minute drive away) and can become
quite expansive about the advantages of being assigned to Israel's
unofficial capital city. "It's a beat that commands world attention,
and ... offers reporters unparalleled exposure," NPR reporter Steve
McNally rhapsodized in the *Columbia Journalism Review.* It is so
much easier to be a "war correspondent" here, he wrote, because
reporters "don't need to travel far"; the West Bank city of Bethlehem "is only a ten-minute drive from Jerusalem." McNally's friend
Jennifer Griffin of Fox News "has managed a feat that would be
impossible almost anywhere else, to be a war correspondent and a
new mother. 'It's a nine-to-five war you can cover and still be home
for dinner at night,' she says, 'I've gone out the door with a flak
jacket and a breast pump.'"

As Jerusalem-based reporter for the *Guardian,* Suzanne Goldenberg spent three years casting the darkest possible aspersions on
her host country, but when she moved on to her next posting she
told *Ha'aretz* that "it is nearly ideal to be based in Jerusalem because
it's small and it's so open. You can wander into the Knesset and talk
to any politician, and they'll talk to you—that's terrific. It doesn't
happen here in Washington. People in Israel will always call you
back—that's great."

Aside from what McNally called the opportunity for "unparalleled exposure," Jerusalem is a favorite destination for young and/or
novice reporters and photographers because, as one lensman assured
another on a discussion board run by freelancecameraman.com, "it's
no problem to get a visa" here, unlike most of the other countries in
the Middle East. Rather quickly one is given access to the romantic
pull of war, which forms a great Panavision backdrop for one's foreign correspondent fantasies.

In 1988, just out of college and in awe of the sexy, Robert
Capa–like war photographers she was meeting in Paris, Deborah

Copaken Kogan—the author of a memoir titled *Shutterbabe: Adventures in Love and War*—decided she wanted to be a photojournalist too. She managed to get an audience with the bureau chief of a Parisian photo agency and when he asked her where she'd like to go for her first assignment, she answered immediately: Israel. "I was just finding my footing and trying to make my mark in a cutthroat profession that favors the easy metaphor (David vs. Goliath, say) over the more ambiguous interpretation of events," she explained to me.

Danger is one of the greatest aphrodisiacs, as Kogan was finding out. She envisioned a future in which she and a Parisian photojournalist paramour would "traverse the planet, bouncing from coup to insurrection, war to revolution, passing our days shooting pictures and our nights under the stars, making love to the gentle thrum of incoming mortar fire."

But Jerusalem provides a backdrop for less carnal sorts of romantic fantasies too. Daniel Seaman of Israel's Government Press Office remembers going to someone's house in 1995 to watch election returns on the night Benjamin Netanyahu was elected prime minister: "They were sitting there, all the journalists invited to this party, and there were quite a lot of them and everybody was all depressed. So I started asking people, 'Why are you so depressed?' The answer was 'Netanyahu' and 'the world is over' and so on.

"I looked at this group and suddenly I saw the Abraham Lincoln Brigades from the Spanish Civil War, the people who came to Spain to fight in the name of Socialism. You have the same thing here now; people coming with this romanticized dream of Palestinian rights. They didn't come to report objectively. They came with their pens to fight."

All these factors seemed to have combined in late October 2000 to draw a great herd of foreign press to the region to cover the second intifada. The first intifada of 1988–89 had been relatively big news in its day, but it hadn't brought in a crowd this size. Things had been relatively peaceful in the area so, as one photographer explained on a freelancecameraman.com bulletin board, "freelancers who have been desperately looking for work over the last few months ... got quite excited at the beginning of the clashes. You could often hear comments like 'Yeah, let's get some action!' or 'This is great

for my bank account.'" There had also been an exponential growth
of news media in the meantime, so there were simply more outlets—like websites (which were just beginning to develop their own
reporters) and many new cable stations fielding correspondents. In
the first months of the second intifada, the Government Press
Office—the body charged with reviewing applications for Israeli
government press credentials—was trying to cope with about 1,500
new journalists all wanting press cards, expecting help finding lodging and other necessities, and becoming irate when their electronic
equipment was held up by border control at Ben Gurion Airport.
Everybody wanted a piece of this story—though conceptions of
what the story *was* varied dramatically.

It was my first trip back in two decades. The last time I had
been in the city, Israel had been in a state of relative peace; but now
the happy, bustling Jerusalem I remembered from my teen years
seemed to have gone into hiding. I decamped to the north end where
Jaffa Road intersects with highways leading to Tel Aviv and the
Galilee. It's a scraggly, stray-cat sort of neighborhood where fluor-
escent-lit warehouses sit next to Crusader-era cobblestone cul de
sacs, which sit next to dilapidated, two-story modern flats with lines
of laundry strung from balconies. Usually the streets are full of
locals: ultra-orthodox Jews in their long black coats and large black
hats, recent immigrants from Russia and Ethiopia, illegal workers
from Mongolia and Africa and the Philippines, and biblical-looking
hippie youth with dusty, sandaled feet and zoned-out eyes. But on
the day I arrived, the streets seemed curiously still except for
reporters—clattering and clacking around in the hydra-headed con-
traption that is a television news crew, or roaring about in jeeps
emblazoned on every available surface with the words PRESS or
TV in big letters.

There was a silver lining of sorts: a brand-new hotel was standing nearly empty. The Isrotel Jerusalem Tower had been built to
accommodate all the travelers who were expected to flock to the
Holy Land to observe the passing of the millennium. Instead, the
intifada had started and the hotel was trying to recoup from the
economic disaster by offering a "Reporter's Special"— a three-star
room and free breakfast for something under $100 a night, for any-
one with an Israeli government-issued press card.

Out of what appeared to be a fit of whimsy on the part of the young Israeli front desk clerks who seemed to be sick of sitting around with no business, I was delegated to an "executive suite" on the ninth floor, which had a panoramic view of the Knesset, a high-resolution TV, and a second wireless phone located over the toilet. I figured if all I did was lounge around on the king-size bed, watch BBC and MTV-Asia (out of India, with many fabulous Bollywood-style music videos), and talk on the handy toilet phone, the trip would have been worth it.

But although the management was practically giving away rooms, the hotel was still like a great, cold, granite-floored sarcophagus. If I saw anybody else on the elevator they were clearly press, instantly recognizable by their ready-for-combat uniform consisting of jeans, rugged Timberland-style boots, and a vest—sometimes merely a down vest but sometimes bulletproof. The completing touch was a neck scarf, often an Arab *keffiyeh*. It's useful to pull up over your nose in the event of dust or tear gas and is also supposed to be a universally recognized symbol of solidarity with the Palestinian people, and thus worn as a sort of talisman by reporters who work in the territories.

The photographers dressed in the same rough-and-ready woodsman style but tended to be larger, burlier and younger, more usually male and more outgoing. News photographers—print or video—are a bit like infantrymen; they are usually loaded down with equipment like pack mules and then expected to function as *de facto* bodyguards for more delicate reporters. Rootless in the world, often without wives and kids at home to worry about, they're generally in good spirits wherever they are as long as they don't have to work in the rain and they're getting "three hots and a cot." They are not asked to think too much about what they're doing. As Deborah Kogan puts it in *Shutterbabe*, "Photographers don't have to be well-versed in the minutiae of a story to do their job. They just have to shoot what's in front of their noses, to understand the conflict well enough to extract the simple metaphor that will illustrate the story for the folks back home."

Producers, editors and writers tend to be older, far more educated, more cerebral and more politically opinionated. Also, perhaps because the hotel had shut down its bar for lack of business, these types seemed even more withdrawn and cranky than usual. The mood was most noticeable in the morning when I charged down to the dining room to collect my free buffet breakfast. After too many Motel 6 "continental breakfasts" during my life "in the field," this was like a shimmering mirage in the desert. The big sunny room was filled with white-cloth-covered tables, each place already marked with a glass of water (with ice cubes!—a luxury in desert countries), orange juice and coffee. Two buffet tables displayed a veritable survey course of breakfast foods from around the world. The line started with the makings of an Israeli breakfast—hard-boiled eggs, untoasted black bread, scallions, tomatoes, cucumbers, avocados, yogurt, feta cheese, leben, olives, herring, smoked salmon, piles of fresh fruit; then American bagels, cream cheese, smoked salmon, then regular American toast, muffins, sticky buns, dry cereals, hot cereals, a vat of oatmeal, scrambled eggs, boiled eggs, sausages. If one wanted, and most people did, one could save costs further by pocketing pieces of fruit and the makings of a sandwich for later.

But the news people sat down taciturnly as if they were determined not to be pleased with anything in Israel, as if they saw this lavishness as a ploy of the foreign ministry to win them over. I tried to empathize. In this era of hyper-competition, news people are overworked, insecure, and often—if they are American—weighted down with their responsibility to the historical record. On the other hand, I reasoned, maybe they were just accustomed to three-star hotels.

It turned out, however, that many were depressed about the recent turn of events: There is a certain exuberance around journalists who feel they've caught the wave and are at the center of the action. Scarcely two weeks earlier, the second intifada had been *the* big story; there was a quivery, breathless sound when the on-air talent gripped his or her mike to say, "Reporting from Jerusalem, this is. . . ." But by the time I arrived in late October, the Sharm el-Sheikh cease-fire had been negotiated. This didn't mean that people had stopped shooting at each other: With a simple visit to the IDF police spokesman's desk, one could read a police blotter of entries about "shots fired at Israeli civilian car in . . ."; "explosive device found under stack of newspapers"; "exchange of fire in . . ."; and so on. What the cease-fire did mean was that large, collective demonstrations in the West Bank had quieted. Except for the occasional pageantry of funerals of *shaheeds,* always a journalistic "evergreen" because of the great visuals (photographers told me it was standard to call the Palestine Media Center in Ramallah to ask if there'd be "any funerals today?"), things seemed quite calm in the West Bank towns. The presidential election in the United States (Bush vs. Gore), now just about a week and a half away, was down to the wire and looking sexier than a dribble of negotiations in the Middle East. Most of the press people had accordingly been instructed by their superiors to "give it a week" and wait around in case "stuff" started up again.

The general attitude among the editors and producers consigned to the snazzy but empty Isrotel was that it was bad enough that they had been put on ice in this sleepy backwater of a region, but they had also been relegated to the least happening hotel! If one was going to sit in Jerusalem waiting for instructions, at least one would want to pass the time having a Real Mideast Experience in a venue where you could pick up a tip for a hot story. (The vast majority of foreign press disdained tips from Israeli government officials because, in the words of one reporter, government officials are "obviously out to spin you.") The more authentic experience, the real contact with real people, the view went, was to be found at the very expensive American Colony Hotel on the other side of the Green Line, in East Jerusalem, which had been continuously booked since the start of this intifada.

Ask where you can find so-and-so journalist who you've just heard has arrived in Jerusalem and the stock answer is "Try the American Colony." It is, as Claudia Dreifus of the *New York Times* once put it, "the place favored by the international press corps . . . a center of activity" where she knew she "would find journalistic comradeship—and gossip." Another American journalist called it "a shiny oasis . . . where you'll find great phone service, wideband Internet, . . . a chauffeured Mercedes driven by an expert who knows exactly where to take you, lounges [that] are filled with laughter in a dozen languages," and a "long shelf of rare vintages of Armagnac." As proof of the enduring bond between the international press corps and the American Colony, the hotel displays a list in fancy script of the most famous journalists (Peter Jennings and Dan Rather, for instance) who have checked in over the years. Ordinary, nonfamous

journalists may sign the guest book as well. "It's good to be home!"
read one entry.

Built by a wealthy Ottoman-era Turk to house his four wives,
the Moorish palace of a building sits in a beautiful, tree-shaded,
tranquil section of Arab East Jerusalem. British administrators of
the Mandate filled this neighborhood after they chased the Turks
out and there is still something very British, very Secret Garden-
ish about the wrought-iron gates and tall stone walls covered with
creepers and moss that shelter lovely crumbling stone houses surrounded by overgrown, once-formal gardens. Many of these grand
residences have gone shabby, in a picturesque, mildewed kind of
way, but instead of housing a British general or a Mandate government official, the decaying mansions have become home to foreign
missions to Palestine and international non-governmental organizations (NGOs), which are ubiquitous on the West Bank. In other
words, the people one sees on the streets around the American
Colony are usually blue-suits of one type or another, often Westerners, certainly not fiery young Palestinian jihadists. If one is going
to have a conversation about the intifada here, it will be in decorous
abstract terms with a professor from nearby Al-Quds University, a
Red Cross or UN staffer, or the administrator of a nearby NGO.

But that's not to say the experience of staying there is completely tame. In fact, everything about the American Colony is an
alternation of the scary and the familiar, of peril and rescue. There
is nothing dramatic about crossing the Green Line. Because the
Israeli government is not interested in vesting this temporary
armistice line (negotiated between Israel and Jordan in 1967) with
any more significance than it is given already, there is nothing particular to mark it. Still, everybody knows where it is and one cannot help but feel that one has "crossed over" some kind of significant
border and is now "on the other side." The feeling continues when
one pulls into the American Colony parking lot—inevitably filled
with vans marked PRESS and TV. Sharp-eyed, unsmiling young
men hang around the front entrance. Are they guards of some kind?
Or just taxi drivers? Maybe it doesn't matter, for the reception room
is full of more emblems of British civility and colonial order. Per-
sian carpets cover the cool stone floors; the sitting rooms are full of
heavy, dark wooden furniture; sepia-colored photographs of

sunburned Westerners in khaki shorts from the Mandate period hang on the walls.

Guest rooms open onto a flagstoned central patio where a fountain splashes in the center and small tiled tables are placed under jade trees. You look up from your table to see the slim, white tower of a mosque next to the building, and when the muezzin comes out to call the followers to prayer, his undulating song is so loud it blots out conversation. Dark-skinned, expressionless waiters in immaculate white coats glide around. "You half expect your waiter to whisper some key bit of intrigue," enthused one journalist who seemed to be having the full American Colony experience.

The legendary bar, where a Coke can go for about $12 depending on the bartender's mood, is in an underground grotto, an Arabian Nights–like series of caves carved into the rock, illuminated only by small pinkish spots on the floor and by the candles on the widely spaced low tables. It is a place that exudes secretiveness, which is catnip to the kind of freelance reporters who pile into the area looking for the big story that will make their careers. Do the bartenders, as is rumored in the journalistic community, really work for Hamas? Is the place really owned by the PLO? Who knows? It doesn't matter if the rumors are true; they send delicious little frissons down one's spine anyway. As Renata Adler put it in her book *Reckless Disregard,* journalism is now full of a certain kind of reporter "who is preoccupied by 'secrets' and the notion that what is obtained in secret is somehow most surely true." There is even a tiny bit of sexual intrigue, rare in journalistic circles these days. Occasionally a genuinely gorgeous French photojournalist type (of the genre that hypnotized Deborah Kogan) will come in, shake the dust off his boots, unwind the sweaty *keffiyeh* from his neck, run his tanned hand through his mop of long hair, and take insolent but intense stock of the women, such as they are, in the joint.

I think the American Colony has become so central to the journalistic community covering Israel and the territories precisely because it teases the nervous system of Western journalists (many of whom are Jews and thus in more peril in the Arab world than their gentile counterparts) in a safe and generally controllable way. Scott Anderson, a freelancer who has covered the conflict for the *New York Times Magazine,* says he would find foreign reporters lounging in the American Colony's bar drawling about having just been "targeted by an Israeli solider" while at work in the West Bank—to which Anderson would reply, "Please! If an IDF soldier had targeted you, you wouldn't be sitting here."

But the hotel is central in a more concrete, logistical way and has been for a long time. As far back as 1988, for instance, Deborah Kogan found that her daily life revolved around the hotel:

> The first story I covered, the Intifada, was more straightforward. Organized, even. I'd take the bus early every morning from my youth hostel in Jerusalem to the nearby American Colony Hotel, where all the other journalists were staying (and where I eventually wound up staying when my clothes were stolen from the youth hostel), and I'd go straight to the restaurant off the lobby. There, I'd ingratiate myself with any photographer I could find who had information about the day's planned demos, his own rental car, and a basket of leftover Danish.
>
> After eating, we'd drive around the West Bank and wait for the Palestinian kids to throw rocks at Israeli soldiers, which we knew they would do only once a critical mass of journalists had assembled.*

And this has not changed since the first intifada. The proprietors, PLO or not, make their anti-Zionist politics clear in the hotel's bookstore window, which displays what might be Noam Chomsky's reading list for an undergraduate survey course on the Israeli/Palestinian conflict—"the very best thinking on Israeli oppression," according to Bruce Schimmel of the *Philadelphia City Paper*.

Since it is already the watering hole of choice for the dozens of twenty- to thirty-year-old UN and NGO workers assigned to the

---

*Kogan told me, "Once I arrived in Israel and saw the reality of the story, wherein Palestinian boys would wait for the appropriate number of news trucks and journalists to arrive before tossing their stones at the Israeli soldiers, I had a much more complicated relationship with the story, understood much more clearly my own implication in the perpetuation of the myth. When I went back to Israel for a second time, I decided to do a more in-depth story, in which I lived for one week with an Israeli settler family, another week with a Palestinian family in Ramallah. I shot quiet photos—the Israeli mother unloading her gun from her purse at the end of the day, the Palestinian mother gazing longingly at a photo of her dead son, Israeli teenagers sitting in a café with an Uzi at their feet, Palestinian boys just being boys. . . . Aside from the one photo of the Uzi in the café, which was used to illustrate a Week in Review essay in the *New York Times*, the story never sold."

territories (who, as one told *Ha'aretz*, do not like to associate with Israelis because it is not "politically correct"), it is the place where their employers, groups like the Red Cross, Human Rights Watch and Amnesty International, often hold their press conferences. When Amnesty International, for instance, held a press conference to announce the publication of their 2002 compendium of "human rights abuses by Israelis in their incursions into Palestinian cities," it was at the American Colony.

All of this combines to make it a political hub, a place where Palestinian activists and academics come to chat up journalists, a place where journalists are introduced to translators and can pick up tips for stories over dinner in the elegant dining room or while having drinks around the swimming pool.

In fact it is so easy to tell oneself that one is doing serious research while hanging out at the hotel that, as one reporter put it, too many press people do little else but "sit around at the American Colony waiting for the call from Palestinian fixers to take them to Jenin or Nablus." The Colony has become such a symbol of "choosing a side" that Scott Anderson says he feels he had a relatively good relationship with the IDF press department because he made sure, in his initial conversations with them, that they knew he was *not* staying at the American Colony but at the Jerusalem Hilton (with its kosher kitchen) on the Israeli side of the Green Line.

■ ■ ■

MEANWHILE, THERE I WAS STUCK on the Israeli side at the Isrotel, where the most exciting thing going down was an evening with MTV-Asia and Ricky Martin singing "Shake Your Bon-Bon" in the original Spanish.

Well, that's not really true. There was something more happening—if you were geeky enough to want to hang out with *Israelis*—and it was actually the thing I was supposed to be looking at. Here on the ground floor of the Isrotel one could observe the tender beginnings of what one could call a post-CNN, post-Dura Israeli press strategy.

The events of the fall had shocked the Ministry of Foreign Affairs into action. Responding to years of charges by reporters that the Israeli government didn't seem to care about reporters, that their officials weren't around when one needed them, the ministry had just opened a press center on the ground floor of the hotel where so many reporters would find themselves staying to cover the intifada. Jonathan Peled, a young (just forty) foreign ministry official who was hanging about on the premises presumably to answer the questions of people like me, explained that the government was attempting to offer visiting press a kind of "one-stop shopping experience"—where they would find all the tools needed to do their jobs: fax, telephone, internet, food, drink, briefing materials, and representatives from all branches of the government. The president of Jerusalem's Foreign Press Association (a trade group for foreign affairs reporters) gave his grudging approval when he said it looked as if the Israeli government "has suddenly woken up to the fact that there are nearly 300 media here, hungry for information, day in and day out." Tracking down information in this city could be wearying because the Israeli press apparatus was famously fragmented. Each of the major divisions of government—the IDF, the Ministry of Foreign Affairs and the Prime Minister's Office—had its own press staff, located in different parts of town, with the IDF press staff in Tel Aviv, which meant that reporters had had to travel a lot to attend press conferences by different government bodies. Since the new press center was all about making things easier for reporters, the foreign ministry had announced that all press conferences would now be held on the ground floor of the Isrotel hotel. As Peled put it, "The press conferences will come to them."

Trying to please reporters was certainly reasonable strategy, but where, I asked Peled, were the images of what so many of us knew as "the good Israel," and why weren't they out there, in the ethersphere, competing with, say, little Mohammed al-Dura and his dad?

Peled sighed. "It is a war of images, we have begun to realize that. Television and still images too have really become key. The Palestinians are good at this and their images are," he hesitated and looked pained, "a little . . . difficult.

"But, we try not to go that low," he said, with a bit of resentment or disdain creeping into his voice. "We have footage of the burning of synagogues. We have the footage of the lynch—that is, the footage that survived, but there is a different standard of using the press here. Obviously we can take pictures of people killed and wounded and try to [get them to editors and producers], but we try to be more rational if you like, not so emotional."

The assumption seemed to be that journalists did not report the whole story because, heretofore, it had been too difficult to get the whole story. The press center was, accordingly, crammed with stacks of backgrounding material booklets with titles like "The Middle East Peace Process: An Overview," fact sheets like the one that listed the résumés of "Prominent Terrorists Released from PA Prisons," and press releases like "IDF reply to Palestinian claims that a Palestinian child was killed as a result of tear gas inhalation." (Apparently an IDF investigation found that a little girl featured in recent news photos and identified as a victim of IDF shooting at rioters had died at a Hebron hospital the day before the alleged incident.) It was, as Peled had suggested, a packaging of the rational, the logical.

On the other hand, it wasn't clear to me that the problem was a lack of information about the Israeli side. A few days into my stay, a piece came out in Britain's *Independent* by Keith Graves, Mideast correspondent for Rupert Murdoch's Sky News network, the third-biggest all-news all-the-time cable network, after BBC and CNN. Graves wasn't finding that he got too little information from the Israelis:

> In Jerusalem, the Israelis have taken over a floor of a hotel next to the bureau of a foreign television station. My telephone rings constantly with offers to put Israel's case. And yet the Israelis still complain that they are misrepresented. It does not seem to have occurred to them that this could be because they occupy Palestinian land in breach of UN resolutions. That they stand condemned by the UN for excessive use of force. Maybe the facts speak for themselves, despite the propaganda blitz.

(The same reporter later told Brit Hume, the Fox News anchor, that he didn't like the Israeli people because they are "arrogant.")

■ ■ ■

IN ANY CASE, ON THE MORNING of my first day I came down to have a look at the new press center. There was an inviting coffee area with soft chairs and polished urns of coffee, plates of cakes and pitchers of juice. A few husky TV cameramen milled around—apparently stoking up to head out into the field. I ventured a little further into the experts' room, where representatives from the IDF, the Israeli police force, the Ministry of Foreign Affairs and the Prime Minister's Office sat at folding tables behind the stacks of freshly minted press releases and booklets. The stacks looked suspiciously pristine and undisturbed, but never one to turn down anything free, I began loading my backpack with them.

The other reporter bait that the Government Press Office had provided at their center was a second room with a line-up of about fifteen computers all equipped with printer and internet connections. In 2000 it was not easy to connect from one's hotel room, so this was a real resource for many reporters. The problem was that to get to the computers one had to walk through the spokespersons' bullpen. And walk right through—eyes straight ahead as if guiltily avoiding eye contact—was what virtually all the newly flown-in reporters who used the center did. Except that they kept up a steady gabble on their cell phones, the young policemen and women, soldiers and foreign ministry types sitting at their temporary conference tables behind piles of backgrounders seemed as lonely as a Maytag repairman.

Certainly some of the people covering the conflict were veteran beat reporters whose newsrooms were probably littered with booklets like these, but it was clear from check-in chitchat I'd overheard that most of the people filling the hotel were what Israeli press spokesmen called "parachuters," reporters who had just flown in to cover a story they had never covered before, and were fairly disoriented. Anyone who'd ever worked as a press rep had stories about these parachuting news commandos. The best one I'd heard had come from Noam Katz, a foreign ministry spokesman who'd had to chaperone an Australian TV newsman to a West Bank checkpoint. As soon as they got there it was clear they'd arrived on a "slow day." This did not deter the TV man, who set up in front of a parked Israeli tank and began his stand-up with "It's the worst day of fighting so far. . . ."

"Mate," said a friend of the reporter's who was standing by, "there is *nothing* going on here."

"I didn't come all this way to say that!" the correspondent replied.

Once one got through the Israeli government's press rep area and into the computer room, the mood was quite gay. A number of these freeloaders of coffee, cake and internet time were photographers—second-class citizens by definition. Apparently grateful for a place to sit down after hours hefting a hundred or so pounds of video equipment, they spent a long time hanging out.

I soon met a young photographer from Britain. He said he was "a freelancer . . . well, actually a student in a photography program at the Hebrew University here in Jerusalem."

Perhaps to repair his image after this embarrassing admission, Chris Dearden, age twenty-five, hastily added that he went into "the territories" all the time with his mates and they were the real thing, blokes who sold stuff all the time to wire services like Reuters, AP and AFP, which all had bureaus next door in the Jerusalem Capital Studios tower. He was really glad he had savvy friends because just yesterday they'd been in the West Bank and had an experience that was "well, really a bit rough."

One of the prerequisites of reporting in the territories is the native guide. Dearden and his mates usually went around the territories with a guy named Yasser, a Palestinian who lived in Bethlehem and spoke "really good English." Yasser was a " journalist and human rights activist" too, although the young Brit wasn't sure whom Yasser was reporting for. Mainly, Dearden said, Yasser was "a really passionate guy who just wants to get the word out." He took them around for free and if they were stopped anywhere in the territories—at the entrance to a Palestinian hospital, for instance—Yasser would just say "they're okay" to hospital officials and they'd be in.

On a trip to Bethlehem the day before, however, Yasser wasn't available and they had hooked up with a new guy, "a local lad" they'd just met on the street.

"He took us down some back alleys where we saw a house on fire," said Dearden. "This was really cool . . . great stuff. Then he takes us through the back alley, where we passed a house that was under construction. On the ground floor that was only halfway built, there was a group of guys kind of huddled together talking— fedayeen types with balaclavas. Without thinking I snapped them. They all dive out, and several of them have guns."

One of the men shoved a gun barrel into Dearden's face. They then strong-armed him and his two friends into a stairwell and kept them penned there while presumably discussing what to do.

"There's a lot of shouting," Dearden continued. "One of the guys was really upset about us and had to be held back by the other men. One of them came over and took my camera. Jeez, I'd just bought it but I said okay.... Then there was a lot more talking among themselves. The interesting thing was there was no unity of opinion, but then they hand the camera back, to my complete surprise. I open it up real fast; take the film out: 'There, it's yours!'"

Dearden and the others were then free to go. "We were just about to walk away, when someone came up and kicked the guy who'd been leading us around. He turned around and gets one in the face and then there's like a complete melee. Hopefully our guy got away but as we were getting out of there, I looked back and saw that somebody got the absolute bejesus kicked out of him."

Dearden felt he had learned an important lesson: "I only know a handful of Arabic words but the most important one is 'Sura.' That means picture. I always say, 'Sura?' If it's 'Sura,' fine; if it's 'No,' I drop it really fast."

That night I had tea with Dearden and his two mates in the Isrotel lobby. I thought they were charming young scalawags and I imagined that young men who hung around ports in the 1800s trying to "ship out" and seek their fortune had been a bit like this. Like many photographers whose work has so much effect on history, they didn't have much interest in the back story of what they were covering, or the possible political ramifications of a shot they sold. They were like the photogs that Deborah Kogan had described. "If they talked about the conflict at all," she told me, "it would only be 'Are we going to see some bang-bang today?' or 'Are we going to see some rock and roll today?'" All they cared about was that it was a good shot, the kind somebody would pay a lot for, and that usually meant blood had to be spilled. Combat was preferred, but in a fix they'd settle for snapping the wounded in hospitals.

The eldest of the three, Renga Subbiah from Singapore, was thirty. None was married, and without dependents or much sense yet of their own mortality, they had the kind of bravura that every photo editor prays for. In their supply and disposability, they are the industry's equivalent of ground troops.

After listening to Subbiah brag about the many war zones he'd covered and the adrenaline high of being in the middle of combat, I tried to get back to my questions about journalistic (and photographic) "rules of engagement."

"Do the Israelis," I was finally able to interject, "put a lot of restrictions on photographers?"

"Are you kidding?" Subbiah chortled in his precise upper-class British accent. "Basically [bice-sic-ahly] you can take whatever you want."

Operating under the venerable TV news slogan "If it bleeds, it leads," the brash young mercenary had filled his film satchel that day with "very good stuff" featuring residents of the West Bank. This included a "dead guy" ("right up in his face I got"), a wounded child, and "a lot of people shooting."

"Awww," I teased, "so you didn't get anybody throwing stones? You gotta get some people throwing stones."

"Of course I got kids throwing stones," he said huffily. "I got a kid who looked like he was fooking eight."

"Eight is good," I kidded him, "but the guy who gets the five-year-old is gonna get the Pulitzer."

They chuckled.

"Are you allowed to take pictures of IDF soldiers? In combat?"

"Oh yeah," Subbiah crowed. "You can get up pretty much in their face as long as you don't interfere with what they're doing. I got one with his rifle pointed straight at my lens. I just ran out in front of this Israeli [soldier] and took a quick snap."

Photographing Palestinians was another thing. As Dearden put it, there was "the unspoken understanding" and they all acted as if it were not unusual to let sources take an active role in directing how they were photographed. The rules were easy enough to follow once you knew what they were—anyway, it's not as if editors were hounding them for shots of Palestinian youths with machine guns. It is not a photographer's job to investigate—just to document what is already considered "the news."

"[Palestinian] civilians don't mind being photographed," Dearden said. "They want the world to know how they are living. They think you are their only hope, otherwise they'd live and die and no one would ever know. But the Palestinian soldiers and fedayeen don't generally want to be photographed; we've done it once but we were friendly with the guys and he said it was okay."

"Basically the ones who are a bit older, they really, really don't want to be photographed ... if they're out in groups," explained Ben Smith, also British and in his mid twenties, "because they are part of [militias], probably they're wanted and they are afraid someone will recognize them from a picture."

"So the Palestinians *have* guns, then?" I asked. (So far, all the TV coverage I'd seen made it appear like all they had against the mighty IDF was stones and slingshots.)

"They only use snipers," Subbiah said matter-of-factly. "It's not like a guy would never walk up to the front lines with an AK-47. You can't see the sniper but he's up there somewhere."

"So it isn't always Israelis who instigate the shooting at these checkpoints?"

"They never instigate the shooting."

"Doesn't that mean that pictures showing Israelis solely as aggressors don't capture the whole story?"

It didn't matter, the three men all said in various ways. There was the physical fact of the blood, the injury on the other side—and the Palestinians had more. There was, they seemed to be saying, a kind of intrinsic moral superiority in simply being the one who'd spilled the blood.

"The general psychological notion of people around the world, people who watch TV," Subbiah began expansively, "is the one who gets hurt is the one who deserves the sympathy. The Palestinians have something the Israelis don't: a lot of dead guys."

"It's sad though," he added, "for many of those kids, it's very much viewed as a game until someone gets killed."

"But then they'll get to be a martyr," Dearden chimed in, "and they'll get respect and they're told they'll go to heaven and all that stuff."

Stories like the one told by Subbiah, Dearden and Smith were everywhere. I didn't have to look for them; they were usually offered up independently and rapidly in a conversation with a reporter or a photographer—if you could manage to get someone one-on-one.

I soon found myself talking to Jean Pierre Martin, a Brussels-based TV producer who worked for a European network called RTL TV1. Before he started his tale, Martin told me emphatically about his deep affection for the Palestinian people.

On October 4, 2000, about a week into the beginning of the new intifada, he had been on his way into Ramallah with his crew to work on a documentary-style feature he'd started about the lives of ordinary—i.e. noncombatant—Palestinians. They were at a check-point where a lot of children were milling around when four young men pulled up in a blue van and began to bark orders at the children. The children began throwing stones at the Israeli guard shack and after a while the men produced Molotov cocktails from their car and began handing them out. (Kids on the scene later told Martin that the men were from Fatah, a faction controlled by Yasser Arafat.) Other crews were on hand, but apparently they didn't see this development or didn't consider it newsworthy, because Martin was the only producer who told his crew to start shooting it.

After a few seconds, one of the young men saw that Martin was filming them (not just the little boys) and he strode over; several seconds after that, all the people on the scene, including the stone-throwing children, surrounded the crew. The men took the camera from the hands of the cameraman and disappeared with it. Meanwhile the crowd of youths began to surge around them, trying to hit them. One youngster got his hands around Martin's neck and started choking him. A Palestinian cameraman who had been on the scene working for an American company came to help them. By talking to the crowd, the Palestinian cameraman was able to calm "this very nervous situation" and get the mob to back off. They were not out of the woods, however. The young men put Martin and crew in their car and drove to PA chief of police headquarters. The men who had seized them vanished into the police shack and Martin was left outside with a guard.

It was one of the scariest experiences of his life, Martin said. He stood in the hot sun outside the police shack under the eye of an armed guard while his fate, or at least the fate of his expensive equipment, was being decided in a language he couldn't understand. Palestinian men and women deemed to be collaborating with Israel— "supplying intelligence" is the usual charge—are often given

summary and very public executions in the West Bank. There are
no known incidents of executions of foreigners, but that was little
consolation to Martin at that moment.

He began punching numbers into his cell phone and calling
people he knew all over the world, anyone who spoke Arabic, virtually anyone he could think of who might be able to intervene, to
put in a good word, to tell the police that he and his crew were not
spies for the Israelis.

Fortunately, the Palestinian cameraman who had saved them
before arrived at the police station. Once again he began to negoti-
ate on their behalf and finally an agreement seemed to have been
reached. The Arabs indicated that he should erase the tape and leave
with their equipment intact. At that point, Martin and company
were very happy to take this deal. Still, on his segment that night,
Martin did an unusually gutsy thing. He opened with a black
screen—"This is what you would have seen if we still had the tape
. . . . ," and then told how the tape had come to be erased.

The incident didn't affect Martin's interest in telling the world
more about the lives of Palestinian civilians, so he returned about
two weeks later to continue work on his documentary. Just after he
and his crew passed through the Qualandia checkpoint before entering Ramallah, however, they noticed a white jeep following them.
UN personnel ride around in white jeeps, as do many TV crews, but
this van didn't have UN or PRESS written in big black letters on
the side. The vehicle followed them to their filming site and when
the film crew parked, the men in the van parked with them. This
time the men (who Martin believed were from Palestinian Authority intelligence services) didn't wait for him to begin filming; they
walked over and began to search his vehicle; again they pulled film
out of the camera and erased it and they smashed one of the still
cameras belonging to the crew. Then they told Martin to leave, and
to make sure that he did, they tailed him back to the Israeli checkpoint. Just as Martin and crew pulled up to the checkpoint, a bullet
fired from the Palestinian side whizzed over their heads.

Martin reported what had happened to Israel's Government
Press Office. GPO staffers must have passed the story along because
an Israeli spokesman recounted it in a daily briefing to the press.
Martin's story was then used again when Israel submitted a

memorandum to the Sharm el-Sheikh Fact-Finding Committee (of the Mitchell Commission), which had been convened by President Clinton to study conditions impeding a peaceful settlement of the Israeli/Palestinian conflict.

By the time Martin finished repeating the story to me, he was fuming, but as in the Cristiano case, his anger was directed almost entirely at the Israeli government, which he said had put him in danger by "exploiting" his story. It was as if Fatah or PA intelligence (if that's what they were) had no role in his problems and as if the Israeli government had been wrong to use his story as an example of the difficulties it faced in its media war with the PA. Because the Israelis had publicized his story, fellow reporters and West Bank honchos now believed he was "allied with the Israeli government." "They," he said with fury about the Israeli government, "have made it very hard for me to go back."

It was always like this in my conversations with press people in those months. If there was any anger it was directed at "Israel" or "Israelis" or "the IDF." Palestinian Authority coercion, if mentioned, was discussed blandly, with a peculiar lack of what the psychologists call "affect."

The *Christian Science Monitor*, for instance, had noted mildly that "in the West Bank and Gaza, ordinary Palestinians on the street display a media saviness. The presence of a camera will intensify rock-throwing, says one TV cameraman for a major US network. He adds that he has been aggressively discouraged from filming Palestinians with guns."

After mentioning "aggressive discouragement" with a seeming lack of curiosity about who did it or what it actually entailed, the CSM reporter immediately informed us that Israel limits the press as well—though their limits "are more formal, as all journalists are required to sign a form at the censor's office, agreeing to submit reports on sensitive military matters for approval."

Most journalists I talked to would immediately counter even mild questions about coercion in the territories by telling you about censors in the Israeli government and requirements that you "submit your copy." "Submit to censors" apparently has a dramatic ring because this phrase appears a lot in stories about the region. In reality, says Baruch Binah, who was liaison to the foreign press for the

Israeli mission to the United Nations in New York during the late 1980s, "the censor's office is quite feeble because in today's world [with the internet and speedier transmission times] this kind of review is unenforceable." And actually, the clause about "censors" comes with a big qualification. It says quite clearly in the agreement one has to sign to obtain a press card that a reporter is expected to submit only materials that are "relevant *to the security of the state*" (my emphasis). In other words, the government is not asking for— and certainly could not cope with—the great bulk of material that reporters generate. The biggest loophole, as far as reporters are concerned, is that the decision of what is relevant to state security is left up to the reporter. Given the chance to self-report, of course, the vast majority of reporters don't bother.

"It's a pain in the ass," Matthew Gutman of the *Jerusalem Post* explained to me. "So nobody does it, and if nobody else does it, why should [my paper]? We do it only with very, very sensitive stuff usually having to do with nuclear policy, things like that. Except that there's nothing in this country anymore that's sensitive. There's very little that is not known And nobody from the foreign press ever submits anything, ever, it's just not done. It's just seen as stupid. What's the point? You can get away with [not submitting]."

He also went on to say that on the rare occasion he had to have something vetted he found that the censors were quite efficient and understanding of time constraints. They'd never hung a story up "more than an hour because they understand you're gonna run it anyway."

I was still interested in the possible chilling effect of getting beaten up by PA affiliates for photographing the wrong thing, so I decided to try talking to people in the bureaus. First on my list was the RAI bureau in the Jerusalem Capital Studios, Riccardo Cristiano's former place of employ. My GPO press card got me inside the office tower. Most bureaus' doors were unlocked and even standing open. Inside RAI's newsroom, a stout man with a white beard turned to me with a rather beatific smile. After doing my usual introduction spiel I said that I had "a few questions about Riccardo Cristiano." The room instantly went silent and people froze as the bearded man seemed to be composing an answer. Finally he smiled thinly and said, "We have nothing to say about that."

Several days later, I was in the Isrotel press office when a GPO spokesman handed me a freshly minted press release. It concerned a new letter that had just appeared on the front page of *Al-Hayat al-Jadeeda*, a daily that is owned and operated by the Palestinian Authority. This letter had been signed by "The Palestinian Journalists' Union" and was addressed to Jerusalem's Associated Press bureau. According to the GPO's translation, the union complained that AP had "an intentional policy of presenting a false picture of the just struggle of the Palestinians against the Israeli Occupation and its aggressive and inhuman actions which contradict all international human rights conventions." If the bureau did not change its coverage, the letter went on to say, the group would adopt "all necessary measures against AP staffers."

Was the Israeli translation accurate? What were "all necessary measures"? What AP stories were they talking about? I had tons of questions and spent half a day trying to speak with members of the Palestinian Journalists' Union, with no success. But how was AP taking this? It was somewhat understandable that RAI had not wanted to talk about the Cristiano affair. Their own reporter had become a global symbol of bad journalism—an international Jayson Blair before the fact. But AP had nothing to be embarrassed about. Why shouldn't they be willing to talk about conditions affecting their reporters? After presenting myself to a series of junior editors and making my pitch to each, I was finally told that Jocelyn Noveck, the bureau chief, would see me.

The front page of *Al-Hayat al-Jadeeda* is prime editorial real estate, I said; the Palestinian Journalists' Union must be a well-connected group. So did she think this memo would have a "chilling effect" on her reporters in the field? She brushed this question away: Publications get threatening letters all the time; neither side in a conflict is ever happy with their coverage; we are bombarded with complaints by both sides. All true, I agreed, but this is not New York; the Italian television stations who had provided the videotape of the Ramallah lynching had apparently taken death threats quite seriously. Two bureaus, the one that actually shot the film and the one afraid they would merely be *seen* as the one that shot the film, had ended up recalling correspondents.

Noveck sighed. "Certainly there is risk—physical risk. From crossfires and such," she added hastily, as she wanted to make it perfectly clear that she wasn't talking about Palestinian Authority intimidation. Lowering her voice a little, she added, "This is a very difficult story to cover ... on both sides, as I'm sure you know." She then asked that everything she said from that point on not appear in print in any form—attributed, unattributed, as background, nothing.

■ ■ ■

THERE WAS ANOTHER FELLOW WHO SEEMED to like the Isrotel press center's free email and cake: a radio reporter from France who carried all the equipment he needed—a shoebox-sized tape recorder and a mike attached with a long, curly cord—slung over his shoulder. Another essential, his boxy European-make rental car, was parked in an underground level of the Isrotel. Like the other foreign press vehicles, it had every available surface pasted with black masking tape spelling out "PRESS" and "TV." As we drove to the American Colony for drinks one night, he watched me struggling to see the street between the huge letters covering the passenger side of the windshield and giggled. "They keep them from shooting me ... sometimes," he said.

I liked that he was a giggler; he had that cute French whimsicality that was certainly preferable to the dead seriousness of the American journalists. Though I'm sure our politics were very different, it felt like we'd found common ground when I groused that political correctness was ruining America. "Zat is so true," he said passionately. "They won't let you smoke *anywhere*."

Only about five-foot-five, with a big nose, a weather-beaten, tanned face and shoulder-length blond hair, he looked like an aging surfer-gnome. He was also the quintessential "parachuter," having just come from Colombia, where he had reported on drug cartels. He acknowledged that it was a surreal existence, and I got a sense of what our information technology has wrought as we clattered along dark streets while he drove and gabbled on his cell phone, taking and making about four calls in the space of half an hour, to friends in Paris, London and Brazil, switching languages when necessary. "No, no, no," he giggled to one friend, "I'm not in Rio anymore. Right now I'm in Israel."

Despite his whimsical *c'est la vie* shrugs and his "what can you do?" moues, he too was unhappy with this new outbreak of peace. He had nothing to do, he said, but his bosses were basically keeping him on ice here just in case stuff started up again. He grumbled about not being able to get a room at the American Colony and about being stuck in Jerusalem where there is "no night life." He sighed wistfully when he thought of Tel Aviv, a mere hour's drive away, where "the women on the streets are the most beautiful in the world."

"So do you, like, have a girlfriend there, any girl you met who you can go visit?" I asked. "No, they won't have me," he grumped. "They say I am a goy. They all want some nice Jewish guy." So he spent his days wandering around the email area looking like a shaggy lost dog.

One day I tried to help him out. "How can you say there's nothing going on?! This is when the interesting part starts!" I crowed. The Israeli and Palestinian Authority governments had just signed the Sharm el-Sheikh cease-fire agreement, but the Israelis were saying they wouldn't stick to it unless they saw that the PA was making an honest attempt to stop members of terror militias or anyone else from firing on Israeli soldiers or civilians. The PA was not known for aggressive crackdowns on terrorist elements, and it would be quite unprecedented if they actually were able to shut down, say, Hamas. (Anyway, the PA's intentions were unclear since within an hour of the signing of the cease-fire agreement, the charismatic young Palestinian Marwan Barghouti, head of the Tanzim militia—an offshoot of Arafat's force, Fatah—had led several hundred in a march through West Bank streets chanting "the intifada will continue." All the way along his route he was assured by shopkeepers that it had "never ended!!")

"Either way," I enthused, "you've got a story: if the PA is out there knocking heads you've got a story and if they're looking the other way and sitting on their hands . . ."

No, he shook his head listlessly, his editors wouldn't be interested in that. He might, he said desultorily, "go back to the territories

... find a widow who'd lost her husband in the intifada. . . . Human interest ... Like that."

"Oh for God's sake; everyone's doing that! Here's one I haven't seen." I started another pitch: "You gotta go to Gilo; it's a settlement on the very southern tip of Jerusalem." (Actually, with a population of about 45,000 in 2000 it looked just like a town.) "It's interesting because the buildings—all these space-agey, modern buildings made out of slabs of white cement—run right up to the lip of this deep valley. There's actually a road that runs along the crest of the valley. Across the way, so close you can see it—almost into it—is a Christian Arab town called Beit Jalla. Anyway, terrorists from towns like Nablus come into Beit Jalla, kind of hold the town hostage, get on the roofs of houses and stuff and shoot into Gilo—not a hell of a lot of shooting, just enough to scare people and perhaps ferment hostility between Israeli Jews and Israeli Arabs, which, of course, is very destabilizing for Israel.

"But Gilo's elementary school is right near the edge of the valley, right in the line of fire," I continued. "Shots come through the window during the day while the kids are in school or at least they're worried that they will come through, because now that side of the school is buried in sandbags. So the kids are sitting there every day trying to study behind these sandbags!

"What a great picture! Oh, I forgot, you're radio. . . . Well, cute story!! Bit of human interest! A 'Neighbors but Enemies' kind of thing ..."

No, he said distractedly, his thoughts apparently far away—probably on the beaches and golden girls of Tel Aviv.

A foreign ministry official named Arye Mekel told me later that "ABC had done a nice feature on Gilo"—a cameraman happened to be on the scene when an Israeli policeman was shot and was given on-site emergency medical care. But in general, he said, the foreign press didn't go to Gilo to talk with Israeli citizens under fire from Palestinian gunmen in Beit Jalla. "They didn't see it as part of the story."

My burst of enthusiasm about Gilo as a subject was probably a result of my trip there the day before. I had decided to go late in the day, with no idea of where the place actually was. I had felt asinine, like the prototypical parachuter, telling a cab driver that I couldn't give him an address or even a street name in Gilo, that I just wanted to go where "they've been shooting at each other. You know, Gilo and Beit Jalla."

"You want to go to Beit Jalla?" he asked, whipping his head around to stare at me.

"No, *across* from Beit Jalla—where the shooting's been going on. I'm sure *anyone* will know," I sniffed, trying to retain a shred of dignity.

After he got into downtown Gilo, he asked for directions until he got to the cliff road, then stopped just long enough to let me get my feet on the ground and sped away.

I found myself alone, on a deserted street, at the lip of a great biblical desert valley where the sinking sun made the Jerusalem stone sprinkled on the hillsides glow with golden light. Across the way, there was a sprinkle of little white houses that were Beit Jalla.

A very nice view, but not the hopping, happening scene I'd expected to find. After the news media's portentous mentions of Israel "sending in the IDF," I'd expected to see the place full of soldiers, tanks, cement barricades and walkie-talkies, but the only sound was the whoosh of wind through the cypress trees. I looked toward the skyline and the rim of the cliff, where one would stand out in backlit silhouette to anyone across the way with a rifle. There was one cement barrier apparently placed there for the protection of a solitary dark-olive military jeep parked next to it.

So there were other people here—people I'd actually, in the line of duty, have to interview. I suddenly felt quite conspicuous. Looking down at my body and taking inventory for the first time that day, it turned out I was wearing a form-fitting white satin-like nylon shell. It would have looked nice at a cocktail party, but here it suddenly seemed inordinately unserious and bourgeois. I supposed I had thrown it in my suitcase because it was sleeveless.

At least I seemed to have done some sensible thinking in the costuming of my lower half. Air circulation was apparently the operating principle. There could be no other reason for choosing to put on a 1950s style circle skirt, in battery-acid green with brass snaps down the front. Air circulation also seemed to have factored into the choice of black platform slides with a toe-cleavage-baring front. The ensemble was topped off by a wide-brimmed straw sun hat. It had gotten a little crumpled in my suitcase but was still serviceable if I punched out the dents. I also wore futuristic-looking black plastic wrap-around dark glasses, which I'd purchased earlier in the fall for skiing. Overall it seemed I had managed to construct the costume of a slightly eccentric, middle-aged British lady, maybe one who had signed up for a tour of "Birds of the Holy Land."

For about the millionth time in my life I wondered why I'd never been able to get the professional-journalist-chick look right. I never looked squared away and serious like Christiane Amanpour. Things were always flying off, coming unbuttoned, hiking up, crumpling like accordions (linen dresses, for instance). My hair was always flying in my face and I always had to pause in the middle of note-taking or question-asking to claw it out of the way. By the time I'd gotten the hair out of my mouth, the Important Public Official would have a bemused look on his face (if I was lucky) or (if I was unlucky) would have turned away and fallen into the clutches of Celia Dugger of the *New York Times*, a relentless, frighteningly methodical and aggressive reporter I had sometimes found myself near when I had covered city schools for the *New York Post*.

So I did what I had done many times before. I took a deep breath and tried to stay focused on the mission. If I'm wearing unserious clothes, this entails assuming a character, an alter ego who matches the clothes but also allows me to get the job done; and that alter ego is usually one of those perpetually cheery, chatty British enthusiasts—Dame Edna on safari, perhaps. She has actually worked pretty well for me. People tend to roll their eyes and snicker when she isn't looking, but she means so very well and is ultimately so unthreatening that you just have to humor her. I pointed my pink shellacked toenails at the jeep and strode forward.

A husky young soldier with a crew cut was sprawled on the hood wearing a disgruntled and defiantly bored expression. He could have put himself behind the cement barricade or inside the jeep, where he wouldn't have presented such an obvious target silhouetted against the setting sun, but he reclined against the windshield with his stiff, booted legs stuck out in front of him and his rifle resting across his lap.

"Hallo!" I said heartily to the men inside the jeep, who seemed slightly more receptive. "Stephanie Gutmann, the *Weekly Standard*

—a magazine in Washington, D.C. . . . um, an important magazine actually, quite influential in Washington . . . doing a little piece about . . . all of this," I said, sweeping my arm in a way that took in Gilo, Beit Jalla, the whole of Israel and the bit of Jordan that could be seen in the haze on the eastern horizon. (I wish I could say I said "Doing a little piece about you chaps over here," but I did not.) The young fellow on the hood set his chin and turned to stare out over the valley. In general the IDF does not have a very high opinion of foreign reporters.

"So how about all this shooting, then?" I asked, soldiering on. "This is where it's all been going on, right?" As the young soldiers in the jeep were now smirking, I found myself addressing a lanky man, mid-forties or so, with a trendy shaved head who was sitting in the driver's seat and regarding me through round, rimless spectacles with what looked like bemusement and even a little kindness. It turned out he was lieutenant colonel in the reserves, an engineer in his civilian life who'd been reactivated and sent here to Gilo several months ago, primarily, he thought, because he spoke English quite comfortably and could talk to reporters.

"No shooting today. I'm sorry not to oblige you," he said in the mock-serious, ironic Israeli way that the English and the Americans (both cultures reared with an expectation of hearty false friendliness) sometimes feel is insolent. "Most of the shooting is now at night. It's become a nighttime intifada."

"Now why's that?" I asked, with an air of someone who's getting down to some serious journalistic brass tacks. "This intifada has been rather a daytime thing, with the rock-throwers and all. . . ."

"It's a cease-fire," he replied dryly. "If they shoot at night, they won't get photographed and they won't get caught. And the PA can still say there's a cease-fire."

From the perspective of a seasoned officer of the IDF, the shooting wasn't terribly serious. Though they had actually zinged bullets through windows of apartments on the cliff-line, the terror militia members who had decamped in Beit Jalla generally missed targets and so the lieutenant colonel had concluded that the shootings seemed mostly designed to keep the residents of Gilo on edge. It was quite bothersome to the Christian Arab residents of Beit Jalla, however, because terror militias had infiltrated their generally

peaceful town and set up shop in its church. Now the terror militias' pot shots at Gilo were drawing return fire and Israeli helicopters sometimes circled overhead to attempt to draw a bead on the
shooters.

"Come back tonight," urged the officer, with an amused and
ironic twinkle in his eye. "Perhaps around 7:30 you'll get to see
some fireworks."

I am sorry to say that I didn't go back that night. By the time
7:30 rolled around, I had staked out a prime barstool at the American Colony, and it seemed much more sensible to stay there with
my new best friend—a Palestinian auto-dealership owner, with residences in Ramallah and Los Angeles, who kept buying me drinks—
rather than head out into the darkness to huddle on a windy ridge
with a tiny contingent of Israeli soldiers. Apparently lots of other
Westerners felt the same way. The place was packed with foreign
reporters and news crews, as usual.

Thinking about it later, I couldn't figure out why news organizations who seem almost vampiric in their pursuit of injury, fear
and suffering had mostly avoided the citizens of Gilo, who by all
TV standards were "embattled." But I gradually realized it was
because Gilo—built on land formerly occupied by a Jordanian army
base, which Israel seized in the Six Day War after being attacked
from that same army base—was what media outlets termed "a settlement." The issue of where international law permits Israel to
build towns and enclaves is too complicated to go into here, but suf-
fice it to say that most media outlets tended to accept the Palestinian Authority's interpretation, which holds that territory Israel
occupied after 1967 is illegally occupied. Accordingly, though a few
outlets described Gilo as "a neighborhood built on disputed land,"
most could not mention the town of Gilo without describing it as
"a settlement," "an illegal settlement," or even, as NPR's Jennifer
Ludden put it in an October 23, 2000, report, "a settlement built in
occupied East Jerusalem." To pay attention to the plight of residents
of Gilo, in other words, might have appeared uncomfortably close
to expressing support for Israeli settlements.

An IDF spokesman I talked to the next day supported what
the commander in Gilo had said: One was seeing what appeared to
be a new strategy, a sort of hybrid built on lessons learned from the

1988 intifada. Kids were used during the day, and the guns came out at night when the press would have more trouble filming them.

But during cease-fires (or at least the relatively quieter periods), a good journalist uses the time to catch up, to explore the history, to focus on interesting arcana. That's when you do a human interest feature, explore "the roots of the conflict," and so on. The soldiers of the IDF seemed to be prime material for a quick feature. Most of them spoke English so there would be no need to pay a translator; they were, almost to a man and woman, gorgeous, tanned, and hard-bodied. Unlike U.S. soldiers, who tended to respond with pre-approved boilerplate, IDF soldiers seemed to say whatever they thought.

So why weren't editors putting these tough-but-thoughtful men and positively epic-looking women on their covers in "On Patrol with the IDF" features? The IDF had recently opened its infantry units to women, so theoretically once they worked their way through the training pipeline, there could be Israeli infantry-women. But nobody was even working this evergreen "First for Women" angle. People were "doing" Palestinian widows and orphans, though occasionally a grieving Israeli wife was thrown in, apparently as a stab at balance. I did eventually find a writer for a Portuguese magazine who, along with his five-foot, perpetually grinning, Sancho Panza-like sidekick photographer, was doing a close-up piece about the IDF. They were quite excited that they would be riding with an IDF unit down to their base in Gaza, where they would stay while putting together their profile. The writer half of the duo said it had been extremely easy to set up and, like me, he was amazed that the material was virtually untouched.

The view from the IDF's side of the barricades wasn't the only good story that nobody would touch. I was hanging out at the spokesmen's tables talking to yet another IDF soldier/spokesman, a guy who had grown up in the United States but made *aliyah* in time to be drafted in the IDF and then get called up again for reserve duty in the second intifada because his American voice was needed at the press center. Since nobody ever approached his table, I monopolized his time. The conversation eventually came around to the subject of what is often abbreviated as "incitement"—a sprawling category that includes inflammatory broadcasts on the PA's television channel, sermons by imams extolling the glory of martyrdom, and school-books designed to instill rage at Israel. Reporters had a weird way of distancing themselves from the "difficult" issue of incitement. When it was mentioned at all, it was as something that Israeli offi-cials "complained" about or "alleged."

Occasionally, reporters wrote about children recruited and trained for martyrdom, but once again, like the riots that "erupted" on the Temple Mount seemingly spontaneously, the training of children just seemed to happen in a vacuum. Reporters appar-ently didn't like to acknowledge that there were adult Palestin-ian persons who strategically, consciously and deliberately conducted a war against Israel with child soldiers. These facts com-plicated the victim vs. aggressor template. In a post-Dura story titled "Palestinian children enact a mock funeral for a 12-year-old boy who was shot to death," for instance, Richard Roth of CBS News quoted a Palestinian boy from Ramallah as saying, "I was waiting for my school to pelt the Israeli army with stones." The next sentence in Roth's report was, "Palestinians are the youngest population in the world ... [a]nd its large youth popu-lation has played a visible role in the latest cycle of violence." At around this time in the segment, viewers might have expected that Roth would explain the boy's comment about "waiting for my school" to start throwing stones again. (What is the involve-ment of the school? Do they practice stone-throwing at recess? Take field trips to checkpoints?) But he never tackled such ques-tions in any part of the piece. Toward the end, Roth hinted at cau-sation by bringing in and making vague statements about Marwan Barghouti, widely known as the leader of the Tanzim, a sort of tiger-cub brigade of terrorists-in-training:

> The man charged with shaping those young minds is 40-year-old Marwan Barghouti, the leader of a youth movement called "Tanzim" or apparatus. Barghouti said the young are critical to the Palestin-ian movement, both as foot soldiers and as symbolic victims of Israeli aggression. "I think our job is to continue in this intifada," he told CBS News, "to work, to continue, to strengthen this intifada."

That, in total, is the Barghouti reference in the piece. In other words, Barghouti has something to do with "shaping young minds," but once again, adult Palestinian action is seen in soft focus from behind the scrim.

One exception to the hands-off treatment of Palestinian agency was an unusually concrete piece by John Burns in the *New York Times,* August 3, 2000, which described the reporter's visit to a Nablus summer camp "run by the men who handle psychological warfare for Yasir Arafat," where 25,000 teenagers (the youngest Burns quotes is fifteen) are "learning the arts of kidnapping, ambushing and using assault weapons." One of the exercises that Burns observes is a mock kidnapping in which a teen is disguised as a reporter in order to get close to and kidnap another teen posing as an "Israeli official." One would have thought Burns would have taken special notice of this training. After all, we know about traditional terror tactics, but teaching children to exploit the special access afforded journalists was a relatively new wrinkle that could have merited a feature-sized piece. But Burns' unusually explicit story disappeared in the tide of words, and did not seem to inform the *New York Times'* subsequent reporting of power dynamics in the second intifada.

In late October 2000, the subject of the PA's incitement became difficult to ignore. Conventional wisdom held that the crowds who had lynched the two Israeli soldiers on October 12 had been goaded to this peak, in part, by frenzied urgings of local imams (who often coordinated with the PA) and that the rumblings from the mosques had only gotten worse. Forced by events, so to speak, the *New York Times* finally broached the subject of "incitement"—very, very delicately.

In an article titled "A Parallel Mideast Battle: Is It News or Incitement?" the *Times'* William Orme said that what some PA officials defended as straight news, some Israelis called incitement to violence. "For Israelis," Orme wrote, "examples of 'incitement' include the standard recitation of long-standing Palestinian political demands by Palestinian cabinet ministers—among them their claim to East Jerusalem and Palestinian refugees' 'right of return' to their former homeland." What were Israelis worried about then? Orme added that "Israelis cite as one egregious example a televised sermon that defended the killing of the [two reservists]," and then he offered a quick peak at the sermon transcript: " 'Whether Likud or Labor, Jews are Jews,' proclaimed Sheik Ahmad Abu Halabaya in a live broadcast from a Gaza City mosque the day after the killings." That, in total, was what Orme allowed *Times* readers to see of the sermon. He left a lot out, such as the sections in which the imam had said:

> Oh brother believers, the criminals, the terrorists—are the Jews, who have butchered our children, orphaned them, widowed our women and desecrated our holy places and sacred sites. They are the terrorists. They are the ones who must be butchered and killed....
>
> . . . .
>
> Have no mercy on the Jews, no matter where they are, in any country. Fight them, wherever you are. Wherever you meet them, kill them. Wherever you are, kill those Jews and those Americans who are like them.

Without these deleted paragraphs, of course, the quoted Israeli officials seem like oversensitive cranks who want to prevent Palestinians from listening to what Orme called "unapologetically nationalistic coverage."

The young IDF spokesman I had been speaking to said he had a lot of material on "incitement." Since nobody else was clamoring for his attention, we walked into the large room, adjacent to the free computer area, where the press conferences were held. He pulled down a feature-film-sized screen that hung against one wall and turned on a VCR. Soon the screen was filled with a compilation of recent images from a PA-owned-and-operated television channel featuring footage of children of about ten training at what looked like a boot camp. The children seemed to have been rehearsed. There were no smirks at the camera or mistakes. Filmed from a low angle, so they appeared taller and more *Übermensch*-like, the children went through their paces, hurling rocks, slinging slingshots, firing rifles, and even doing a drop-and-roll maneuver that any Hollywood stuntman would admire. The black-and-white newsreel-type footage was accompanied by martial music and a frenetic Arabic speaker who, the English subtitles (added by the Israeli government) informed, was calling for a jihad in which "streets would run with blood of the Americans, the Jews and the Israelis."

Seeing real incitement (as opposed to talking about it as an abstract concept) is ... inciting. *"Have you sent this anywhere?!"* I asked the reservist/spokesman. "To CNN," he said, but the person that press officials had spoken to there had been dismissive. The Israeli press officers had continued to push the issue as the months went by and CNN had finally said they would have someone look at the tape—as if they were doing the Israeli Government Press Office a favor. CNN didn't want to rely on an Israeli government translation of the Arabic, and they would have to call in their own translator, which all meant that they didn't think they would get around to the tape for a while. A year had gone by and the GPO hadn't heard anything else from CNN or seen a piece on this subject.

Indeed, it would be about a year and a half before major outlets began doing stories about the training of children and financial awards to the families of young "martyrs," but those stories were often like Richard Roth's exercise in the use of the passive voice, in that they simply stated that such things happened without linking them to the Palestinian Authority (in the case of the training) or to Saddam Hussein (in the case of the financial awards). And the stories didn't run in the beginning of the second intifada, when children were the primary soldiers, but later in the news cycle, when older suicide bombers took over. In other words, the context of the stone throwing was not supplied when it would have helped make some sense of the pictures that people were seeing.

But I was left to wonder how CNN could have ignored such explosive, newsworthy material. Perhaps they had a good reason, I figured, so for days afterward I tried to set up an interview with a CNN producer, and for days I was repelled by CNN flacks at different levels—told to submit an interview request here, or there, or somewhere else, or in triplicate—until I gave up.

■ ■ ■

ON THE DAY BEFORE THE 2000 presidential election in the United States, the Israeli Ministry of Foreign Affairs held a press conference in the same large room. It was to be a general briefing conducted by Nachman Shai, who was acting as the chief spokesman to the foreign press until a permanent one was appointed.

Everything on Shai's résumé seemed to recommend him for the job. He had been a reporter himself for the Israeli Broadcasting Authority (IBA), Israel's state-owned radio station, and had covered the Yom Kippur War from front-line tank units. His beautifully written columns, which appeared in the *Jerusalem Post,* were often about the media and showed an insider's understanding of the subject. Most important, he had a proven record of winning the public's trust. During the first Gulf War when Saddam Hussein loosed a barrage of Scud missiles at Tel Aviv, Shai, who by then was a senior official at the IBA, had become Israel's version of Walter Cronkite—the calm, informed voice telling Israelis when to go to their "sealed rooms" and when it was safe for them to come out.

Broadcasters at the IBA had been caught by surprise on the night of the first missile attack. Details like who would take the central role of "chief spokesman" and where the broadcast center would be located had not been straightened out yet. But "into the vacuum of the first night burst the soothing voice of Nachman Shai at 2:48 am," as *Ha'aretz* put it. "When Shai [who began his broadcast from a cell phone in a car riding to the studio] first went on the air, he knew only a little more, if anything, than his millions of listeners . . . he simply understood that someone had to say something." One of the things he advised was "Drink lots of water." It was Shai, not Prime Minister Yitzhak Shamir, who developed what one Israeli writer called a "personal dialogue with the public" while they waited for instructions in their sealed rooms. Shai had even been able to finesse a compromise between the IDF and the press corps. The IDF wanted no reporting of Scud damage whatsoever (so as not to reveal information that would allow the Iraqis to adjust their targeting), an idea that made the foreign press corps indignant. Shai mediated a compromise: Reporters were allowed to file daily stories, but each was assigned his or her own personal censor—usually just some hastily called-up army reservist—who looked over the reporter's shoulder as he typed to catch any security breeches. Shai announced this policy to the press in a take-it-or-leave-it manner, with a now famous statement: "If you want to commit suicide please do it somewhere else."

In 1990–91, the late journalist Michael Kelly had traveled to Saudi Arabia, Iraq, Egypt and Israel to write a series of dispatches about the United States' attempt to liberate Kuwait, which were eventually put together in a book titled *Diary of a Small War*. Kelly was in Tel Aviv during the Scud attacks at the height of Shai's popularity and watched him conduct a press conference. At first Kelly found the spokesman "an unlikely heartthrob, a slight smallish man with sloping shoulders and mousy brown hair that fell in a thick and unruly shock over his forehead. He had a modest, pleasant smile and wore wire-frame aviator-style eyeglasses and a green uniform that was, in the Israeli fashion, purposely casual—no jacket, no tie, the sleeves rolled up." Kelly eventually understood that "a flashier type would have made everybody nervous . . . by his very blandness and reticence Nachman Shai reassured."

But whatever had endeared him to Israelis ten years ago did not seem to be working its magic in the fall of 2000 on foreign press come to cover the second intifada. For one thing, Shai was not working in his native language as he had on the IBA radio. His English is generally very good but he has a heavy accent (his th's came out as z's, so "with" came out "wiz," and "sealed rooms" was "sid rhums," as Kelly put it) and occasionally he didn't make the best word choices. For this the Israeli press—which is unremittingly critical of its own government—had already begun to gang up on him. *Ha'aretz* reported that journalists "mocked Shai for consistently mispronouncing the word 'hostilities' and for saying that missing businessman Elhanan Tennenbaum [who was thought to have been taken hostage by Hezbollah in Lebanon] had 'disappeared at his own initiative.' "

Another possible factor was Nachman's appearance. His superstar run was now ten years old. Shai is a Germanic sort, with a thin, angular face. As he had aged, his cheeks had sunk in and the corners of his mouth had drooped. His hair was now white and shorn very short against his skull, and he wore rimless eyeglasses. With his impassive gaze and ramrod posture, he looked like central casting's version of an SS commander—a perfect image for the narrative, increasingly popular among some journalists, that Israel was conducting a Nazi-like ethnic cleansing on a helpless population. One Israeli journalist seemed to be talking about Shai when she groused that while Palestinian spokespeople were accessible, Western-educated and fluent in English, "Israel's various speakers appear at times as grim white men—mostly security types and power lawyers—mumbling monotonic vague statements that often sound like orders being issued."

In front of foreign press, who no longer gave Israel the deference accorded to victims, and after a prolonged period of battering since early September {both from Israelis who didn't think he was doing a good job and from foreign press who are reflexively suspicious of Israeli officials), Shai seemed to have retreated into a kind of bunker behind his spectacles. On the other hand, I thought on November 6 as I watched the foreign press enter the press conference area, perhaps it was the kind of job that would leave anybody battle-scarred.

People had begun to fill the row of folding chairs in front of the podium. In a row toward the back, slouched in his chair, his arms thrown over the seats next to him, sat a tall, beefy, red-faced man with a blondish beard. Flanking him on either side were two much smaller, thinner, paler and worried-looking people, who seemed to hang sycophantically on his every word. As reporters filed in, the three bent their heads together and whispered.

I had just chosen a seat near the front where my tape recorder would get decent quality when I heard the low voices of two men speaking in English behind me: "Anyway, he's got this olive orchard. It's been totally destroyed. They used bulldozers," one said in an excited, breathless tone. "He's really articulate, very open to interviews. It's a *really* good story, trust me."

"Wow! Great! Can you give me his number?" whispered the other.

An Israeli press office aide began passing out the GPO press release I had seen earlier in the week about the Palestinian Journalists' Union threats to journalists at the Associated Press. Copies were passed to the two men, but they didn't break their conversation to look at it and didn't bother to stop their conversation when Shai launched into his preliminaries.

"So, where do we stand today?" Shai began in a conversational tone. He listed some news items to convey the-state-of-the-state: Prime Minister Barak was on his way to Washington for a meeting with President Clinton. The Palestinian Authority was still not keeping to their end of the Sharm el-Sheikh agreement.

After a few more bulletins, he said, "There was another item I want to draw your attention to." Holding up the release about the threats to the AP, he began reading the part that said "the [Palestinian Journalists' Union] will adopt all necessary measures against AP staffers as well as against the AP bureau." Suddenly a booming voice from the audience broke in: "But Israel, but Israel does this too; why don't you talk about that?" It was the big beefy man I had noticed when I entered the room and he was very red in the face.

"Yes Conny?" said Shai rather weakly, as if trying to pretend that the man had actually raised his hand and then asked a question, as is usual practice.

"But Israel does this too, why don't you talk about that?" stormed the man. "We have proof. I think you should cover that also, we have crews who are threatened by IDF."

"Conny, if you have specific examples and you want to tell us about them, they will be investigated," Shai said.

Shai started to talk again, but the man bellowed, "And the state of Israel should stay out of this."

When another journalist asked the beefy man to identify himself, Shai smiled thinly and said, "This is Conny Mus, someone I know very well."

I didn't know it at the time, but after some research I found out that Shai (indeed, the entire Government Press Office) was on first-name basis with "Conny" and "knew him very well" because he had been based in Jerusalem since 1982 as a correspondent for Dutch TV. Mus was a past president of Jerusalem's Foreign Press Association chapter; he had bought a house in West Jerusalem and had become a sort of grand old man of the Middle East journalism scene. Indeed, if one wants to track Mus's career on the internet, he pops up with regularity, as a sort of fixture in dispatches from reporters and photogs who've just come back from the Middle East. Mus is usually seen sailing past IDF and Israeli police barricades with newly arrived journalists and photogs in his wake—as in this account written by an evidently awe-struck young photographer, who goggles when Mus and the rest of his crew "come across several Police check points turning back the traffic. These are expertly bypassed by Conny. . . . We approach several cordoned–off sections at full stretch, David and Conny briskly sliding the barriers aside themselves and waving their accreditation as they go."

Before the PA came to the territories, Mus had been fairly sanguine about Israel's restrictions on the press. In 1993, for example, he told a journalism newsletter, "Every journalist signs an agreement on the censorship law. You have to show the army every story that is leaving the country, but of course this is not how things work out in practice." In the same article he went on to complain about the dangers of working in the Gaza Strip: there were threats "by phone, [and the danger of] being beaten up or nearly killed by bullets.... If you go into the Gaza strip or one of the other areas, you should always go with at least two persons. [Accordingly] most images of violence in the occupied areas are shot by Palestinians. They use 8 millimeter handycam videos. Their pictures go around the world."

But during Yasser Arafat's regime with its vigorous repression of a free press, Mus had become a zealot on the subject of *Israeli* suppression of media. In 1997, for example, the AP reported that "three Palestinian cameramen (ABC, AP-TV and Reuters) were shot and slightly wounded with rubber-coated metal pellets as they filmed a demonstrator burning Israeli flags." Mus, as chapter president of the Foreign Press Association, was asked to comment and he said, "The soldiers appeared to be targeting journalists.... It is clearly no coincidence that six of our colleagues were shot down in recent days."

And now, at the press conference, Mus was bellowing again: "Every reporter for French TV is going around with security because they get threats from Israel!"

"Conny, I have no such reports," Shai replied evenly. "I can't do anything about them if I am not told about them. Of course there should be no threats to the media...."

"Make an investigation," Mus broke in.

"I'll do my best to find out what happened but I can't do it if I don't know what happened and where. For us the freedom is something very basic," said Shai, apparently trying to turn the conference back to the subject of de facto Palestinian censorship.

Mus continued to break in.

"You've told me about these cases three times already; if you want me to say my line a fourth time, I'll do it again," Shai said finally.

"I would love it," said Mus, settling back in his seat with a grin.

"If you bring me specific facts—times, places—I will do an investigation, but I am not familiar with any union of Israeli journalists sending such a letter; if Israeli military or civilian should threaten you it is something . . ."

But now Shai was interrupted by another voice. This time it belonged to a very young man speaking broken English with an Arabic accent. As Mus looked on like a doting parent, following every halting word with encouraging nods, the young Arab asked why "people" were "taking press cards from the Palestinians who work for the foreign press." He hadn't finished describing the situation before Mus, who was halfway out of his seat, interjected, "People with valid GPO cards are not being allowed to do their job!!"

"I don't know of anybody taking away press cards," Shai said. "But we do have a closure applying to Palestinians right now. Is that what you're talking about?"

Bending toward the young Arab to be heard over Mus's interjections, Shai told him, "Palestinian journalists or photographers carrying GPO cards are not allowed to enter Israel. Nor is any other Palestinian, because this is the situation now; this is the closure, the closure applies to everyone. Carrying a press card doesn't give you any advantage over others." The young man sat back, apparently at the end of his English, or satisfied with the answer.

Now there was finally quiet at Mus's end of the room, and there was a new question. "Do you have any comments on the investigation of the death of Mohammed al-Dura?" asked a reporter who was apparently American. (By now, everyone had dispensed with the formal practice of stating one's affiliation before asking a question.)

"It hasn't been finished yet," said Shai. "It takes time. The IDF is in the middle of an investigation. I encourage the IDF to come to their conclusions."

There had been a few more questions about other matters when a natty white-haired man in a crisp checked shirt spoke up. "Nachman," he asked, in a British accent, "can I ask you a follow-

up on the investigation of al-Dura? If *Ha'aretz* has done its home-
work it seems clear that the two technical experts had reached their
conclusion before they started the investigation and the investigation was designed to prove that he was killed by a Palestinian.... Is
that reeeally," he drawled in a voice heavy with sarcasm, "a professional way to conduct an investigation?..."

At that point Shai could have offered a generic defense—that
Ha'aretz was only one of Israel's five daily newspapers, or that it
wasn't at all "clear" (except possibly to *Ha'aretz*) that the investigation had been "designed" to prove anything and that Israel had
done fairly unflinching investigations of its military conduct before.
Instead he said stiffly: "As I said before, this investigation is being
handled within the IDF."

Now an American woman spoke up, asking whether the Israeli
government had anything to do with a recent explosion in Lebanon
that had demolished the house of a suspected terror militia leader.

"There was a stage," said Shai, "when anything in this area—
and maybe all over the world is attributed to Israel—and sometimes
it's true, but in many cases it's not. Maybe it was just an accident.
The guy is an expert with explosives. Anyhow the northern border
continues to be very tense. We know that Hezbollah is planning to
hit all the way from Lebanon into Israel." Shai was referring to
recent news reports alleging that Hezbollah had developed new,
longer-range missiles capable of hitting Haifa or Tel Aviv instead of
being limited to kibbutzim in the Galilee region.

"What about the complaints about the violations?" the same
woman asked sourly, referring to Lebanese government charges that
Israel had flown into its air space.

"Of what, by helicopters? I have not heard about any complaint. We will investigate it. But there was no military action under-
taken by Israel in Lebanon that I know of...."

At the use of the phrase "we will investigate," there were tit-
ters around the room and knowing looks were exchanged.

A French reporter wanted to know who had allowed Yigal Amir,
the Jewish extremist who was serving a life sentence in jail for assas-
sinating Yitzhak Rabin, to do an interview from his jail cell with
Israel's Channel 2 Television. Shai allowed that he didn't want to
talk about "this person who we all hate" but "no one knows for the

time being who actually made it possible for him to give such an interview...."

"And you'll be doing an investigation of that, I suppose?" piped the British man. It got a big laugh.

Shai didn't seem to get the joke. "Yes, but an internal one, without international involvement."

"Do you subscribe to the conventional wisdom that President Clinton will have less leeway [to continue his attempt to broker a peace agreement in the last months of his presidency] if Bush gets elected?" asked another.

"Now here is something I really can't speak about," said Shai coldly. "I cannot predict who will be president of the United States some 24 hours from now or what his policies towards Israel will be...."

"That's just bullshit," the guy behind me muttered.

The press conference was over. At times it had been painful to watch. Most of the crowd had seemed like they had not come to listen to what Shai had to say or to learn anything new, but on the off-chance that he would commit some kind of gaffe. It had felt like watching a bearbaiting.

Shai hadn't growled or raked anybody with his claws, but he had let opportunities to educate and contextualize go by. The question that had hung in the air, for example, while the French reporter tried to find out who had allowed Yigal Amir to do a television interview was whether hawkish, conservative forces in the Israeli government (a group to which many in the foreign press ascribed great sinister powers) could have surreptitiously allowed the interview as a way to help Ariel Sharon, who was then in the running to become the new prime minister and whom the foreign press generally saw as akin to Attila the Hun. It may have been a farfetched idea, but it was the kind of conspiratorial angle that some reporters seemed to love. An adept press spokesman would have sensed this subtext and defused the notion, perhaps with a joke that would put the blame for the error on ratings-hungry TV executives—something like, "Well, we know Channel 2 is concerned about their ratings but I think I would have tried for an interview with Monica Lewinsky."

As soon as the room began to clear, Helene, my new French magazine-writer friend, and I jumped to our feet and hurried over to Shai. As with everything in this miniaturized country, this important man turned out to be too easy to get to. No guards or flacks sprung to block us as we scurried toward him. He made no moves to hustle out of the room, and he didn't haughtily scan my jacket for my credential to see if I was worth talking to. (Perhaps because we were the only people trying to talk to him anyway.)

Unable to resist the opportunity to tell somebody what to do, I bellowed to him over the din of the departing press herd. "Look, you've got to say more than just 'We'll investigate.' You've got to talk to the underlying agenda. Couldn't you see that ultimately they were asking you 'Did you guys kill al-Dura? Did you kill him on purpose?'? You could have made some generic comment about the fog of war. Most of these people have no idea what combat is like."

"We've said that already," Shai muttered.

"But zeez are new people," Helene practically shrieked. "What eef zay joost come yesterday. You have to say it again!"

"No, no, no," he kept shaking his head. "They would not understand."

"God, they can be frustrating," I said to Helene as we walked away. "They just don't get it."

"No," stormed Helene, who had been around the Israeli press apparatus much longer than I had, "they are stooopeed."

I often got in arguments with Israeli press spokesmen when I said I thought they didn't explain enough—that they didn't use a reporter's question, any question, as a taking-off point to "educate" the just-parachuted-in press people. After all, the Hebrew word *hasbara*, which is often used as a substitute for the phrase "public relations," actually describes a more subtle combination of education, persuasion and representation. So where was the education part? It often seemed like the Israeli officials naively assumed that any reporter who appeared on their shores had been following the continuing conversation, the fine points of the Israeli/Palestinian conflict. Israeli press reps had a habit, for instance, of saying things like "the Sharm el-Sheikh agreement calls for Yasser Arafat to end incitement and he hasn't done that," an answer that takes for granted that reporters have a full sense of what "incitement" in all its gory specifics really entails.

In contrast, Palestinian spokesmen had a way of turning this most complicated conflict into an extremely simple story line, one that could be transformed easily into headlines. Fielding the kind of questions that Shai had been dealing with, they would sidestep specifics and offer broad contextual answers. If a reporter, for instance, were to ask something like "Why did the Palestinian Authority [screw up in some way]," a PA spokesman would come back with something like "This would not have happened without Israeli occupation" and so on—a response that would put the focus back on Israel. As Israeli journalist Fiamma Nirenstein wrote in 2000, "Palestinian spokesmen . . . like Saeb Erekat or Hanan Ashrawi . . . never miss an opportunity to begin their story from the top: this is our land, and ours alone, and the Jews who are occupying it are employing armed force against an unarmed people."

I often wondered why Israeli press people seemed uncomfortable making "sound bite" answers directed at the viscera, not the mind. Maybe one reason is that Israeli culture has been shaped by military exigencies and so has adopted military values, which stigmatize complaining, wool-gathering and even, to a certain extent, explaining. In the field, explanations for failure or success—and lessons learned from them—can come later. Explanations, going over the past, are a luxury. In the immediate crisis state of military action, only the question "What are we going to do now?" is useful. The ubiquitous Israeli expression "Nu??" which translates directly to "So?" but in practice means "Spare the histrionics and cut to the chase," is an expression of this sense of impatience and focus on utility. Unfortunately, visitors to Israel often experience this curtness as rudeness.

Another part of Israeli culture that has hurt their ability to win media wars is, paradoxically, the disputative, verbal, parsing culture of the Jewish religion. People who take words seriously do not like to be imprecise and are frustrated by the limitations of the sound bite: Hence the long, qualified, clause-ridden answers one hears from Israeli spokesmen.

There was yet another reason underlying what I saw as a fundamental Israeli discomfort with explaining, and that was that explaining oneself to the world may have felt, to stiff-necked Israelis, too much like begging for approval. Of course it is the older generation, those old enough to remember 1948, who feel this most strongly, but Israel had been created for a "new Jew" who would not have to explain, to rationalize, to ingratiate, to bargain for his patch of earth. Survival would no longer depend on someone else's whim, someone else's sufferance. Getting your own house, so to speak—getting out of the land controlled by the czars or the Nazis—must have felt like a liberation from the opinions of others. Maybe that is why Israeli founding father David Ben-Gurion famously declared, "It's not important what the goyim think, only what the Jews do."

In the mid-1970s, Saul Bellow had dinner with Prime Minister Yitzhak Rabin and found himself pushing against this Israeli attitude when he tried to persuade Rabin, the first "Sabra" or native-born Israeli prime minister, "that Israel had better give some thought to the media intelligentsia in the United States."

Bellow was concerned that Israeli leaders like Rabin didn't realize the extent of American ignorance about Israel. "Very few Americans," he pointed out, "seem to know, for instance, that when the UN in 1947 proposed the creation of two separate states, Jewish and Arab, the Jews accepted the provision for the political independence of the Palestinian Arabs. It was the Arab nations which rejected the UN plan ... [but] the Arabs have succeeded in persuading American public opinion that the Jews descended upon Palestine after World War II and evicted the native population with arms."

"Israel has not been effective in its publicity," Rabin replies tersely.

"Yes, but Arab propaganda has become extremely effective!" insists Bellow.

Clearly bored with the topic, Rabin says airily, "They have a talent for that sort of thing."

The attitude continued. At the beginning of the Oslo negotiations in the early nineties, Foreign Minister Shimon Peres remarked, "If you pursue good policies, you do not need *hasbara*, and if you pursue bad policies, no amount of *hasbara* will help." When Israel elected Benjamin Netanyahu in 1995, they elected a prime minister who was intensely interested in *hasbara*, but he did not last long in the office. Then came Prime Minister Ehud Barak, who made cuts in the government's *hasbara* apparatus, perhaps because he thought he was going to win the *hasbara* jackpot of all time by negotiating a two-state solution with Yasser Arafat at Camp David. He briefly won the world's approval when it appeared to most that Arafat rejected a historic opportunity, but Arafat regained his footing and launched one of the greatest public relations campaigns of all time, the very camera-dependent second intifada.

But these were the experiences of the old guard. It was also clear that there was a young guard waiting in the wings, men who were less ambivalent about explaining. They were men like Jonathan Peled of the foreign ministry (the one who had talked to me on my first visit to the press center) and Danny Seaman of the Government Press Office. Both were forty or thereabouts, old enough to have participated fully in Israeli life—with military service, for instance—but young enough to be more conversant in the language of imagery, which has come with television and the internet. Men like this seemed to have no great love for *hasbara* but they saw it as a necessary chore of government and, at the very least, winced openly when their elders made *hasbara* mistakes. As I got ready to leave Israel, I wondered who would win out—the older generation of former generals who disdained explaining themselves to reporters, or these young men who were willing to coordinate the media war with the ground war.

The problem was that even if the old guard suddenly got out of the way, these younger men would still be stuck working with the pittance that Israel budgeted for *hasbara*. From 2000 to 2004, for instance, the Israeli budget (admittedly strained by defense costs and recession) allocated only $9 million, less than 1 percent of the yearly total, for the Ministry of Foreign Affairs' press division, supposedly its flagship press department. In theory, the MFA could call on the help of three other press staffs (for the IDF, for the Prime Minister's Office, and the additional one called the Government Press Office), but these brother divisions were separated from the MFA and from each other by geography, operating philosophy and a network of old political feuds. Put another way, the four parts of the *hasbara* whole needed each other but did not share their marbles well. As the agency that manages the more than one hundred embassies around the world, the Ministry of Foreign Affairs' press staff was mandated to be the brains of the press operation both abroad and within Israel. This made sense in theory. MFA staffers are specially chosen because of their intelligence, their language abilities, their diplomatic ability, polish and charm. But a good MFA staffer is rewarded for competence *by being moved out of Israel*— to head a consulate in another country. Therefore, as disgruntled staffers of the other three press divisions sometimes put it, the MFA "was always reinventing the wheel." Just as a new crop of fresh, young faces had figured out how to deal with the often combative, demanding and suspicious foreign reporters that come to Israel, they were transferred out to run the embassy in, say, Argentina. This impermanence—and a tendency to starry-eyed "Peace Now" politics—was one of the reasons that the IDF's press division, which is responsible for state security, was not in a hurry to work with the foreign ministry.

And therein lay another central problem. The IDF press division was given the most attention and the most difficult questions (Why did you demolish that house? Why did you shoot into the crowd?), but the rights of a free press and the needs of an effective military are eternally in conflict. It's extremely difficult to find a balance between giving out too much information, which endangers lives in the field or puts the kibosh on upcoming operations, and giving too little information—the terse IDF standbys like "We are investigating the incident" or "Our investigation showed the soldier involved acted within guidelines." The IDF needed spokesmen who could find that balance, who could improvise good, generic, informational statements when military news first broke—and they were not finding many of them. Still, ever mindful of state security and the fear that civilians in, say, the MFA would blurt out something dumb, the IDF leadership continued to demand that other divisions defer to it when questions about military matters came up.

To throw a wild card into the mix, the prime minister had his own hand-picked press representatives with offices just outside his own. These spokesmen had high profiles and were known to most reporters, but their jurisdiction was unclear; so they represented another leg in this four-legged race to the *hasbara* finish.

About a mile away from the MFA was yet another division and another factor in *hasbara* power-sharing: the Government Press Office, the much-maligned poor cousin of the operation. This division had a few brain-related functions: providing summaries of the Hebrew-language press to visiting foreign reporters and offering them a menu of background briefing sessions. But overall, they existed to serve the body of the press beast. GPO staffers issued press cards (or at least reviewed the applications for them), rescued visiting media's electronic gear stuck at border control, rescued reporters held up at border control, obtained street clearances for TV or radio people who needed to, say, tie up a city block for a live broadcast, helped reporters with visas, assisted the spouses and household help and child-minders of the reporters with visas. They found wheels—at one point the GPO supervised the importation of twenty-five bulletproof cars—and helped reporters locate housing.

The GPO, as I saw it, was also a sort of dark horse in the operation. Others in government dismissed them as clerks, as logisticians, but ultimately journalism lives or dies by logistics. Also, since most of that division's staff were civil servants—not political appointees who came in and out with every change of prime minister—the GPO was actually the division with the best institutional memory and the longest-term relationships with reporters.

In any case, the parts of the *hasbara* apparatus may not have been meshing well, but by late 2000 it was clear that Israeli citizens were going to storm government barricades if the situation didn't improve. Israel is served, on the print side alone, by no fewer than five dailies (running the political gamut from the very liberal *Ha'aretz* to the very conservative *Hatzofeh*), and prescriptions for fixing the *hasbara* problem filled the opinion and editorial pages of these papers. Everyone seemed to have a diagnosis. The editorial board of the *Jerusalem Post*, for instance, pointed out that:

> Israel is losing the war of words once again. Since the start of the current troubles, bundles of Israeli spokesmen, speakers and various advisers have been taking turns at making jumbled statements on Israel's striving to live securely. Yet Israel's information campaign is ever more confused and confusing. Prime Minister Ehud Barak's media adviser, Nahman Shai, for instance, welcomed the final statement of last month's Arab summit; then Barak soon proceeded to

call it "threatening." Following last week's car bombing Shai acknowledged Palestinian efforts to curb the violence, then Deputy Defense
Minister Ephraim Sneh went on to blame Yasser Arafat for the
bombing.

I wanted to stay and watch Israel grapple with this new, wired
intifada and a Palestinian Authority that was using the media with
such skill, but my funds were running out. I had to go back to the
United States, where I could write up what I had just seen, collect
my fee, pay my rent and struggle to understand the conflict just like
everybody else—except that now I'd have to struggle to understand
from afar, through the filter of the *New York Times* and network
and cable television. I had to hope those reporters would do their
best to ascertain and report the truth.

FIVE

JENIN AND THE
MASSACRE THAT WASN'T

I'm working in a press center we've set up. A guy comes in; he's a photographer for some news organization; his office is someplace in Europe; he himself is, I don't know, Chinese maybe. I ask him if he needs some help. He says something to me in very bad English, something I can't understand. We're just at an impasse. Finally he says: "Where blood? Blood: Where I go?"

—Arye Mekel, government spokesman for Israel
during Operation Defensive Shield

At least in New York you can keep talking to the people who construct this product we call "the news." You can't roll a bowling ball down Broadway without knocking out a couple of writers, but it was the photographers I really wanted to talk to. Everyone agreed that in an image-driven conflict, these were the guys with the power.

I asked the news photographers I knew if they knew anybody who'd been working in Israel and the territories recently. They had no idea where he was, they said, but the guy I should talk to was a rising young star named Chris Anderson. Supposedly there was a small hierarchy of guys who always got the work, the best assignments, and he was at the top. Indeed, when I went to track Anderson down, it turned out he had just been awarded the Robert Capa Gold Medal Award from the Overseas Press Club of America for excellence in war photography, and as coincidence or the zeitgeist would have it, he had just been in the territories photographing the second intifada for the *New York Times Magazine*.

He had touched down briefly in New York and I was able to reach him on his cell phone as he was barreling down a busy midtown sidewalk. Weaving in and out of pedestrian traffic, he was clearly distracted—which probably had something to do with the direction our conversation soon took.

I started with the question I'd asked his colleagues: "What was it like to shoot out there, in the Israel/West Bank nexus?"

"Well it was okay," he said, "except for the Israelis, who were absolutely barbaric. They shoot at children, in cold blood."

Where had he seen this? I asked.

At demonstrations around checkpoints, he said, and it was "at children whose only crime was to have thrown stones."

"But isn't it true," I asked, "that soldiers work from tear gas, to rubber bullets, going to live fire only if they are in mortal danger from someone in the crowd?"

"You sound just like the Israeli government," he said in disgust. He knew the Israelis shoot real—not rubber—bullets at civilian crowds, he said, because he'd had one "go right by me when an Israeli soldier had targeted me."

"How can you know he was targeting you? Were you in a combat zone? On what side were you standing?"

Well, he admitted, he was in the line of fire and on the Palestinian side of the shootout, "but the soldiers could see very well that I was press, with my blue helmet on and my obviously Scandinavian features." He never took his accusation to the Israeli foreign ministry, which could have started an investigation that might have ended with the discipline of a soldier, because, he explained, "I'm here with bullets going every which way and one seemed to have been targeted at me, and sometimes they are deliberate but it would still be very difficult to prove."

He went back to railing about the brutality of the IDF: "In four weeks of intifada I have watched, all the gunfire came from their side—except at night," when he would see Arab men with arms.

"Did you take any pictures of those guys at night?"

"No, first of all because it was at night," he said. It would have been hard to photograph without flashes and such, which tend to alarm the photo subject. "There *was* shooting on their side then, but if you see a Palestinian with an automatic weapon, you're not going to take his picture."

"Weeeeell, why not?" I pestered.

He made a choking "duh?" kind of sound as if he couldn't believe the stupidity of this question, and after a pause he said primly, "Because he doesn't want you to and I don't take people's picture if they don't want me to.

"Anyway," he continued "it isn't like Palestinians don't want you to take pictures. In general the Palestinians are usually happy to let you take their picture; at funerals they say 'Please take this!' and 'Please take that!' They want you to take a picture of the body; they'll push you forward so you can see it, like 'See! Here!'"

I said something quite mild in defense of the Israelis—along the lines of Israel had a right to accurate coverage and a stream of pictures showing one side without their guns and the other side with guns distorted reality.

"Then you are in the minority, if you think that," he shot back. "Then you are the only one! Virtually all of the European press agree with me!!"

"Oh yeah?" I replied. "Well, why is it that when I was there, one of the people most fired up about unbalanced coverage of Israel was a French magazine writer?"

"A Jew," he said.

"No, I don't think she was."

It was a ridiculous point to argue—as if one reporter more or less changed anything about the general bent of the European press.

"What was her name?" he asked in a mocking tone. The conversation had gotten quite childish, but we seemed to be locked in.

"Um, Helene Keller-Lind. That's K E L L E R hyphen Lind, L I N D. I don't think that's a Jewish name; that doesn't sound Jewish to me."

Anderson made a skeptical noise.

I couldn't believe it. We were scouring the names Keller and Lind for Jewish content. Why did it suddenly seem so important to prove that a name was "not Jewish"? What was this, 1938? He must have also realized at this point that the conversation had strayed into a sensitive area, because we soon mustered some pretend cordiality and said stiff goodbyes.

But I have never forgotten this exchange. First of all, there was his charge that he'd seen the IDF "target" children. Even if one knows that the terror militias put children on the front lines, it was a horrible image and if it was true, as he claimed, that he'd seen a child die at a demonstration, it explained his seething tone. On the other hand, we'd never settled on a definition of "child" (someone under eighteen? that would include half the armies in the world) and when I'd mentioned the Palestinian Authority's recruitment of "martyrs," he'd snorted and indicated that this was just more Israeli government propaganda.

But what really bothered me was that, once again, I was seeing a journalist (a photojournalist in this case) who seemed to live very comfortably with dual standards on the issue of press censorship. In other words, it was okay for Palestinian fedayeen to virtually dictate how they would be covered ("they don't want to be photographed with guns, so I don't do it"), while Israeli soldiers and government officials weren't given the right to a choice. He also demanded that these people, to whom he gave the barest respect, protect his life in the middle of *their* hazardous and crucial war—simply because he was engaged in the holy work of journalism. He seemed to assume that IDF soldiers could simultaneously defend a border, try not to get killed themselves, avoid hitting civilians who were liberally seeded amongst fedayeen, and keep a running inventory of the whereabouts of the various press people in the combat theatre. But if the soldiers messed up, if they got slightly addled in handling all these jobs at once and zinged a bullet past a photographer's cheek or even hit one (as has happened), the IDF was "targeting photographers" as part of some dark conspiracy against a free press.

And it's not like the photographers made the job of protecting their lives any easier. It was clear from Anderson's photos of that period (for which he was soon to win another award, this time from Kodak) that he spent most of his time on the Palestinian side of the barricades, usually up close and personal with rock-throwing and slingshot-wielding subjects, sometimes in the middle of—or at least very close to—angry mobs. An Agence France-Presse article made this point pretty plainly: "Chris Anderson gets within a couple of meters of the young Palestinians. He says he does not want to die and does not consider himself brave, but if he is not in the front line he will not get what counts."

Meanwhile, as Anderson had put it, "virtually all of the European press" agreed with him that Israeli soldiers target journalists—as an expression of government policy. A piece in the English newspaper the *Observer* appeared shortly after our conversation. It was titled "The First Casualty" (as in "the first casualty of war is the truth") and it described a meeting of Jerusalem's chapter of the Foreign Press Association that had been called to discuss "harassment of reporters covering the intifada." *Newsweek* bureau chief Josh Hammer, an FPA member, had recently been "detained by Palestinians while working in Gaza." When Hammer was released after a few tense hours by the armed Fatah members who had seized him and another journalist to send a message that they were "ready to kill Americans" if the U.S. didn't change its policies, *Newsweek* management released a statement expressing relief that the journalists were safe and decrying what they called "a kidnapping." The FPA wanted to talk about this incident, but they weren't especially concerned with the "kidnapping" or "detainment" part. The group was far more disturbed, the *Observer* reported, by "the Israeli government's use of the incident as an opportunity to accuse the Palestinian Authority of harassing journalists":

> If journalists were facing any intimidation during the present intifada, it was from the Israeli army, which [the FPA] accused of directing gunfire at them.... That harassment is psychological as well as physical and at its worst has smacked of the tactics of the Soviet Bloc.... [D]ossiers of alleged anti-Israeli bias have been sent to editors ... and correspondents who have fallen foul of the authorities have complained of being targets of humiliating searches when they leave the country.

Why would Israel resort to such tactics? The *Observer* had a sinister explanation:

> A new front is opening in the intifada. Faced with increasing international criticism of its handling of the new Palestinian uprising, the Israeli government of Ariel Sharon and its allies in the powerful and influential pro-Israeli lobby, have stepped up their efforts against

international media reporting the current crisis. News organizations that fall foul of Israel are accused of being pro-Palestinian or at worst anti-Semitic.

Ideas of this kind were a bit more muted on the U.S. side, but nonetheless they dominated discussions about press freedoms in the Middle East. At around the same time, early 2001, for instance, the *Christian Science Monitor* titled a piece "Israel Launches Image Management Campaign." According to the *Monitor*, Israeli-style image management involved "strictures placed on the media as well as mounting danger faced by journalists, [which] promise to significantly curtail the flow of information for shaping opinion."

The *Monitor* reinforced its implication that Israel was censoring the flow of information and covering up dark deeds by then quoting a *Ha'aretz* columnist who had said, "When a city is occupied horrible things happen." Then the *Monitor* quoted the Committee to Protect Journalists, which had recently stated that "gunfire from the Israeli Defense Forces was the most dangerous and immediate threat to journalists in Gaza and the West Bank."

■ ■ ■

AFTER SEEING THE PROBLEMS ISRAEL faced in getting its side of the story out, I was not comforted to read shortly after coming home to New York that the Israeli government was actually cutting jobs in its press offices. Prime Minister Barak felt that the entire Government Press Office—the arm of the press apparatus that handles logistical matters—could be severely downsized and eventually eliminated. He made staff cut after staff cut, so that by November 2000, director Daniel Seaman found himself heading a department of one. Seaman's sole employee was a young man named Andy Luterman, who was having trouble keeping up with the announcements of press conferences and the digests of Israeli media that he was supposed to be supplying to permanently based and visiting non-Israeli reporters. When Luterman went on vacation in November, emails from the GPO announcing press conferences and such suddenly stopped. "I wouldn't be surprised if [the downsizing] is a reason Israel hsan't had good PR during the [early months of the second intifada]," Seaman told *Ha'aretz*. "We have two hands and a foot tied behind our backs." Luterman was scheduled to come back in December but would have to leave again in January to do army reserve, just as the country would begin preparing for May elections.

By late November, I found myself reading in the Israeli press that the press center on the ground floor of the Isrotel had been shut down as well. "It was barely used," said Nachman Shai, "and each organization and [foreign] press division has its own ways of retrieving information. We did not need to waste funds on such a facility." Shai looked on the bright side. The exercise had not been wasted. The country had "jumped into the cold water," he said. "We had to build a whole operation from scratch, but now we are really ready."

Maybe Shai was right. All the resources they had piled on seemed to have been mostly ignored, from what I'd seen—the spokespeople who sat by themselves, the press releases that lay in stacks unread. On the other hand, it was better to have something like this around than not, if only as a kind of placeholder. If there was a vacuum, Palestinian Liberation Organization and PA spinners were quick to fill it with themselves, their lines, their written handouts, their quotes-for-publication. Which, according to media analyst David Bedein, who runs a Jerusalem-based organization that tracks coverage of Israel, was exactly what was happening. He visited the Isrotel one day in November and "found some of Arafat's press representatives ... sitting in the lobby, talking to reporters. I sent a query to the [Ministry of Foreign Affairs] and the answer was, 'The Israeli government does not have the budget for such things.' Arafat can now rule the roost of the media in Jerusalem with no competition."

■ ■ ■

THE ISRAELI/PALESTINIAN MEDIA WAR was a gripping, emotional subject, but it became harder to concentrate on as urgent things began to happen at home. By January 2001 the economy in New York City had begun to slide into recession. Competition for small scraps of writing work was reaching surreal levels. Then the slowing economy got a real body blow: September 11, 2001.

While my neighbors and I spent September 12 trying to get our phones to work, and to understand what had just happened to our city, another significant battle in Israel's media war with the Palestinian Authority was beginning:

On that day, people poured into the streets in several West Bank towns to fire guns in the air, cheer, dance, wave flags, hand out candy and generally celebrate the attack on the United States. The biggest demonstration—about three thousand people, according to an estimate in the *Times* of London—occurred in the terror militia stronghold of Nablus. An AP reporter/photographer filmed the huge demonstration for AP's television wire service and bounced it to the bureau in Jerusalem. Just as AP was about to put the footage on their wire, however, bureau staffers got a phone call from their photographer in the field. He was standing in the office of Nablus's governor; gunmen on each side of him held guns against his skull and had been ordered to shoot him if the video of the demonstration went on the wire. AP's Jerusalem bureau chief, Dan Perry, called New York. There was, one assumes, a *brief* conversation and then AP agreed to let the governor's men destroy the film.

But Danny Zaken, a reporter for the Israeli Broadcasting Authority, who is married to an AP reporter, heard the story of the cave-in from several sources and reported it on his radio show. In the meantime, other outlets—the *Times* of London, for instance—reported on the demonstrations and, following the venerable journalistic principle of never passing up an opportunity to celebrate the failures of a competitor, they also reported that AP had bowed to pressure and destroyed its own videotape of the event. AP's Jerusalem bureau was soon deluged with calls from enraged Israelis. Ra'aan Gissin, chief spokesman for the recently elected prime minister Ariel Sharon, called AP to demand release of the tape, and told the press that the affair was "journalism under terror." But soon AP's Jerusalem management got another call, from the PA minister of information, Yasser Abed Raboo. Raboo is reported to have told AP bureau chief Perry that such nasty events need never arise again if his reporters and photographers were "more careful." In fact, he said, he "could not guarantee their safety" in the territories unless they learned to be more "careful." Bureau chief Perry has said that he had yet another meeting with Raboo sometime later in which Raboo apologized for threatening the wire service. (And perhaps he did apologize—after he had been assured, even just through implication, that AP reporters had indeed learned to be "careful.") In any case, it was not the last time AP would be threatened by the Palestinian Authority.

All of this was a kind of tipping point for Danny Zaken. He put his frustrations in print in an Israeli journal of media criticism, where he derided the "peculiar behavior of the foreign media in Israel," which were "critical and bitter toward Israel but cowardly forgivers toward the Palestinians." He explained,

> There are more than 600 Palestinians employed by the different foreign tv stations, news agencies and newspapers in Israel and the territories and they are manipulated and directed by the Palestinian Authority ... as "Tanzim" [i.e. as a kind of militia] to deliver censored information usually by using threats and violence.

Soon another example of media bias occurred in which another major story was almost consigned to oblivion. This time, however, PA intimidation was not involved. This time, the culprit was an odd marriage between journalistic mistrust of Israel and Israel's party politics.

Israeli intelligence had been tracking a 4,000-ton freighter called the *Karine A* for some time; they observed it stop in an Iranian port to take on cargo and then sail into the Red Sea in the direction of the Gaza Strip. The Israeli Navy waited till the ship was in international waters and then a unit of commandos boarded it on January 3, 2002, at 4:45 in the morning while the crew was still asleep—which allowed them to seize control quickly and with little physical coercion. When Israeli naval special forces operatives searched the hold, they found fifty tons of weaponry—rockets, anti-tank missiles, mortars, rifles, RPGs, and hundreds of pounds of C-4, the powerful, highly moldable plastique explosive that had been used in the bombing of the USS *Cole* and the Khobar Towers barracks and as a lining in the shoes of would-be plane detonator Richard Reid. The commandos interviewed the captain, who told them he was a senior officer in the Palestinian Authority's naval police and that the weapons had been ordered by PA officials.

If the weapons had indeed been ordered by senior PA officials, their mere possession would have been a contravention of the Oslo Accords and an indication that the PA was talking peace while

covertly supplying terror militias with very deadly arms. The Israeli
Navy made the catch on a Thursday, but apparently afraid that the
story would leak, and trying to beat the Shabbat deadline (sundown
on Friday), when much of Jerusalem grinds to a standstill, the IDF
press division called a press conference for 2 P.M. on Friday afternoon. The Sabbath hadn't officially started, but this was tantamount
to calling a press conference late on a Saturday afternoon in the
United States.

Most of the local Israeli outlets sent reporters, but as Lt. Col.
Miri Regev of the IDF spokesman's office explained tartly, many in
the foreign press "apparently wanted to rest on the weekend."

Big audience or not, IDF chief of staff Lt. Gen. Shaul Mofaz
was ebullient. "In a daring and complicated mission carried out by
navy commando troops, air force pilots and the intelligence, the IDF
took control of the ship, which is now in our hands," he told the
reporters who had shown up. "This operation, executed about 500
kilometers from the shores of the State of Israel, was professional,
precise, coordinated, and a complete surprise done without a single
casualty. . . . From the weapons we examined, it appears that most
of [the cargo] was Iranian and included both short- and long-range
Katushas [rockets] . . . and many other weapons.

"Use your imagination," said Mofaz. "If, God forbid, they had a
122mm Katusha inside the Palestinian Authority, with a range of 20
kilometers, just where they could reach Tel Aviv . . . it would have dramatically . . . widened the scope of terror against us for a long time."

He insisted that "the link between the staff aboard the ship
and the PA and its leaders is, without a doubt, clear and undeniable."

But many reporters there were highly skeptical. What were
the "clear and undeniable" links? The IDF produced no documents
in this presentation; the ship was still at sea and the captain was in
the custody of the Shin Bet, the state security agency, for interrogation. A French reporter asked if the whole affair hadn't been cooked
up by the IDF "so as to dictate" to Gen. Anthony Zinni, who was
trying to broker Israeli/Palestinian cease-fire talks, "the agenda
which Israel seeks." Another foreign journalist reminded the assembled that a previous disclosure of the capture of a weapons ship had
been made just a few hours after reports circulated about the death
of an infant girl by IDF shelling in Khan Yunis. "Are such sequences

mere coincidences?" an American journalist chimed in. "I don't think so," he continued, answering his own question. "We have the impression that Israel is trying to ... divert affairs away from the peace process and Zinni's mediation efforts, and toward the mantra cherished by Sharon and Mofaz, which holds that ... there is no way to forge an agreement with [Arafat]."

In other words, with the hard evidence still in the *Karine A* and not available for viewing, reporters were being asked to accept a tale of daring commandos, a nonviolent seizure of a ship, and blatant proof of Palestinian evil-doing, entirely on the say-so of Israeli military men, precisely the people that the foreign press are most reluctant to believe. "Israel has the most political army chief of staff in its history," a British journalist (who wanted to remain anonymous) explained to *Ha'aretz* in a piece that the newspaper published about why the *Karine A* story got little coverage in Europe. "Mofaz doesn't speak like an army chief of staff in a democratic state, where the political echelon has clear superiority and the military officers take a back seat.... The opposite is the case."

Soon after the press conference, skeptical reporters checked Lloyd's List, a source for shipping records, and found an Iraqi—not a Palestinian—listed as the owner of the *Karine A*. Soon European newspapers, with an air of "gotcha," were running stories accusing Israel of getting its most basic facts wrong—which, they implied, cast doubt on the entire *Karine A* story they were trying to sell.

But the reporters' skepticism in this regard was highly selective. The average dock-worker could have told any one of them that a ship's papers mean next to nothing. People who want to escape high taxes and regulation imposed by their country—or smuggle contraband—often "flag out," i.e. pay a citizen of another country to sign on as owner of a ship. According to an International Transport Workers' Federation 2001–02 report on "flags of convenience," the practice is "characteristic of the maritime industry as a whole." Honduras is a popular "flag." Panama is another. "If one counts the number of ships bearing its flag and the gross tonnage of those ships," the report said, "Panama is one of the world's great maritime powers."

In fact, in shipping industry and Homeland Security circles, the *Karine A* ("owned by an Iraqi who had registered the ship through Tonga under the kingdom's flag-of-convenience registry which was run by a Greek company in Piraeus, Greece," as a shipping industry pundit put it) became a sort of "case study for why a shipping register is generally useless," according to industry column nist Michael J. Marco. Reporters for major media didn't look this far, however, and the cries of "gotcha!" continued.

Meanwhile, the ship itself had finally docked at the Israeli port of Eilat on the tip of the Negev Desert, and the IDF press department, undeterred by the skepticism exhibited at the press conference, was getting the arms cache ready for its big moment in the spotlight—without any help from the division that had the best rapport with foreign diplomats and the press, the MFA. "[The IDF] just didn't trust us," explained a foreign ministry official. The rift between the two agencies was painfully obvious to the journalistic community when one of the reporters who had been at the Friday press conference called Gideon Meir, head of the MFA press division, for a statement about the significance of the *Karine A*, and Meir had to tell him that he hadn't heard about any ship capture and had no idea what he was talking about. It was another incident that made the Israeli government look inept—and therefore perhaps untrustworthy in its claims about the ship as well.

A direct look always helps, but if reporters were going to look at the big fish that Israel's navy had caught, they would have to get to Eilat, a six-hour drive from Jerusalem across the Negev. Obviously, planes would be needed to transport dignitaries and press to the captured freighter. By then it was Saturday, when many observant Jews don't answer the phone and most businesses in Israel shut down. Stymied, the IDF conceded partial defeat on the planes project and called in its old rival the MFA for logistical help. MFA staffers were able to find a plane for the diplomats, but somehow in the general confusion a second plane promised for the press never materialized. Foreign ministry spokesmen tried to shoehorn as many foreign reporters as they could into the diplomatic plane but they were unable to find spots for everybody and, in the end, major media like CNN apparently decided it wasn't worth the trouble and just didn't make the trip.

Indeed, many of the reporters who did somehow make it to Eilat for the Sunday press conference may have wished they hadn't bothered. Workers had laid the huge cache of captured weapons on the deck of the freighter. But IDF officials also wanted the top tier of the Israeli government, people like Ariel Sharon and Shaul Mofaz, on risers behind the weapons, which meant that press photographers, for security reasons, had to stay a safe distance away. Given that an RPG, disguised as, say, a boom mike could have decapitated the Israeli government in one go, this was a reasonable precaution, but it also meant that photographers could not get a usable shot of the weapons cache. The main ceremony and briefing then began, and to the bewilderment of the foreign press it was conducted entirely in Hebrew. The IDF promised its foreign guests that the briefing would be repeated in English, but then cold winds began to rake the deck, so government officials herded diplomats and reporters into a room that turned out to be too small to contain all of them. Would the editors and producers who had made the trip then finally get to take pictures of the cache or at least be given some good close-up shots of the weapons? No, Israeli government officials insisted that press people would be given shots that their own photographers had taken of the weapons cache—except that the pictures, for some reason, were still at the IDF press office in Tel Aviv. Press people were reassured that they could pick them up there when they returned from this trip to Eilat.

When everybody was back in their respective homes in Tel Aviv, Jerusalem and Haifa, the upper tier of Israeli government continued to proclaim the significance of the capture. Reporters dutifully recorded these statements but, still wanting more evidence, they inevitably followed Israeli government remarks with disclaimers saying that Israel "had not so far provided any hard evidence of its claims." The PA continued to deny any involvement with the ship, calling the Israeli claims propaganda and a fabrication; and the U.S. State Department continued to issue noncommittal statements. Press accounts began to play the thing as just a particularly big case of "he said/she said." The story now became "the row" over who was right—just another example of those eternally scrappin' Israelis and Palestinians—instead of the fact that a Palestinian ship loaded with C-4, possibly ordered up by Yasser Arafat, had just been found on its way to the Gaza Strip.

"Both sides are squabbling over who is telling the truth," wrote Jon Immanuel of Reuters.

[A] row continued to rage between Israel and the Palestinians over the Israeli military's seizure of a ship which it said was carrying Iranian-supplied arms to the Palestinian Authority, an allegation the Authority and Tehran denied....

With the ship as a backdrop, Sharon told a showcase news conference in the Israeli port of Eilat Sunday that Arafat was irrelevant and an enemy of Israel....

The Palestinian Authority, denying involvement in the alleged smuggling attempt, accused Israel of "magnifying the incident" to avoid honoring a cease-fire.

A few weeks later, Immanuel seemed to sneer openly when he wrote:

Israel thought it had a blockbuster on its hands in the tale of a commando raid to seize a boat full of arms in the Red Sea. Prime Minister Ariel Sharon even gave it a title worthy of Hollywood: "The Ship of Terror." ...Yasser Arafat, Israel's ostensible partner in the search for peace, was cast as the criminal mastermind and paymaster of a crew linked to his Palestinian Authority. But to the directors' dismay, critics poked holes in the plot.

Immanuel then—once again—virtually transcribed Arafat's denials, without any sort of commentary.

Fed up with the skeptical and even derisive coverage, Sharon himself overrode the Shin Bet, ordering it to make the *Karine A* captain available for interviews whether the security service was finished with its interrogation or not. On Monday, January 7 (three days after his capture—ages in newspaper terms), Captain Omar Akawi was interviewed from his Ashkelon prison cell by reporters from Israel's Channel 1 and Channel 2 television, Fox News and Reuters. Appearing calm, healthy and unruffled, Akawi said that he had been a member of the PA's Fatah organization since 1976, that he was an officer in the PA's naval police force, and that Adel Awadallah, head of arms procurement for the PA, had told him to "ask where there are ships for sale." He said that he took most of his orders from Awadallah, but knew only that "the arms were going to Palestine ... to be used ... for the Palestinian people to protect themselves." Apparently not terribly afraid of Israeli government reprisals while in jail, he took the opportunity to speechify a little, saying, among other things, that "the Palestinians should have their own arms. There is no justice that Israel has all the sophisticated weapons and we have nothing."

Apparently convinced by the interview, or by other evidence it may have been shown, the U.S. State Department finally got off the fence. Soon, spokesman Richard Boucher was telling reporters, "We do believe there is a compelling case to say that senior Palestinian officials, as well as officials from Fatah, were involved in this arms smuggling operation." The State Department's pronouncement seemed to force a kind of split in the reportorial ranks. Michael Kelly, for instance, then a columnist for the *Washington Post*, wrote that there was now "compelling evidence … of PA involvement." Outlets like CNN and the BBC took a middle-ground position by sidestepping the question of the PA's possible culpability in the recent past, focusing instead on Yasser Arafat's immediate remarks, his vows to get to the bottom of the matter, find the miscreants and so on. Outlets like Reuters, which tends to be suspicious of the United States and Israel, dealt with Akawi's jailhouse confessions by implying that they had been coerced out of him by the Shin Bet and were therefore of little value. This opinion was signaled to their readers with the repeated and pointed use of the qualifying phrase "Akawi, who was in Israeli custody when he told reporters that. . . ." At one point in the story's run, Reuters even permitted a reporter, in a piece marked as a news story, to segue into near-editorial mode by writing snidely that "Boucher said the United States, which gives Israel about $2 billion a year in weaponry used to kill Palestinians, objected to the $100 million shipment to the Palestinians on the grounds that it contributed to the escalation of violence."

Gradually, however, perhaps because of the U.S. State Department's interest, the idea that senior PA officials were involved in the arms smuggling began to work its way into the central assumptions governing most stories. Since this quietly became an assumption, journalists could (and logically, should) have moved on to the question, "What did Arafat know and when did he know it?" Once again, however, journalists showed an uncharacteristic delicacy around the *Rais* ("king" or "leader" in Arabic and a sometime fond nickname for Arafat). PA statements were, for the most part, reported straight, transcription style, with none of the speculation or qualification that accompanied every statement by an Israeli official.

Actually, if one looks back on the progress of the story day to day, one sees Arafat's statements about how much he knew change with the day and the outlet he was talking to. But this wasn't commented upon either.

Finally, on February 14, 2002, there were quiet newspaper stories reporting that Colin Powell had received a letter from Yasser Arafat in which, in Powell's words, Arafat "took responsibility" for the arms smuggling.

Former IDF spokeswoman Col. Miri Eisen shudders when she talks about the *Karine A* affair, which she calls "the biggest [*hasbara*] flop ever." It was caused, in part, by government infighting over who would get to the *Karine A* trophy first and be seen on Israeli TV with a foot planted on the dead lion's head, so to speak. "You had the [IDF] chief of staff [who had held the first press conference] and another, the defense minister. Both of them wanted to be politicians," she explained. "Both of them wanted to talk, both of them wanted to show it, each wanted their Israeli constituents to hear them [so] both of them wanted to talk in Hebrew." The press conference in Eilat had been first and foremost a photo op made for Israeli television. The world audience had not been their first concern.

■ ■ ■

DID THE WORLD'S GREAT YAWN over Israel's *Karine A* claims encourage the PA and the terror militias to step up their jihad against Israel? It's possible. In any case, soon after this event the intifada moved into a new phase that terror militia leaders called "the armed struggle," a focus on deadly attacks on civilians within Israel, with less focus on the choreography of rock-throwing little boys. Attacks on civilians have been a feature of Israeli life since the beginning of the state, and while there were a number in 2001 (on one day in January, for instance, there were five bombings in the city of Jerusalem), their pace accelerated in 2002, reaching a peak in February and March.

Leaving out attacks on soldiers, attacks on settlers, and aborted attacks—which also have great impact on citizen morale—here is the ledger of completed attacks on civilians inside the Green Line during March of 2002:

March 2: Eleven civilians, mostly women and small children, were killed and 50 injured, 4 of them critically, when a bomber blew himself up in an ultra-orthodox neighborhood of Jerusalem where a crowd had gathered for a bar mitzvah celebration.

March 5: An 85-year-old woman was killed by a suicide bomber who boarded a city bus as it pulled into a bus station in the Israeli town of Afula. That night, a Fatah gunman opened fire on people seated at two adjacent restaurants in Tel Aviv, killing 3 and wounding 30. In Jerusalem, 11 people under the age of 31 were killed and 10 seriously wounded when a suicide bomber (later claimed by Hamas) pulled his detonation cord in a crowded downtown café.

March 8: Gunmen dressed as IDF soldiers opened fire on vehicles on a road in the Galilee near the Lebanon border, killing 6 civilian residents of nearby kibbutzim, most of them women.

March 17: A gunman opened fire on passersby in the center of the town of Kfar Sava, killing an 18-year-old-woman and wounding 16 people.

March 20: Thirty people were wounded and 7 people ranging in age from 19 to 75 were killed by a suicide bomber who boarded a city bus carrying people from Tel Aviv to Nazareth.

March 21: A suicide bomber (claimed by Fatah) detonated himself in the middle of a crowd of shoppers on King George Street in the center of Jerusalem, killing two women and one man and wounding 86.

March 27: A huge crowd was sitting down to begin a Passover seder in the banquet hall of a Netanya hotel when a suicide bomber pulled the detonation cord on his belt. Thirty people were killed and 140 injured, twenty seriously. Victims ranged in age from 20 to 92, with most in their seventies.

March 29: Two Israelis, age 17 and 55, were killed by an 18-year-old female bomber recruited by Fatah's Al-Aqsa Martyrs Brigade.

March 31: A suicide bomber (claimed by Hamas) detonated in a restaurant near Haifa, killing 15 people ranging in age from 16 to 67.

If victims were the currency to buy coverage and moral capital in the television age, Israel was catching up. The news coverage of its nightmare month of March was generally grave and sympathetic, though the *New York Times* continued to run pieces introduced with what I have come to think of as the "two worlds collided" lead. This lead features two people who have been pushed together by vast forces beyond their control and have had an encounter in which, as the *Times* has put it, the lives "of both are changed forever"—usually because one has done something very life-changing, like killing the other.

The *Times* produced one of these in its coverage of the March 29 suicide bombing in which an eighteen-year-old Palestinian woman detonated herself outside a downtown Jerusalem supermarket, killing the store's middle-aged male security guard, who had tried to stop her, and a sixteen-year-old girl who was on an errand for her mother. The piece was titled "2 Girls, Divided by War, Joined in Carnage." The "two girls" were "joined in carnage" when "The vastly different trajectories of their lives collided for one deadly moment mirroring the intimate conflict of their two peoples." It might be hard from this description to tell that one woman blew up the other. The life of suicide bomber Ayat al-Akhras was sketched out and she seemed to be as wholesome as a Girl Scout. Indeed, writer Joel Greenberg seemed to be tying himself in knots to avoid saying anything that might seem mildly judgmental. Even her deliberate act of murder—after leaving behind the "martyr's" traditional farewell video spelling out her intentions—is drained of any quality of agency:

"As Ms. Levy walked up to the supermarket . . . a little before 2 P.M., Ms. Akhras also approached. They walked to the door, where Ms. Akhras was stopped for a check by a security guard. Then, an explosion."

Granted, such morally relativistic coverage was better than coverage that didn't humanize Israelis at all—coverage that represented "Israel" as faceless soldiers or inhuman lumbering tanks. But did this mean that Israelis had to keep dying in order to keep their human face in the news? At the onset of the second intifada, an Arab leader had said he expected that his side would win this new low-intensity war because "Our ability to die is greater than the Israelis' ability to go on killing us." I don't think he was talking just about attrition war here—the ability to take casualties. I think he was also referring to the Palestinian Authority's ability to deploy civilians ready to die on camera.

If success in this new televised war depended on who could "die better," the state of Israel—founded around an informal manifesto of survival—was in trouble. Benjamin Netanyahu was alert to this when he told an audience of diplomats in the summer of 2002, "We appreciate your support when we are down but we would appreciate it also when we fight to defend ourselves." In other words, the true test of news coverage of the conflict would be revealed by how outlets reacted to a large Israeli military maneuver. The news media had the habit of using the same generic heading "violence" to describe any event in which blood was spilled—as in "Violence flared again today in Israel"—as if all acts of violence were equally immoral. Would the news outlets now be willing and able to make the distinction between different kinds of death and different kinds of killing? Would they be able to separate acts of self-defense (acts of aggression by soldiers in the course of a war) from the indiscriminate targeting of civilians?

That real test came at the end of March 2002 with Operation Defensive Shield, the IDF's bid to stop the suicide bombings. The operation was originally designed to be a kind of lightning strike on terrorist enclaves in Ramallah, Nablus, Qalqilya, Hebron, Bethlehem and Tulkarem and especially the refugee camp section of the town of Jenin, which Fatah documents called "the capital of suicide bombing." Israeli intelligence had compiled a very specific "get" list of men in each town who they believed were militia leaders, but along the way, men with, say, Hamas tattoos on their bodies would be rounded up as well.

And it might have been a lightning strike, over in less than a week as first envisioned, if the IDF had relied on air strikes. Instead, because of reports from the United Nations, Amnesty International and Physicians for Human Rights condemning Israel for use of "excessive force" during the first two years of the intifada, Operation Defensive Shield employed mainly infantry and some light artillery.

The least surgical weapon is a bomb dropped from an airplane, which takes out everything below. The most surgical (also the most vulnerable) weapon is a man on foot, armed with a gun, and there was no doubt that fine surgery was needed in places as densely populated as the Jenin refugee camp.* Though the IDF warned the civilian population via bullhorn and announcements in Arabic that the

---

*For a very short period over fifty years ago, when Arabs left Israel and moved to the West Bank and surrounding Arab countries, refugees lived in camplike housing—tents with communal shower facilities, etc.—but the United Nations Relief Workers Agency,

camp would be invaded, and despite the fact that troops massed outside the camp were held back a day because of heavy rains, it is estimated that 1,200 people remained in this dense urban terrain of narrow streets and sandwiched buildings. (How many were determined fighters and how many were unaffiliated civilians will probably never be known.) Ironically, Ata Abu Roumeileh, a Fatah leader who remained in Jenin to fight the IDF, told a *Time* magazine reporter that they had expected air strikes and that "it was only when his forces saw the Israelis advancing on foot that they decided to stay and fight."

Once the IDF had surrounded the camp and blocked its exits, three units moved in and began the painstaking work of going house to house in search of fedayeen and weapons. Walking in the streets was extremely dangerous given the snipers in the buildings above and the explosives that had been hidden underground—some of them 250-pound bombs, ten times the size of an average suicide bomber's belt; so IDF units much of the time avoided the streets and moved house to house by blowing holes in connecting walls between units. Though it is "surgical" in the extreme, a house-to-house search operation is not pretty. Even if they make their approach via a front door, explosives are often involved. IDF procedure stipulates that troops must knock and say "Army, Open up!"* If the house is uninhabited—and often, residents have fled in advance—the IDF then attempts to open the door, working in stages from the least invasive technique, a crowbar, to the most damaging, a small "finger" of explosive that knocks it down.

Occasionally, journalists have accompanied IDF soldiers on this type of mission. When soldiers storm into a home and handcuff the men (teenage boys included), children and women cry. There has been a lot of film of children and women wailing and beseeching IDF

UNRWA, a UN division created specifically to serve Palestinian refugees, built permanent structures very quickly. Since then it is more accurate to describe most "refugee camps" as looking like villages or as dilapidated neighborhoods attached to towns and cities, but the term "camp" has stuck.

*The IDF sometimes used "human shields" —a civilian neighbor who is asked to go to the door instead of the IDF, but it is very hard to determine how often the practice was used in Jenin because of the flood of rhetoric, contradictory reports, claims and counterclaims that have been published since. The practice was banned by Israel's High Court a month after the completion of Operation Defensive Shield.

soldiers searching their belongings to stop, and the isolated image is immediately symbolic of the weak at the mercy of the strong. But in life, as opposed to on television or other picture journalism, there is no such thing as an isolated image. The image itself is nothing without context; it wouldn't have been created without the context of people using such homes to store weapons and build bombs, but how does one represent back story on the screen?

One of the problems with the reporting of Operation Defensive Shield was that many journalists had little familiarity or visceral understanding of the contextualizing exigencies of urban combat and tended to react reflexively and emotionally to these images. I remember John Gibson of the Fox News Network remarking indignantly on his talk show that the Israelis certainly seemed to have the habit of using excessive force. "What was all this about them blowing holes in walls?" he fairly bellowed to a guest, a retired Marine general who worked for a think tank in Washington, D.C. The general replied calmly, "Moving through a string of houses by blowing holes in the connecting walls has been used by every force in the world, in virtually every war, as a way to move through a village while avoiding sniper fire."

The difficulty in urban warfare is finding the balance between giving one's forces some protection and attempting to separate the "good guys" from the "bad guys" in a situation where a bad guy is often disguised as a good guy. Urban combat does not look like old-style combat with clearly delineated forces, but news media in general seemed unwilling to adjust their eyes to see the challenges for soldiers of urban guerrilla warfare. *Time* magazine stood apart with its extremely well-reported, balanced, and unemotional wrap-up of Operation Defensive Shield. The most significant thing about the piece was its title: "The Battle of Jenin." It was the only acknowledgement I have seen in the mainstream media that this was a prolonged bloody fight between *two* determined forces—not a "Jeningrad," as Yasser Arafat described it in interviews, or an "incursion," as the press tended to call it. *Time* wrote: "It was real urban warfare as a modern, well-equipped army met an armed and prepared group of guerrilla fighters intimately familiar with the local terrain."

But being "modern" and "well-equipped" didn't give the IDF any particular advantage in this case. There is a "home-field advantage" in guerrilla war that mitigates technological superiority. Fighting devolves to an almost primitive level, where one's chief tools are eyes, ears, reflexes and marksmanship. An Israeli company has recently invented a radar device that can "see" through walls, giving a three-dimensional picture of what's on the other side, but it will be years before the device is standard issue for infantry units. In the meantime, the average infantry soldier is stuck not knowing who or what waits on the other side of a door. The most advanced pieces of standard equipment the IDF used in the infantry phase of Operation Defensive Shield were cell phones, but of course the other side had those as well.

Accordingly, once inside the camp, IDF units moved extremely slowly and cautiously to avoid drawing sniper fire, tripping booby traps or triggering sudden conflagrations in which it would be difficult to tell combatants from civilians. One unit, for instance, moved only seven hundred meters in five days. *A Psalm in Jenin*, based on accounts given by Jenin's combat veterans, conveys the difficulty of the "surgical" operation:

> Stu watched as two Naval Commando soldiers went to place an explosive brick on a door. Just as they were about to blow in the door, they spotted a woman sitting with two children nearby. They approached the woman and her children to . . . move them out of harm's way. A sniper bullet caught one of the soldiers in the leg, severing his femoral artery. Immediately afterwards, an exploding booby trap sprayed the other soldier with shrapnel.

Toward the end of the operation, gunmen had left most buildings or been captured, but on April 9, a platoon of IDF soldiers blundered into an open clearing between two houses that had been seeded with booby traps. Thirteen men were killed and seven severely wounded by the explosives or by the snipers who appeared in the building windows overhead to administer a coup de grâce. A loss like this is felt throughout a small force like the IDF, so the commanders called an end to house-to-house searches and brought in huge armored bulldozers to level the buildings that were providing cover for the remaining booby-traps and snipers. The IDF has said that soldiers armed with megaphones instructed anyone inside, in Arabic, to get out and waited until they were reasonably sure that buildings were empty before the D-9 Caterpillar operators began their slow, clumsy bludgeoning. Nevertheless, the airwaves were soon full of reports—drawn from "eyewitness" accounts—of innocent civilians who had been trapped in buildings as they were being destroyed.

As the IDF struggled with its military operation, its soldiers also had their hands full responding to the demands of the international press that had been deployed from all over the world. The second intifada had taken an exciting new turn and 1,100 new journalists had arrived in Israel to cover it, adding to the hundreds of press with permanent billets in the area. The "incursion into the West Bank" promised international significance coupled with good pictures (violence, destruction, conflict, yelling) coupled with—as the majority of reporters, editors and producers saw it—the always popular Strong versus Weak story line, all set in an area where reporters could retire at the end of the day to lovely hotels with all the amenities one finds in a modern democratic country like Israel.

The problem was that when the convoys of reporters got out into the field, they began to find out that the sexiest venues, those that promised the most action, had been closed to reporters by the IDF. Some areas, like Ramallah, were only closed for a period; others, like the refugee camp in Jenin (the site of most of the terror militia organization and preparation) were closed to press until the IDF was done with major operations. The decision to exclude reporters became extremely controversial in Israel's press circles after Operation Defensive Shield was over, but IDF spokeswoman Miri Eisen says that within the IDF, the decision was not taken lightly:

> The press people said "Listen, the journalists aren't going to like it" and the operational people said "We don't care about the journalists right now and about the image, we don't want them inside." It had to do with the way we were working operationally inside the camp. We had infantry coming in from 360 degrees which means that you're firing in all different directions. It's not like a journalist can be [safe] on one side or another. It's a very difficult type of combat to coordinate with the forces, let alone with somebody you don't know who's inside.

"It wasn't that we told journalists to leave," she pointed out to me. "If someone had been in there already, he would have been in there. It was that we didn't let them in once the fighting started."

Many of those in Israel's *hasbara* apparatus say they would have preferred to allow reporters complete freedom of movement, but they acknowledge that it's a difficult call. Having reporters traipsing around "disrupts operations," explained Ilan Sztulman of the Ministry of Foreign Affairs—one of those who would, nevertheless, have permitted reporters complete freedom. "You're aiming a shot; a photographer gets in the way of a shot; you have to shoot; you have to remove him."

Daniel Seaman of the Government Press Office, on the other hand, sided with the IDF in keeping press out of combat zones: "We are concerned about our soldiers and we wanted them to concentrate on the mission at hand and not worry, 'Is that a terrorist? Is that not a terrorist? Is that a journalist?' Despite what the press say— 'Oh we're responsible for ourselves. We're big kids'—anytime they're in an area and they're shot, eventually—even if it comes out that it wasn't our fault—they still accuse us of doing it."

In any case, reporters hanging around the edge of closed areas weren't about to go home. Honor comes to the person who gets the story, by any means necessary, and it is not good form to obey government directions too slavishly. It was possible to embed with the IDF and see lots of action—as Scott Anderson did for the *New York Times Magazine*—but nothing is as tantalizing to reporters as a closed door, and "hundreds of journalists," as *Ha'aretz* put it, began to do "their best to elude the army, [making] their way into the territories by taking roundabout dirt paths, accompanied by Palestinian escorts," to get into the closed zones.

In many cases, "getting in" became the point of the story beamed to the folks back home. Ashleigh Banfield of MSNBC, for instance, filmed herself and her crew sneaking past IDF guards into Ramallah. Broadcasting from inside the city, she breathlessly told her viewers that she had trekked across fields and along back roads in order to "bring you the story the Israelis don't want you to see." Then she pointed her cameras at an IDF unit that was preparing to raid Yasser Arafat's headquarters.

Other journalists also seemed to consider IDF regulations an affront. ABC producer Deirdre Michalopoulos told Sara Leibovich-Dar of *Ha'aretz* that while she and her crew were trying to get near IDF action in Ramallah, two jeeps came toward us, then honked their horns and shot rubber bullets without any warning. I'd been in many war zones. I was in Afghanistan, Pakistan, Albania and Bosnia. I was in Israel in October 2000. Soldiers had never opened fire on me before. It's hard to work when you find that you've become a target. There was a moment when I was very frightened. I didn't know how far they would go. The worst part was that they didn't say anything. They didn't order us to leave. They just shot without any warning.

But an IDF spokesman had a different version of events:

At this time, a group of journalists is trying to break into the Muqata compound in Ramallah in contradiction of the order declaring it a closed military zone that was given by the military commander in the area, in keeping with the instructions of the political echelon for isolating the area. IDF forces are attempting to keep the journalists away by tossing a number of stun grenades in their direction. The IDF Spokesman wishes to make clear that the stun grenades were used not just to keep them away, but also to reduce to a minimum the chance that they would be injured. No rubber bullets were fired at the journalists as has been reported.

As the fighting went on, reporters just kept trying to get in and lower-ranking IDF soldiers posted as guards just kept trying to follow orders to keep them out. The constant friction didn't improve either group's opinion of the other. NBC's Dana Lewis complained that the "soldiers were very aggressive this time. They shot endless warning shots in the air." Keith Miller of NBC said that IDF soldiers were "haughty." He told *Ha'aretz:*

They made a contemptuous gesture telling me to go away. They could have politely told me that it was forbidden for me to enter because the army is concerned for my security. If someone would take the trouble to give them a 15-minute course, it would all look different. And then when the Palestinians scream that there was a massacre, you ask yourself—If the army treats you like a threat, how does it treat someone who could really be a threat?

At least the "aggressiveness" of the IDF soldiers kept members of the foreign press entertained at the end of the work day, as *Ha'aretz's* Leibovich-Dar revealed:

As they go about covering the war, the foreign journalists are vying
with each other for prestige as well as for scoops. This calculation
includes things like: Who is staying in the more elegant hotel, who
has the best bulletproof transportation, who brought the biggest stars
to Israel, who got into the Jenin refugee camp first, and who is suffering more at the hands of IDF soldiers.

The perennial subject of "being shot at by Israeli soldiers"
fueled many a conversation over a glass of wine at the American
Colony, but one of the problems, according to Scott Anderson, who
has worked in numerous war zones, is that "80–90 percent [of these
reporters] had never been near combat before and could not distin-
guish between a bullet shot over their heads as a warning shot and
one aiming at them." Often, he told me, reporters would witness
the IDF firing warning shots and report that the IDF had "fired into
the crowd" or that the IDF had "fired at reporters." In fact, he heard
a CNN reporter doing a live report say excitedly into her mike that
the "IDF fired into the crowd, wounding two journalists." But Anderson had seen the sequence: The IDF had fired warning shots over a
crowd to disperse it. As for the two journalists, they hadn't even
been on the scene. (In the heat of the moment, the CNN reporter
had conflated the shooting "into the crowd" and the wounding of
two journalists.) Anderson knew that one of the journalists had suffered damage to his eardrum because he had been near the explosion of a flash grenade (a nonlethal crowd-dispersion tool). Live fire
had not even been involved. On two occasions, Anderson said, he
had seen IDF soldiers who looked as if they were targeting a journalist, but overall he had been very impressed by IDF soldiers'
restraint. He had reported from "many war zones," he said in a 2002
panel discussion in New York that I attended, "and given the same
circumstances another army would have had ten times the civilian
casualties, the Russian Army a hundred times."

Reporters tend to move "around in a pack," Anderson said in
that lecture, so "the more people" covering a story, "the worse coverage gets." A vast, interdependent press pack inevitably creates its
own informal information network and its own rumor mill. Soon
it is hard to know whether something you pick up from another
reporter is rumor or fact, and in Jenin, according to Anderson, "rumor

was reported as fact." Reporters who didn't feel like trying to "get in" that day hung around together in a large huddle outside an Israeli blockade, waiting for tips, personal accounts, anything to send to bosses back home. Whenever a Palestinian spokesperson showed up (or merely someone who claimed to be an eyewitness to events inside the camp), Anderson said, "reporters were on them like flies." And thus as the operation dragged on, claims about what was happening "inside" grew more and more lurid. Palestinian Authority spokesmen like Saeb Erekat, for instance, had a habit during this period of calling CNN headquarters from a town outside of Jenin, such as Jericho, and rambling virtually uninterrupted on his cell phone about a massacre he claimed was under way in Jenin. Reporters for the majors claim they had no choice but to report these allegations. And the colorful allegations were given far more space than the inevitably terse IDF rebuttals. On April 13, four days into the invasion of the Jenin camp, the *Washington Post*, for instance, reported that "Palestinians have said that Israeli troops killed hundreds [in Jenin]. . . . Palestinians compared the killing in Jenin to the deaths of Palestinian refugees at . . . Sabra and Shatilla."

As Professor Mohammed Dajani of Al-Quds University in Jerusalem pointed out, the Palestinian Authority was eager "to turn Jenin into an 'Alamo episode.' Here the press was a willing partner [as] they aspired to make Jenin a symbol of resistance to Palestinians." On April 12, for instance, James Bennet of the *New York Times* reported that "Palestinians here describe bodies cut in pieces, bodies scooped up by bulldozers and buried in mass graves, bodies deliberately concealed under collapsed buildings. They describe people drinking out of sewers and people used by Israeli soldiers as human shields." Once the bulldozers began their work, stories about people trapped under buildings began to proliferate. "All my nine children are buried under the ruins. . . . [C]ome back in a week and you will see their corpses," a man named Abu Ali told reporters. *Le Nouvel Observateur*, an influential French weekly magazine, didn't wait a week to substantiate Ali's claim. It soon appeared with photos in a two-page spread in the magazine under the title "The Survivors Tell Their Stories."

Ordinary, reportorial common sense should have triggered skepticism about the claims that hundreds had been killed as

buildings were demolished, but again, *Time* magazine was one of
the few to keep its head, pointing out that:

> Undoubtedly, the D-9s destroyed houses, but they certainly didn't
> bury as many people as Palestinian officials have alleged. It takes the
> D-9 at least half an hour to fully wreck a building. Israeli soldiers
> say they always called to residents to come out before the bulldoz-
> ers went in. But even if the innocents were too frightened initially
> to leave, most would surely have done so as soon as the D-9 started
> its work. A senior Palestinian military officer tells Time it was prob-
> ably the gunmen's own booby traps that buried some civilians and
> fighters alive. There were bombs that were certainly big enough to
> wreck a cinder-block refugee house more devastatingly than a D-9
> ever could.

By the end of the operation, most of the fedayeen and their
families had left that section of town, but once the massacre rumors
got started even the *absence* of civilians on the streets was used in
news reports to imply IDF dark-doings—as in this report, a coop-
erative venture by CNN and TF1 of France:

> (CNN reporter voice-over): One of the few journalists to have made
> it into the camp is Michel Scott, of the French TV network, TF1. This
> is what he saw on Friday. In crowded alleys, evidence of heavy fight-
> ing. Israeli bulldozers leveling buildings in the center of town and
> very little evidence of human life until a young woman appeared in
> a doorway.
>
> "Endeera Harb [a phonetic spelling] does not know where her
> brother is. She has been trapped for nine days in her house with her
> mother and three small children.
>
> "'I didn't see anyone killed in front of my eyes, but in my sister's
> house across the alley, there are five people dead.'
>
> "The bodies lie in two rooms. No one has been able to move them.
> It is not safe to try to take them out. The neighbors say they were
> not fighters.
>
> "Another woman called out. In a nearby courtyard, the body of
> her brother-in-law shot by an Israeli sniper, she says, six days ago.
> Her family has had to leave his body in the shed where he crawled
> to die.
>
> "'He went to get water for his children from the well,' she says,
> 'and he got shot. They did terrible things to us.'"

Once again, there are lacunae in the text where the acts of grownup Palestinians should be. The only *actions* that are attributed directly are attributed to Israelis. The Israelis "have leveled buildings" and an Israeli sniper has allegedly shot someone's "brother-in-law." Then the reporter uses the passive voice to report that civilian residents say they are "trapped in their houses" and are "afraid to move dead bodies." Trapped by whom? Afraid of whom? Since the Israelis are the only actors shown to be moving in this landscape, it's natural to assume they are to blame for these problems as well.

But of course while the IDF was busy "leveling buildings" and the like, Palestinian fighters (such as Ata Abu Roumeileh, the Fatah leader interviewed by *Time*) were busy supplying the other half, the unseen half, of this battle. For instance, one of the reasons why the woman in the interview may have been afraid to move dead bodies was because "The Palestinians wouldn't let anybody take the bodies out," according to Ilan Sztulman, an MFA official and an officer in the IDF reserves. "They manipulate the imagery. That's how they fight," he said. "There were bodies decaying on the street. They stank. But if anybody approached the bodies they would get shot.... They booby-trapped a lot of the bodies. Some [IDF] soldiers got killed before they figured this out. So to get them out the IDF soldiers began using a sort of anchor. It's called a sapper's anchor: You throw it; it gets stuck on flesh and if it doesn't explode, you can come close."

The conspicuous corpses had the desired effect on the foreign press. On April 14, Phil Reeves of the *Independent* got into the combat zone and wrote a story that his paper titled "The Camp That Became a Slaughterhouse":

> A terrible crime has been committed by Israel in Jenin refugee camp, and the world is turning a blind eye. Colin Powell, the US Secretary of State, visited the scene of a suicide bombing that murdered six Israelis in Jerusalem, but he did not visit Jenin, where the Israelis admit they killed at least 100 Palestinians. The Israeli army claims all of the dead were armed men, that it took special care to avoid civilian casualties. But we saw the helicopter rockets rain down on desperately crowded areas: civilian casualties could not have been prevented.

> The Israeli army sealed off the entire area around Jenin yester-
> day, arresting journalists who ventured into it. That is because they
> have something to hide in Jenin: the bodies *

Australia's Channel 9 Television announced that its reporter Jim Whaley had also managed to "slip into the refugee camp, or what was left of it, in the West Bank city of Jenin this week ... avoiding the Israeli military on the outskirts of Jenin by using back trails to walk into the city [where Whaley] discovered for himself ... that the devastation of Jenin was 'horrifying beyond belief.'"

"It's the smell you notice first," Whaley said in his report. "The stench of rotting corpses is overpowering. It clings to your clothes for hours."

They have to be photographed and they have to be described, but corpses have a way of ending rational discourse about cause and effect—which is clearly what happened in the Jenin coverage. Photographers also contributed to the confusion by keeping their cameras low. In effect, they didn't allow the viewer to "escape" this lunar landscape of rubble and twisted metal and to see the destruction in context. Destruction filled the camera frame and the news segment. Without larger, orienting shots it was natural to assume that an entire town had been destroyed.

Very late in the Jenin coverage, someone in the Israeli press operation was able to interest a few television producers and newspaper editors in an aerial shot of the whole city of Jenin that an enterprising Israeli press official thought to snap while flying over the town in a helicopter. The photo showed that an area of about one hundred square yards was indeed pulverized, but the remainder of the town appeared undisturbed, for according to an Amnesty International report published long after Operation Defensive Shield ended, "the siege of Jenin" had actually involved an area that was "about the size of a soccer field or about one-tenth of the town."

For anyone who had imagined a sort of Hiroshima-by-bulldozer, the photo was a revelation, but only a few outlets picked it

---

*In August, after a UN report finding no evidence of a massacre, Reeves published an apology for his Jenin coverage with a column that began: "One of the hardest aspects of covering the Middle East is admitting to a mistake."

up. Besides, it was too little, too late. So was the UN investigation of the massacre charges. Finally completed in August 2002, four months after the fact, it found no evidence of a "massacre" and allowed that IDF claims of about forty-five Palestinian dead, mostly fighters, were correct. The final numbers indicated that three children and four women had been killed—and Abu Ali's nine children, whom *Le Nouvel Observateur* was so quick to suggest had been buried under a building, were not among them.

Indeed, even with the UN report and one by Amnesty International that also supported IDF casualty estimates, the "massacre" story has never really died. Two weeks after IDF soldiers had left the area, a young Arab-Israeli filmmaker named Muhammed Bakri came to the camp to collect footage for a film he would title *Jenin, Jenin*. Usually referred to as a documentary, the film has been shown at film festivals, at universities and on public television stations around the world. It relies almost entirely on interviews with residents done several weeks after the incursion, who tell a litany of atrocities along the lines of Nazi concentration camps. One of Bakri's interviews, for instance, is with the director of the hospital in Jenin, Dr. Abu-Rali, who says on camera that "the western wing of the hospital was shelled and destroyed," and that "the IDF purposely disrupted the supply of water and electricity."

But when the film was screened in Jerusalem, a doctor with the IDF reserves named David Zangen was in the audience. He had been called up for Operation Defensive Shield, had treated injuries in Jenin, and found the film so ridden with falsehoods that he wrote a piece for the Israeli newspaper *Ma'ariv* detailing them point by point. Dr. Zangen noted that the Dr. Abu-Rali making this claim in Bakri's film had also told Al-Jazeera during the incursion that there were casualties "in the thousands." As for Abu-Rali's claim that an entire wing of his hospital had been "destroyed," Zangen said, "The truth is that there never was such a wing and, in any case, no part of the hospital was shelled or bombed." (Another documentary, shot at the same time, shows the hospital undamaged.)

"IDF soldiers were careful not to enter the hospital grounds, even though we knew that they were being used to shelter wanted persons," Zangen wrote. "We maintained the supply of water, electricity and oxygen to the hospital throughout the course of the fighting, and helped set up an emergency generator after the electricity grid in the city was damaged."

Zangen was also surprised to see that Bakri had filmed an interview with a seventy-five-year-old resident of Jenin who, "crying bitterly, testified that he had been taken from his bed in the middle of the night and shot in the hand, and, when he failed to obey the soldiers' orders to get up, was shot again in the foot." Zangen recalls:

> This same elderly man was brought to me for treatment after a cleanup operation in one of the houses used by a Hamas cell in the refugee camp. He had indeed sustained a slight injury to the hand and suffered from light abrasions on his leg (although certainly not a bullet wound). IDF soldiers brought him to the station for treating the wounded, and there he was treated, including by me.
>
> One of the army doctors diagnosed heart failure, and we immediately offered to transfer him for treatment to the Emek Hospital in Afula. He requested to be treated at the hospital in Jenin since he was not fluent in Hebrew. After the Jenin hospital refused to admit him, we transferred him to Afula. He was in the internal medicine ward for three days and received treatment for heart problems and anemia, from which he suffered as a result of an existing chronic disease.

Many more came forward to challenge the accuracy of the film, and after about a year of fielding challenges, Bakri began to temper his defense somewhat. In an interview for *Ha'aretz* a year or so after the film's premiere, he dodged the question of whether the film is a documentary, describing it instead as "a 50-minute movie of the subjective truth of people who were there after the army conquered the city."

Often lost in the hand-wringing over the battle of Jenin was that Operation Defensive Shield accomplished its objectives with relatively little human cost. Hundreds of arrests were made, illegal caches of terror weapons captured, and key militia funding streams identified by material captured in raids of PA buildings. The operation left Israelis, and the Palestinians menaced by terror militiamen in their midst, much safer. But no one forgot how Jenin "looked." In the ramp-up to the American attack on Iraq in 2003, when observers predicted that the United States would soon find its troops fighting house to house in Baghdad and elsewhere, Col. Yoni Fighel of the IDF, a military governor of Ramallah and Jenin, advised Americans to "take a lesson from our invasion of Jenin. And have full TV coverage on the points of friction between military and the population—even have soldiers with cameras." And indeed, the United States seemed to have learned the lesson of Jenin. It launched the embedding program, which has graduated a new generation of war correspondents who understand war a lot better than several decades' worth of American reporters before them.

■ ■ ■

THERE WAS ANOTHER SILVER LINING to Jenin, in addition to military successes. The media debacle—symbolized by the image, now frozen in amber, of the IDF's "siege" of a helpless "refugee camp"— created greater urgency in Israel about the government's handling of media war. In the months after Jenin, the government comptroller's office began to prepare a report on the state of the country's *hasbara*. (Government officials already had a pretty clear idea that the report was going to criticize the fragmentation of the operation, the lack of cooperation between divisions.)

As I watched from the United States, I spotted small stirrings of action, more initiatives on this level, indications that the Israeli government was rallying. In June of 2002, for instance, the Israeli Broadcasting Authority launched an Arabic-language satellite television station that would be available in the territories as an alternative to satellite channels like Al-Jazeera. The point was to go over the heads of PA-controlled media and attempt to bring the Israeli side of the story to the Palestinian masses—which ultimately, it was hoped, would convince Palestinians of the benefits to them of living next door to a democratic, prosperous and secure Israel. The government had also begun work on a center that would monitor major world media (including Arab satellite channels like Al-Manar and Al-Jazeera) around the clock so that press spokesmen could react to negative and/or inaccurate reports faster. Even the generally *hasbara*-averse IDF press division seemed to be acknowledging the media war. It was debuting a new chief spokesperson, the first woman to hold that position: Brig. Gen. Ruth Yaron, who was born in Algeria in 1957. Young, female and Sephardic (Israel's version of "black") instead of old, male and Ashkenazi (Israel's version of "white"), she was the perfect face for a kinder, gentler IDF.

There were, in another words, stirrings on Israel's side of the second front. Would they change the balance in the media war? It seemed like a good time to go back to Israel and take a closer look.

SIX

JERUSALEM
THE BATTERED

*The Intifada is a success. We have thrown the flourishing
Israeli economy into a real recession. This is even causing a
reverse immigration. Thousands are leaving the country
every year.*

　　—Dr. Mahmoud al-Zahar, Hamas leader,
　　　　in an interview in the *Jerusalem Post*, October 3, 2002

W HEN I RETURNED TO JERUSALEM IN AUGUST 2002 the recession that had just begun when I was there last was now two
years old. The City of Gold was still golden at twilight when
the setting sun was reflected on the ancient walls of the old
city and the white Jerusalem stone apartment buildings in the hills,
but most everything else seemed to be covered with a patina of
grime. To cope with a recession caused by reductions in tourism and
in foreign investment, the worldwide tech bust, and higher defense
costs, the government was laying people off and cutting services.
This drive to downsize government came as a shock to those parts
of the population that had become hooked on cradle-to-grave sub-
sidies (like the vast public health care system that paid for everything from a bottle of aspirin to surgery), and public workers' unions
were outraged and threatening strikes. Garbage handlers had just
begun a slowdown and garbage bins overflowed onto the sidewalk,
where the wind lifted the Cadbury chocolate wrappers and torn
newspaper pages and made them skitter fitfully in the streets. The
garbage handlers only went back to work when the government
pointed out that the twenty-foot mounds of trash that sat on every
street were ideal places for terrorists to hide bombs.

The service cutbacks showed all over. Jerusalem is a city of surreally diverse architecture, where buildings left by the Ottoman Empire sit next to Bauhaus and Saarinen-esque experiments. Moorish buildings with facades of carved stone can take a little patina of dirt, but Bauhaus and Saarinen are all about the beauty of intersecting planes of glass, concrete and steel. They have to be kept immaculate and gleaming or they look like dour, boxy Soviet public housing—which is exactly what had begun to happen. Jerusalem's buildings of "the international style" were built in the 1940s and 1950s by recent immigrants from Austria and Germany who must have felt besotted with the light of the place and by new expanses of space. Building for a socialist utopia, these designers probably never envisioned a future in which striking workers would let their beautiful structures languish like this.

To top off the feeling of a gathering apocalypse, Israel was undergoing what one aid group called its "worst drought cycle in recorded history." Lake Kinneret, for instance, the source of one-third of all Israel's fresh water, had gone below its "red line." With sprinkler use restricted, the grass in Independence Park, which I walked past nearly every day, had baked in the desert sun and turned to straw. The fountain at the corner of the park, on Hillel Street, which had once given passersby a refreshing misting, had been turned off and its concrete basin was exposed, revealing a crack in the stone and a sort of bathtub ring of baked-on pond scum.

There was something unsettling to me about the sight of this rudely exposed fountain basin—and the sight of so many things drying up and turning ugly. The irrigation of the desert was one of the great achievements of the state; the lushness of its agriculture was an early symbol of success and stability. I had never known an Israel that was not full of merrily whipping sprinklers and blooming trees, and now it seemed as if the country could sink back into the desert from which it had risen.

A newspaper columnist in the *Jerusalem Post* summed up the country's situation: "Owing to security and economic issues, social welfare and unemployment, and feeling of international alienation, ... the last two years have probably been the worst in Israel's history."

But at least people were out and about this time around. Israelis seemed to have adjusted to life in the new intifada and were clearly determined to live normally again. Because sidewalks downtown were clogged with people once more, it was now possible to see how much the population had changed in the last decade, how much Israel had become a global soup, like the streets of midtown Manhattan. Instead of faces that were mostly either Sephardic or Ashkenazi, there were now workers from countries like China, the Philippines and Africa, who had come to replace Palestinians no longer working in Israel. But there were many new permanent residents, new Israelis, as well, and I found myself doing a double take at, for instance, the man from Somalia or Ethiopia (recognizable by his oval face, high hairline and almond coloring) who was wearing a kipa and talking in fluent Hebrew on his cell phone. Between 1990 and 2000 the state had tried to digest about one million immigrants; they continued to come in at a rate of about thirty thousand per year in the next three years after that. Many were Jews and thus eligible for instant citizenship—or Jewish enough, given what one columnist called "new accounting tricks worthy of Arthur Andersen." The biggest influx had come from the countries of the former Soviet Union. "The Russians," as Israelis called them, were everywhere and especially visible because they seemed to carry their Russian-ness with them. A whole section of Jerusalem had become a little Russia, with shop after shop signed in Cyrillic offering Russian goods. The Russians seemed generally to be young, strong, healthy and quite beautiful in a high-cheekboned, blond Tartar way, but most were also without language skills or capital of any kind.

But all these people, whatever their other problems, have bodies, and bodies was what Israel was using to plug the hole in the dike, so to speak. It was fighting the intifada with what looked to me like an unprecedented call-up of citizen soldiers. Although there were countless news stories about a relative handful of IDF "refuseniks," nearly 100 percent of the reservists called up for the second intifada had responded, even those who had reservations about Israel's strategy. Those older, more experienced troops—in their thirties, and including doctors, lawyers, engineers and everything else—were generally used to man checkpoints on the far perimeters, but with younger troops being used for guard duty inside the city, at any given time approximately one-third of the population of downtown Jerusalem appeared to be made up of green-

uniformed teenage soldiers of the IDF, slung with rifles that sometimes (mostly in the case of the girls) looked as big as they were.
On their way back to base or home for the weekend, jabbering on
their cell phones, lounging in boredom at public bus shelters, or clattering down the street in small groups, they sometimes looked more
like high school kids than members of the legendary IDF. Still, the
sheer numbers were reassuring and their energy seemed to be keeping the ancient, crumbling city alive.

Older, more specialized security operatives were everywhere
too—if one looked carefully. The Mahane Yehuda market is a souk,
an old-world catacombs of narrow stone alleyways lined with stalls
displaying piles of fruit and vegetables still dusted with dirt from
the fields, heaps of spices, slowly asphyxiating fish, shoelaces and
gray-market batteries. Packed with people much of the day, it is a
perennial bomb target and so it was seeded with sport-jacketed men
with squiggly things coming out of their ears who talked into their
shirt cuffs a lot. Sometimes one would see other men, in proletar-
ian dress, lounging against a bin of tomatoes watching the human
parade with eyes that were just a little too intent, and I figured they
must have been security guys too. Any private businessman who
wanted to stay in business hired his own guards. These jobs were
usually taken by young men from Africa and the recently opened
Balkan countries. It was monotonous work, searching purse after
purse and wanding waist after waist, but lapses in attention could
be deadly. Security guards are "the first line of defense against terrorism," as one Israeli mayor put it. Spotting a suspect meant confronting him—asking him to show an identity card, or to submit
to a closer search—and that's the exact moment that a terrorist,
sensing that the game was up, would reach under his shirt and pull
the detonation cord. There was perhaps, at most, a two-second window during which one could pin the bomber's arms down to prevent him from touching the cord, and there had been remarkable
displays of heroism when security guards tried to take advantage
of that window. Sometimes they succeeded in actually apprehend-
ing a bomber without any loss of life; sometimes they died as human
shields, in the act of pushing the bomber away from the door so he
killed fewer people.

It was these stories—like the new immigrant bus driver who sensed something and threw himself on top of the bomber who had just stepped onto his Egged bus on Dizengoff Boulevard in Tel Aviv— that helped keep Israelis afloat during this period. That and what seemed like a determination to carry on as before. Checkpoints and metal scanners at virtually every entrance and the surreptitious assessment of any new arrival into, say, a café had become the new normal. But to talk about this stuff more than absolutely neces- sary—to worry, to vent—was seen as profoundly uncool, something only hysterical tourists did. Yossi Klein Halevi called it "civilian Israel's decision to pretend the war wasn't happening" and the "abil- ity to simultaneously inhabit a state of emergency and a state of willful suspension of emergency."

By early September 2002 it appeared that the government's strategy—"flooding the zone" with soldiers, and making surgical hits on key terrorist leaders in the territories—was working. A month had gone by without a successful suicide bombing inside the Green Line and the international press had begun referring to "a period of calm in the Mideast."

Of course, the extent of this calm depended on where you were standing. Calm meant only that nobody had been successful *lately*. *Attempted* car bombings and suicide bombings continued at their usual daily rate during this period. They were not noted in news- papers outside of Israel, but every day in the local newspapers one saw, in effect, the record of a war: brief, matter-of-fact listings of exchanges of fire on the borders and of bombs found in bins of flour on their way to a Jerusalem market, or buried in the bedding of a baby carriage, or packed around the waists of young men dressed like Israeli soldiers or Yeshiva students. Generally these bombs were taken away and given a "controlled detonation" by IDF sappers near the place where they had been discovered.

A city dweller could be vaguely aware of this constant batter- ing at the perimeter, the way one half notices rain pelting a roof or insects buzzing outside a screen door. The sound and fury were *out there*—outside the walls. And most of the time, the "wall" of IDF green and police force blue held. We are adaptable creatures. The mind adds additional layers of insulation if additional insulation is

needed. As soon as something did break through the seams—when
there was a suicide bombing in Tel Aviv, or in Haifa, or in a Jerusalem
neighborhood that was not mine—I found my brain rushing a
rationalization to the site of anxiety the way white blood cells speed
to heal a cut. "It happened on a bus at rush hour. And I would never
take a bus at rush hour." Or: "It happened at a packed nightclub;
you'd have to be crazy to go to a packed nightclub." Or: "There is
a pattern to these things and they can be avoided if you keep your
wits about you."

■ ■ ■

THE LOVELY ISROTEL HAD long since closed for lack of business, and
the next best lodging deal I could find this time was in a huge "residential hotel" (long-term stays welcome and condos available) in
the center of the city, where I could walk to most places rather than
take a bus. The Lev Yerushalayim had been hit hard by the tourism
drought, and its occupancy rate was hanging at around 15 percent.
It was a bit creepy, this ghost hotel with its expansive 1960s-style
lobby and the unused dining room where no one sat except the
hotel's Arab workers when they had their morning coffee. There
were maybe one or two other visitors on my floor at any given
time—usually a lone, black-hatted Hassid, invariably from Brook-
lyn, New York, who would stare past me as if I were a ghost too.
      Of course, to stave off the alienation and the loneliness of a
hotel room there is always the familiar nattering of cable television,
which I reflexively switched to CNN. But the ubiquitous news network only increased my feeling of alienation and vague anxiety.
The CNN on the other side of the Atlantic is a very different ani-
mal from the CNN that comes to us from Atlanta, Georgia. Head-
quartered in London, staffed and anchored mainly by Brits,
CNN-World resembles a kind of dumbed-down BBC—especially
in its politics, which in the summer of 2002 were anti-American
and anti-Israel almost to the point of parody. When I switched to
Sky News and BBC, I found the same thing. It is no exaggeration
to say that English-language news stations, especially BBC and
CNN-World, that summer seemed to regard the United States as a
kind of evil colossus striding around the planet leaving devastation
in its wake.

Arriving in late August meant landing in the middle of the cable networks' virtually minute-by-minute coverage of the 2002 Earth Summit in Johannesburg. This brought a parade of stern-visaged environmental reporters warning of "declining resources," worldwide drought and a parched future in which, as one conference speaker put it, "small quantities of water would be traded like gold"—problems that could all be traced back to the United States' failure to sign the Kyoto Protocol.

Mercifully, the conference concluded in early September, but then the producers turned their attention back to what they seemed to consider the ongoing world crisis of Israel's occupation of the Palestinian territories. Things were relatively quiet in the first week of September; it was, after all, the week before the high holidays. But if there was nothing dramatic going on between the Israelis and the Palestinians, the BBC seemed determined to come up with some "thumb suckers" to continue the sense of crisis.

One day I watched a segment featuring a BBC reporter who had gone to a West Bank town where pot shots were being exchanged by fedayeen and IDF soldiers. She turned her camera on boys playing in the street nearby and announced, "The sound of pitched battle a few blocks down doesn't send anyone running. People here believe this is the beginning of full reoccupation, tacitly backed by the United States. Even if it isn't, Palestinians say they won't accept the peace terms dictated by Israel—not even if they're imposed by military might."

Was there a "full reoccupation . . . imposed by military might" that week or any week thereafter? No, she was posing a theoretical scenario, and then getting upset about her own invention.

Meanwhile, the West Bank was full of great investigative stories going uninvestigated. That fall the Palestinian Authority was the recipient of "the highest per capita aid transfers to a developing country in the history of foreign aid," as International Monetary Fund Mideast director Nigel Roberts put it, yet the infrastructure—schools, hospitals and such—was dilapidated. Where was the money going?

The BBC didn't ask that question. Instead, they blamed the poverty and general dishevelment on Israel. The point was made with constant juxtaposition of images (the cut from the faceless IDF

soldier to the barefoot Palestinian child) and a very liberal use of
opinion interjected as fact: Curfews imposed on towns are "collective punishment that is crushing their economy." One West Bank
town was "a man-made disaster" because of checkpoints, its "agri
culture withering under Israelis' restrictions."

School season was coming to the Palestinian territories, and
to the BBC that was more catastrophe waiting to happen. A reporter
placed herself in front of residents of one town and stated, "Their
future, their children and that of the Palestinian school system as a
whole is at the mercy of the Israeli military." She then turned to an
Arab woman identified as a UNICEF representative who was speaking agitated Arabic. According to the reporter, the rep was "implor-
ing Israel to lift curfews just during the day so children can go to
school. School is a place of peace for the children. There's no harm
in letting them go to school."

The thing that made pieces like this particularly hard to watch
was that these great storms of near-invective were "pegged," as they
say in the newspaper business, to one or two verifiable, indisputable
facts. In the school season piece, for example, the woman identified
as a UNICEF representative probably really was one—though BBC
coverage in general relies too much on the employees of West Bank
and Gaza-based NGOs, who are highly politicized, usually far left,
and often have a material stake in a continued sense of crisis. The
translation of what the UNICEF rep said for the cameras was probably basically correct—though translators who work for Western
news crews have a habit of regularly translating Arabic speakers as
referring to "Israelis" when they have actually said "Jews," apparently because "Jews" sounds so . . . racist. And the town under curfew was indeed under curfew at the time—though neither the length
of time it had been under curfew nor the IDF rationale for the curfew was given. But the piece as a whole was another example of
what Bret Stephens, then the editor of the *Jerusalem Post*, called
the foreign press's way of "getting it right while getting it wrong."

It is true, as journalists kept pointing out, that occupation is
toxic—for the occupiers and the occupied. (A top Israeli official had
just made headlines that fall for describing the continued occupation
of some West Bank towns as "corrosive" to Israeli society.) But it is
also true that the Israeli government had been trying all summer to

get out of the occupation business with a series of pull-backs, cease-fire agreements and so on, which were broken with heartbreaking regularity by the terror militias, who seemed perversely determined to keep IDF soldiers in their towns so they could keep fighting them. A pull-out from Bethlehem that fall, for instance, was followed within days by a suicide bombing carried out by a terrorist from Bethlehem. International media never remarked on this pattern, if they noticed it at all; one could observe it only by reading the local press every day.

It is true that IDF checkpoints and the occasional complete closure of towns like Nablus, a terror redoubt, had reduced trade within the West Bank to a trickle. But it is also true that the Palestinian economy was withering at least as much because Yasser Arafat was channeling foreign aid donations into his own bank account instead of the infrastructure, seed capital and job creation for which it was dedicated, and he had given control of key commodities, like gas, to one or two cronies. And where was any mention of incitement in Palestinian schools, which made them not such "peaceful places" (as the BBC's UNICEF worker had put it) after all? Where were the statistics about the number of food and medical supply trucks that did pass through checkpoints into curfewed towns? Where was it noted that curfews were temporary and usually lifted after one or two days? Or that the Israeli economy was hardly thriving either under the new intifada, or that crushing the Israeli economy was in fact one of the stated aims of Hamas—along with the complete reoccupation of all lands "from the river to the sea"? If journalists were going to discuss the plight of Palestinian refugees, where, in the coverage, was any mention of the hundreds of thousands of Palestinian refugees living in what Amnesty International called "abject poverty" in Lebanese refugee camps, forbidden by the Lebanese government from owning property, attaining citizenship or taking anything other than menial labor?

It was not necessary to believe that any of these factors justified or explained Israeli policy; one could mention them and still hate Israelis and Israeli policies. But these facts are part of the reality on the ground, and without them, reporting is incomplete, unbalanced and ultimately unfair.

■ ■ ■

A VETERAN NEWSPAPER REPORTER I KNOW who was transferred to
Jerusalem to take over his paper's Israel/Palestine beat found that
among his new colleagues, "There is only one narrative and that is
Palestinian suffering." The line is seductive, he said, because it is
"easy to write and it's what's expected by news desks." But it was
also enforced in a way he had never seen in any other expat journalist community. New to the Middle East and full of questions, he
tried to discuss issues with other reporters, sometimes by taking a
devil's advocate (or pro-Israel) position, only to find that he had to
"work hard to avoid getting in an argument when even expressing
a tentative opinion." The attitude among the Europeans was "if
you're not with us, you're against us." One of his first backgrounding experiences had been a lecture sponsored by the local Foreign
Press Association chapter featuring a top Palestinian Authority
spokesman who had explained the conflict to the crowd, largely by
"blaming everything short of the weather on Israel."

He found "a small world of journalists who mostly hung out
with people from the EU, the UN, with diplomats, all of whom rein-
force views." Very few of the media people he met "know any
Israelis." He had asked an American journo he'd met if she knew
any Israelis and she had said she "really didn't" because Israelis—
as opposed to Palestinians, who were open and welcoming—"aren't
much fun."

Around this time I found a particularly blatant example of
more of this "template enforcement" in the British magazine the
New Statesman, in a review of an anthology of photographs of
Gaza. The reviewer approved of one photographer for he had gone
"on night manoeuvres with the Israeli occupation forces and shows
how these jollies have become a highly ritualised form of brutality." Another photographer started off well in the reviewer's opinion by showing us "buildings shorn in two, walls so scarred with
bullets that one can scarcely believe there is so much firepower in
the world," but then he blows it with other photographs of "uninhabited areas" in Gaza. "Where is the truth?" the reviewer
demanded. "[The photographer] is in Gaza, the most densely populated place on earth, yet his landscapes are empty.... This is not
truth, it is artifice, the kind a photojournalist grabs when he is reaching for profundity."

But in fact, Gaza is far from being "the most densely populated place on earth," and if the reviewer had ever been to Gaza he would have seen that there are expanses of empty land. That is a truth about Gaza as much as "walls scarred with bullets" are.

Another photographer attracts the reviewer's ire because he "comes from the 'chirpy incongruity' school of photography." In other words, his photographs are of "Palestinian youths wearing T-shirts with pictures of Diana, Princess of Wales, or stepping out of beach huts and going for donkey rides."

But there are many narratives in the West Bank and Gaza. And one of them is the clash of Western modernity and traditional Islam—as personified by the goatherd wearing a Princess Di T-shirt. Would the reviewer have minded the Princess Di T-shirt if the boy were also throwing a rock at an Israeli soldier?

As for another photographer, the reviewer grouses that he can't understand why his work was included in the book at all:

> [The photographer] argues that depicting violence only perpetuates the situation.... But given the title and proclaimed aim of the exhibition, it seems odd to include photographs that have nothing to say about the conflict. His series is called Twenty in Jerusalem; it might easily be retitled Jewish and Arab Girls Who Are Quite Foxy.

So apparently during an intifada, girls aren't allowed to be foxy. But maybe this photographer's pictures show that spirit and beauty continue to bloom in the middle of war—or some other point outside the usual Occupiers vs. Occupied template. On the other hand, as my newspaper acquaintance put it, among the British and European press there was "only one narrative."

One morning that fall I received an email invitation to a lecture at the beautiful King David Hotel about the resurgence of anti-Semitism in Europe. The invitation had gone out to anyone with an Israeli government-approved press card and a buffet was promised.

About sixty journalists were seated around a great circular table to listen to Abraham Foxman, the director of the Anti-Defamation League, who had come all the way from the United States to be the keynote speaker. After talking about the rising incidence of synagogue torching and such in Europe, his lecture came around to press coverage. Foxman said he had seen great improvement in

Israel's coverage by U.S. outlets since the first years of the intifada.
Europe, on the other hand, was another story and he said that
Europe's demonizing coverage played some part in the new surge
in anti-Semitic incidents.

The lecture had mostly attracted Israeli journalists, but there
were a few European representatives at the conference table, among
them Simon Wilson, a senior producer in the BBC's Jerusalem
bureau. Wilson spoke up in an earnest, Hugh Grant–like manner
to say that the BBC was truly perplexed when groups like the Anti-
Defamation League accused them of blatantly anti-Israel reporting.
"We have tried very hard to understand this," he said in a sincere
manner. "We have scrutinized our coverage carefully, and we just
can't see it."

We soon adjourned to a canapés-and-drinks table, where I
seized the opportunity to corral the poor man. His deeply engrained
British politeness forced him to suffer me for a few minutes.

"You must be able to see that you have a rather dramatic lean
in one direction," I said. "Can't you see it in your copy? The words
you use, for instance, they are so leading, so loaded...."

"That is just sort of how we *do* journalism. It's just a different style than the American," he said. "I'm sure if you'd check you'd
see we cover everything that way."

"Maybe," I said. "But there's also your story selection. It's like
Israel is under a microscope—everything exposed, everything subject to criticism—but their failings are not balanced by anything on
the other side. And we all know terrible things are happening on
the other side, don't we?" I said, searching his face for some clue
that he knew what I was talking about.

He nodded.

"It's like you hold Israel to a higher standard than the Palestinians," I pressed.

"I guess we do hold Israel to a higher standard," he mused.
"After all, it's a Western country, a modern country...."

"Isn't it a little condescending not to hold the Palestinian
Authority government to any sort of standard, as if they're a bunch
of primitives, or as if they're children?" I asked.

"Interesting idea," he said, with what may have been forced
heartiness. "I will have to give that some thought."

■ ■ ■

IN THE FALL OF 2002, the Ministry of Foreign Affairs press division, along with the rest of the ministry offices, was housed in a British army barracks left over from the Mandate era. A month or so after Operation Defensive Shield, the *New York Times* had made a reference to Israel's "vast [press] apparatus" that "rolls out press kits with every tank," so I was interested to see if Israel's press operation had in fact become much more vast and efficient since I had last seen them in action. The *Times'* description, of course, suggests something large, cold and slightly fascist. Certainly, one could experience a tiny Inside-the-Third-Reich frisson as one approached the compound from the street. Young men with shaved heads (*à la* Vin Diesel) and wraparound dark glasses prowled on the sidewalk, cradling semi-automatic rifles. The thick black stone wall that surrounds the compound itself was topped with rolls of concertina wire, and before one could walk through its heavy, electronically controlled gate, one had to check in at a glass-walled guard shack to go through a metal detector, have one's bags searched, and wait while sotto voce phone calls were made.

But once inside the wall, I felt as if I'd slipped into a little paradise under glass. Here was a cluster of sand-colored stucco bungalows—seemingly unchanged since the 1940s—covered with flowering vines, shaded by cypress and orange trees, and connected by tiny, meandering stone walkways. At lunchtime, MFA staffers strolled on these paths, jacketless, greeting each other by first name and stopping in pools of shade to chat. Something about the scene seemed very "Israeli"—something I couldn't put my finger on, until I realized that the MFA compound felt like the relaxed, small-town life of the Galilee-region kibbutzim I lived in and visited as a teenager. Whether they had intended it or not, the Israelis had taken one of the most central divisions of their government and replicated the informal, agrarian feel of the kibbutz. Staffers were a bit sad because later that month this historic compound would be razed, and, in the interest of a much-needed consolidation of press operations, the entire division would move to a new, modern building closer to the Knesset and Prime Minister Sharon's office. "There has always been a democratic feeling here," MFA official Baruch Binah told me. "You

were never called 'up' to see somebody, because there is no real 'up'
to go! Everyone is on the same level."

The alternation of high security on the outside and pastoral
atmosphere on the inside made me think of something a wire serv
ice reporter had told me about the difference between the Palestinian Authority and the Israeli government's treatment of the press.
"When you go to the Mukata [Arafat's headquarters], some guy
just waves you in," he said, "but once inside, you better be on your
best behavior. If you value your life and your career you wouldn't
say 'Arafat sucks' because it's a dictatorship. It's the exact opposite
if you go to interview Sharon. You go through three checkpoints,
but once in those halls you can say whatever you want."

Still, it was obvious from just hanging out at the compound
that people there—while not exactly showing Germanic efficiency—
had grown more serious, less lackadaisical about *hasbara*. For one
thing, when I asked to speak to the people in charge of the *hasbara*
effort, there was no hesitation, because people knew exactly who
those people were. I was directed to an MFA official named Arye
Mekel. Maybe because he was actually just leaving Jerusalem, and
on his way to New York to head Israel's mission to the United
Nations, he came across as the greatest optimist of all time. He
brushed away my comment that Israel still seemed to be having
problems with its image:

"The whole operation became a lot more sophisticated since
2000. We looked at our experiences then and drew conclusions. You'd
be surprised how scientific and systematic our operation is. We have
practically turned it into a science," he said, flinging himself back
in his chair and throwing his plump arms in the air like a magician
who's just pulled a rabbit out of a hat.

"We have created a high level of coordination," he continued
with gusto. "For instance, the minute that Prime Minister Sharon
made the announcement that they were beginning Operation Defensive Shield, we got going and by 8 A.M., 11 A.M. . . . something like
that . . . the next day, we had this thing together—a very large-scale
media center. It continued for twenty-five days, until the last day
of the operation. It was much better than the one in 2000. We really
created a situation that they couldn't live without. There were top

military spokesmen, top foreign ministry spokesmen who could be interviewed on the spot, all kinds of information, videos ..."

"But you laid on a great array of information the last time and the foreign press simply ignored it," I interrupted.

"Aha, but any journalist who comes to Israel wanting to work has to get a press card, right?" he said with an air of triumph. "So, we made [the press center] the place they had to get the card. They *had* to come there first."

To address the problem of erudite, experienced Israeli spokesmen whose erudition and experience were lost in thick accents, the MFA had also "created six to eight spokesmen who are interchangeable. Each have enough information, skills and clout with media." And impeccable English. As far as what the polished new talking heads would actually say, gone were the days of every-man-for-himself, improvisation and anarchy: "We have created a sophisticated system of creating the message; the message is being crafted by professionals," Mekel explained. "First we have at least daily meetings with top-echelon people to decide what it is that we want to say; then we have very professional all-American-born people to craft it in the form of a sound bite."

By around 10 A.M. each morning, Team Israel would thus be ready to go, equipped with the sound bite of the day. All spokespeople were now hooked together by pager and cell phone, so they could stay in close contact and coordinate a consistent government statement when news broke. MFA spokesmen thus seemed to live with cell phones wedged against their ears. One day I watched MFA staffer Jonathan Peled doing a series of live interviews with international broadcast hosts and reporters as he stood in a cafeteria line and then while he was attempting to wolf down a sandwich—which he left half-eaten. Minutes later he "conferenced" with the rest to discuss what he had said.

The MFA was also trying to be more proactive; thus they had maintained an archive of video backgrounders and had embedded a staffer in the Jerusalem Capital Studios. If news broke, that staffer would be ready to offer tape to frantic, picture–hungry producers. The new media monitoring center I'd heard about was now completed and had been filled with banks of televisions tuned to the planet's major TV stations—Al-Jazeera, Al-Arabiya, Al-Manar (otherwise known as the Hezbollah channel), BBC, ABC, CNN, etc. The idea was to catch inaccurate statements early, before they descended much further down the media food chain and became "fact."

Certainly I sensed a sincere new energy about *hasbara*, but I still had not seen the "vast operation" that the *New York Times* had referred to. The entire MFA press staff received less than 1 percent of the national budget. Thus the fancy new press monitoring center, for one example, was run by a staff of about three: one or two recent college graduates and a perpetually harried director.

I had other misgivings about the improved *hasbara* initiatives. It is important for a government staff to stay "on message," but the Israelis seemed to have responded to the new mandate a little too dutifully. The ever-optimistic Arye Mekel had said that "9/11 showed Americans that we and they are in the same way in respect to terrorism. Our battle and their battle are part of the same big battle." He was repeating an idea that had been turned into a major theme for MFA press spokesmen. There was nothing wrong with the message per se, except that every time I saw MFA spokespeople on television that fall, they were hammering the "same big battle" sound bite—making this point whenever possible, often making convoluted twists in conversations to work it in. To turn on, say, BBC was to see an otherwise brilliant man like former Israeli ambassador Dore Gold address a direct question about, say, water rights to the Wazani River (which Israel shares with Jordan) with an answer about the global war on terrorism. It made Israel's spokesmen look evasive, like they were trying too hard, or even like they weren't listening to their interviewer.

There was another new trend that I had ambivalent feelings about: a new embrace of victimhood. The day in the fall of 2000 when Jonathan Peled had said, "Obviously we can take pictures of people killed and wounded and try to push them through but we try to be more rational, not so emotional" seemed very far away. Israeli officials had ceded the fact that the language of television is almost completely emotional. If the Palestinians felt they would win this new war because they could "die better," as a Palestinian spokesman had put it two years earlier, Israel was now pushing its bloody children and its keening widows in front of the cameras too.

But perhaps the new approach was necessary. Israelis had long commented with dark irony that they were losing "the media war" because their emergency services were too good at cleaning a street of all traces of a terror bombing and opening it to traffic within a few hours. By the time reporters got to the site of an attack, there was not much to see. Even if the reporters did jump into their vans and drive to local hospitals to get film of victims, Israeli hospitals enforced a policy based on a victim's "right to privacy"—so snaps of the recently wounded or dead were not allowed.

By April 2002, in the aftermath of "Jenin," there had been a growing feeling among government people that, as Miri Eisen put it, "enough was enough. It was time to show the victims."

"We decided we have to go on the initiative," Eisen said. "And we all—the IDF, the MFA, the GPO, the Prime Minister's Office, the police spokesmen—came together and it was decided to bring out the Israeli victims, by approaching people and asking them if they wanted to be a part of the initiative to show the other side." Hospitals were asked to open their doors to reporters and most did so.

One thing had not changed: The IDF and the Ministry of Foreign Affairs may have come together briefly in the crisis atmosphere post-"Jenin," but by now they had gone back to scrapping. In the summer of 2002, Israel's civil defense branches were preparing the citizenry for a supposedly imminent American invasion of Iraq and the new barrage of more accurate Scud missiles this would probably trigger. So that this shouldn't be a total loss, the MFA wanted to put videos of brave Israeli citizens stoically making preparations into the hands of the world's television producers. The problem was that the IDF operated "the home-front command" and thus had access to footage of sealed room preparation and such, and they were refusing to allow MFA staffers into their compounds.

"People are interested in [the issue of] Iraq," explained an MFA official, who insisted on anonymity lest he damage relations between the two divisions any further. "They should be seeing scenes of how the [IDF] is getting ready, how the protective equipment against gas works, stuff like that. But the army says 'we don't want to talk about that. If we talk about that there's going to be panic in Israel.' They have meetings about how they're going to talk to the media but they don't invite us."

The IDF was even known to keep secrets from its own press department—a tendency that had made for some very bad headlines. Earlier that year, one of the IDF's most elite and secret Special Forces units (something akin to Delta Force in the United States) had determined that one of its "most wanted" would be entering a specific abandoned building in Rafah, a town in the Gaza Strip, at a specific time. They set an explosive booby trap that they believed only the wanted man would trigger. Instead, three Palestinian boys came to play in the building and were killed. When reporters asked MFA spokesmen to explain the incident, MFA officials called the IDF spokesmen's office and were told that the boys had been hit by a tank shell—because that is what the IDF press officers were told by the unit commander, who was possibly trying to preserve the whereabouts and M.O. of his elite unit. But BBC reporters went to the building, where it was obvious that the boys had been killed by an explosive. The BBC soon after reported, in its habitual "Gotcha!" style, that Israel had killed three little boys and its foreign ministry had tried to cover it up. The special ops unit was finally forced to explain what had actually happened to its own bewildered spokesmen.

The number one complaint about the IDF spokesmen's office has been that it takes too long to comment on events. The safest and most accurate explanation is that "an investigation is under way," but a terse "we are investigating" creates a kind of news vacuum, which the Palestinian Authority took the opportunity to fill with the words of its most florid spokesmen. On the other hand, incidents like this, in which the IDF came out too soon with the wrong information, seemed to have made the press division even more phobic about issuing any statement other than "an investigation is under way." As the foreign ministry official—himself a current officer in the reserves—charitably pointed out, investigations take days to complete because first one has to track down the soldiers involved, and they are usually on the move to somewhere from somewhere else.

To me, the incident illustrated the irresolvable tension between a free press and the waging of an effective war: It's easy to see why the special ops unit didn't want to publicize that it was working in a specific area and using a specific method. As soon as a quarry learns it is being tracked, it will change its movements, and in a flash, weeks, even months of intelligence work is made useless. Nonspecific but educational, contextualizing answers are needed (see Donald Rumsfeld's 2003 press briefings as he painstakingly educated a mostly militarily illiterate press corps about the exigencies of war); but the best people to supply these answers to an impatient, suspicious press are currently in the MFA.

But chances that the IDF would get over its longstanding mistrust of the civilians in the MFA seemed slim, and it was unlikely that the Prime Minister's Office would step in and force them to cooperate. My MFA source remarked glumly, "[We are] much less important than the army in Israel because we are in a continual state of war. Our job is to coordinate and run all the media activities to the outside world, but you can't expect [MFA director] Gideon Meir to go to the IDF chief of staff and slap him in the face. It doesn't work this way."

SEVEN

BEHIND THE VEIL

Most of the correspondents of the Arab TV and radio sta-
tions need to be educated politically and culturally about
the internal situation [of the Palestinian Authority]. The
task of educating these journalists should be the responsibil-
ity of the Palestinian Journalists Syndicate, although some
of its heads also need to be educated. The Ministry of Infor-
mation should also be entrusted with educating these corre-
spondents by telling them which phrases are used in our
political life. We don't understand, for example, why some
Arab satellite stations are no longer using the term "mar-
tyr." How is it possible that some Palestinian journalists are
capable of making harmful remarks against their leaders at
a time when even foreign journalists are careful not to
alienate the Palestinians?

  —Yussef al-Qazzaz, senior official with the

  Palestinian Broadcasting Corporation, January 12, 2004

In the sea of newsprint I scanned every morning as I drank my
coffee in my Jerusalem apartment during the fall and winter of
2002, one byline became more and more important to me. A
Jerusalem Post reporter named Khaled Abu Toameh did something I had never seen before. (In fact, my newspaper industry contacts think he may be the only person doing it in the world.) Toameh
writes on a daily basis about life on the other side of the Green Line
(and life in Arab East Jerusalem) without the habitual neo-Orien-
talist condescension of Western reporters—just matter-of-factly,
with concrete detail, the way one should cover any other area with
a sprawling government, a legislature, hospitals, a number of universities and just about everything else that other countries have.

Born in the West Bank town of Tulkarem in 1965 while it was still occupied by the Jordanians, raised in Israeli-controlled but primarily Arab East Jerusalem, and educated in Israeli West Jerusalem, Toameh is a Muslim Arab with Israeli citizenship who is fluent in Arabic, Hebrew and English. His mixed background made him something of a permanent outsider in both worlds, and thus an ideal observer. Toameh's writing was unemotional and spare, but his reporting felt like a "window-pane" (as George Orwell once said journalism should be) between a reader sitting in West Jerusalem and life in the territories. I learned about the Palestinian legislature, the West Bank universities and other day-to-day stuff from reading his work, but what I mostly learned about, sadly, was the way violence saturated the territories—not the Israeli-versus-Palestinian violence that is always reported, but Palestinian-on-Palestinian violence. I do not think that Toameh went out of his way to cover daily brutality, but that in covering the normal ebb and flow of Palestinian politics, he could not avoid it. "There is a lot of violence in our society, unfortunately," Toameh told me. "People believe that through violence they can solve problems."

The dead formed an endless daily procession in his stories. They were members of feuding Arab tribes, rival factions and warring families. They were wives deemed immodest, girlfriends deemed treacherous, daughters deemed disobedient, and always, always there were those executed in gruesome ways for having collaborated, in some loosely defined way, with Israel. It was always strange to me that the press which so loves blood turned a blind eye on the death of these innocents.

"Yesterday members of Fatah's military wing, the Al Aqsa Martyrs Brigades, shot and killed a mother of seven in Tulkarem after accusing her of collaborating with Israel. Ikhlas Yasin, 39, was shot in the town's main square," Toameh wrote in a typical dispatch one day in August.

In a story in September he reported that "masked men opened fire at the home of Nabil Amr, a former Palestinian Authority cabinet member who has openly challenged PA Chairman Yasser Arafat and called for wide-scale reforms in the PA."

In November, Toameh described his conversations with a nineteen-year-old terrorist who told him, "I am not afraid of the Jews. . . .

We will kill them wherever we find them," and then just as quickly described how, with "his own hands," he had "strangled to death" a local village leader (a *muktar*) who was suspected of collaborating with Israel. "He was about 70 years old," the nineteen-year-old told Toameh with a smile, "and it wasn't a problem to kill him."

One of the subjects that reoccurred regularly in Toameh's reporting was what he called Arafat's "complete control over the media inside the territories." This was a regime, he said, that "believes a [journalist's] role should be limited to serving as faithful spokesmen for the Palestinian leadership as is the case in most Arab countries." And journalists got it from both sides—Hamas, which is a rival of the PA, believed that local journalists should be "faithful spokesmen" for them as well.

On November 3, 2002, for instance, Toameh reported that "a large number of Hamas activists and supporters attacked . . . local journalists who arrived at [a funeral], beating them and destroying their cameras. The attacker accused the journalists of collaboration with Israel and threatened to shoot them." A senior Hamas leader personally "cocked his automatic rifle and forced the Palestinian journalists [representing the Associated Press, Reuters, Agence France-Presse and Palestinian TV] to hand over their videotapes."

When the PA regime wanted to ensure loyalty, it often resorted to violence as well; but sometimes just the threat of violence, or the reminder of how violent the regime could be, was sufficient to ensure that the local and visiting press corps remained tractable. In August 2002, Toameh had an experience that became emblematic for him of how docile the foreign press corps working in the territories had become.

It was a hot, sticky day. Toameh was waiting with a group of reporters outside Arafat's headquarters in Ramallah for a cabinet meeting to break up, when two men emerged from a building dragging another man whose face was covered with bruises.

"It must have been the strange look in his eyes, a look that will haunt me for many years. I fe[lt] as if this young man [was] begging for help," Toameh wrote:

> I decide[d] to follow him and see where he [was] being taken. The two men [took] him to the back of a building north of Arafat's office. What happened next is hard to describe. The man was blindfolded

and made to stand against a wall. Three policemen, standing about three meters away, sprayed him with bullets from their rifles. He was hit in the head and chest and fell to the ground.

One of the policemen then walked up to him and fired one more shot into his head. "Take him away," came the order from another police officer.

I couldn't believe my eyes. The executioners did not notice that I was watching. When the rest of the journalists heard the shots, they rushed to see what was happening. Nervous policemen charged at the reporters and ordered them to leave the area.

I asked a police officer what happened and he replied, "A criminal has been executed. What's the big deal?"

"What did he do?" I asked another police officer who was trying to block cameras with his hand.

"He murdered two elderly women and raped his grandmother," he answered.

"Was he ever tried?"

"I don't know, but the president this morning approved the execution."

An ambulance that had been waiting nearby took the body away before anyone else had a chance to see it. As it was leaving, ministers continued to arrive. I asked three of them if they had heard about the execution which just took place a few meters away, and all replied that they had no idea what I was talking about.

A few hours later the PA confirmed that the execution did take place, identifying the victim as Bashir Attari. Palestinians described him as mentally retarded.

What was most notable about this was that no one else wrote a story. The press "saw no evil, spoke no evil, and heard no evil," Toameh concluded. And he grew to understand that "many foreign journalists avoided writing stories because they didn't want to embarrass the PA, risk their lives, or ruin their relationship."

The docility of local Palestinian reporters was a little more understandable than that of the Western press. After all, Western reporters got to leave the territories at night. (If they went in at all. Too often, Toameh said, people thought they could cover the territories by "staying in Tel Aviv and making a few phone calls.") Most rotated out after one or two years of this "difficult" duty. Palestinian journalists, on the other hand, were surrounded by the repressive environment and had had nearly ten years of reminders of what happened to those who "collaborated," even journalistically, with Arafat's enemies.

The lessons began in 1994 when Arafat took power as part of the Oslo Accords. In Western media, the history of what followed is mainly a chronicle of a PA struggling under the yoke of Israeli occupation; but the reports of the human rights organization Freedom House, along with one scholar's monographs and Toameh's reporting, present a parallel history of a systematic crushing of the free press that existed before Arafat's move to the territories from Tunis in 1994. Fatah, Arafat's enforcer arm, moved from newspaper to newspaper (there were five feisty and independent newspapers based in the territories when Arafat came in) and from radio station to television station, beating, jailing and threatening anyone who reported anything that would reflect badly on the new leader. When papers were driven out of business or their editors jailed, Arafat quickly replaced them with his own mouthpieces—the Voice of Palestine radio network and the Palestinian Broadcasting Corporation. By 2002, the three daily newspapers covering life in the territories—*Al-Quds* (the largest), *Al-Ayam* and *Al-Hayat al-Jadeeda*—all sounded, as Toameh put it, like "the Palestinian versions of the now defunct Pravda."

Even when a story was not clearly political, just bad, Palestinian reporters were loath to report it because of the hypersensitivity of the Arafat regime. When a six-year-old Palestinian girl disappeared from her home, Israeli police began a search and tried to enlist the Palestinian media. According to Toameh, the Israeli police said they "literally had to beg the editor of *Al-Quds* to do a story." The next day, the paper ran a brief item, without a picture, saying only that "Israeli police are searching for missing Arab and Jewish Girls." A Palestinian editor explained to Toameh that he hadn't wanted to do more because "journalists are afraid to cover stories that could get them into trouble and most of our journalists believe this is not the right time to deal with stories that might reflect negatively on Palestinians." The girl was found dead in a drainage ditch several weeks later.

In the fall of 2002, Toameh, who lives in West Jerusalem, had a personal experience with the kind of intimidation that Palestinian journalists in the territories had been enduring at the hands of the PA. He had written a fairly routine news story on legislative activity in the West Bank for the *Jerusalem Post*. Included in passing was a mention that Ahmed Qurei—then a speaker in the Palestinian Legislative Council, later appointed prime minister of the Palestinian Authority—had requested a meeting with Ariel Sharon in order to ask the Israeli prime minister to take IDF troops away from Arafat's headquarters in Ramallah, where they were stationed to retaliate for suicide bombings near Tel Aviv. That Qurei had sent a request to Sharon (instead of, say, waiting for Sharon to call him) might seem like a small detail, but according to one of his aides, this detail "harmed Qurei's dignity and presented him as someone who is humiliating himself in front of the Israeli prime minister." The night the story appeared in the *Jerusalem Post*, Toameh began receiving calls on his mobile and home phones from a Qurei aide, who said things like "we'll show you" and "we'll deal with you." Toameh was forced to call the Israeli police. The aide is an Israeli Arab who lives in West Jerusalem, so he was not hard to find. The Israeli police held him for several hours until he was released on bail. In the end, Toameh allowed the matter to drop without charges because, he says, he wanted "just to give him a warning and stop the harassment."

Other journalists in Jerusalem regard Toameh as a hero, but they speculate about how long he will be able to keep risking the ire of Fatah and Hamas. One thing in his favor may be his very innocuous, everyman appearance. He is around five-foot-nine, in his early forties, with a round face that is quick to smile, and he usually wears casual clothes and a baseball cap. He does not look stereotypically Arab, but neither does he look particularly Anglo-Saxon.

Toameh comes from a middle-class, politically neutral family—the type one hardly ever sees in coverage of the West Bank. He learned to speak English as a child. When he was ten, his family moved from Tulkarem to East Jerusalem so his father could take a job as the principal of an all-girls school there. As East Jerusalem was now part of Israel, Toameh automatically became an Israeli citizen.

Many years earlier, though we never met, we had both been students at Jerusalem's Anglican Church School—a little island of Masterpiece Theatre style Britishness in the middle of Jerusalem, with chilly stone-floored classrooms, morning hymns, and Anglican nuns who taught subjects like Latin. I *had* to go there because it was one of the few schools in Jerusalem where the instruction was in English, but when it was time for him to go to high school Toameh chose the Anglican Church School because it was (and still is, he says) "the best school" around.

After graduating from the Anglican school, Toameh went on to Jerusalem's Hebrew University, where he graduated with degrees in English literature and international relations. While still in school he worked at a PLO-financed newspaper that had an office in East Jerusalem. It was a clerical job, but it convinced him that he wanted to go into journalism and he began to accept freelance assignments for English-language, generally pro-Israel publications like the *Jerusalem Report*. Eventually he became the Palestinian affairs correspondent for the *Jerusalem Post* and he covers the territories as a daily beat while freelancing on the side for publications from *USA Today* to NBC News.

The Israeli reporter Danny Zaken calls Toameh "a *yahid beminoh*—one who comes once in a generation. He writes without fear, he writes what he wants, and he is reliable." Zaken thinks it is this mixture—"speaking in Arabic, being an Arab, but also having the Israeli *protexia*," friends in Israeli government—that has allowed him to survive so long. It also helped, Zaken thinks, that Arafat and Company didn't worry too much about what was printed in the *Jerusalem Post:* "If Khaled wrote for the *Washington Post*, things would be different."

"Some people think I'm mad," Toameh told me. "Some people think I'm risking my life, because in the Arab world you don't have freedom of the press; our culture is antidemocratic, it doesn't understand the real meaning of freedom of speech."

Toameh is not optimistic about peace because of what he—along with writers like Bernard Lewis and Fouad Ajami—see as a tendency in Palestinian culture toward self-pity, fatalism and self-justification: "There will be a lot of talk in the Arab press about IDF raids, IDF killings, IDF checkpoints, closures, seizures, but they never say why. They are always searching for someone to blame. There's rarely an attempt at self-criticism."

But he is not a mouthpiece for the Israeli government either. He blames the Israeli government, in part, for the reign of Arafat.

"I always said from the beginning that this so-called 'peace' was just a contract between ten thousand or so Palestinians from the PLO and their families and businesses [and the Israeli government]," he told me, referring to the Oslo agreement of 1993. "It was just a deal. People on the ground were not part of it." The Israeli government "made the mistake of thinking they could turn Arafat into a policeman by bribing him and several thousand Palestinians around him. So the PA police have been acting more like militias with criminals taking over senior jobs." (Of course, Israel was under its own pressure. For a long time the international community treated making nice with Yasser Arafat—shaking hands, agreeing to meetings, funding the PA—as the index of Israel's desire for peace.)

Journalists in Israel speculate about how Toameh continues to go into the territories almost every day to report; he says he gets his stories because "there are many people inside there who are trying to get things out. There's a growing number in the Arab world, especially among the Palestinians, who disapprove of dictatorship, who don't want this to continue."

Anyway, he said, "This is my job. If bad things are happening, then they're happening, and the fact that many journalists ignore them is a problem." Toameh regards intimidation of the local press and murders of "collaborators" as "a major story within the PA," and asks, "How can you ignore it?"

EIGHT

FIXING THE NEWS

f I was to revisit the territories myself, I needed, at a minimum, an Arabic-to-English translator. Everybody has them. They are fixtures at the sides of Western reporters working in the territories. It's true that the bigger towns in the West Bank are full of English signage because of past tourism, and virtually all top PA and PLO functionaries speak good to impeccable English because many were educated in English-language countries like Canada, Britain and the United States. So, in a pinch, one could probably grope around the West Bank relying on English. The problem is, as an Israeli reporter put it, that Jenin and the like are not places where you should "go groping around" armed only with a map and a smile. In other words, one's translator becomes also a native guide, a driver, a maker of introductions—"a fixer."

Journalists employ fixers in every part of the world. (A Columbia School of Journalism alum I heard of is trying to set up a sort of international "fixer" listing service.) But when reporters come to Israel to cover the conflict it is assumed, despite the number of Israelis who can speak Arabic and who would be allowed to "cross" into the territories, that one is looking for a genuine Palestinian fixer. For years, probably as long as there have been foreign press in Jerusalem, each foreign bureau has had its unofficially attached Palestinian fixer. One more or less "inherits" them, as a newspaper reporter I know put it, the way one inherits a gardener, an old family retainer.

Paul Adams of the *Toronto Globe and Mail* explained the particular benefits of a Palestinian fixer in an October 2002 article for his paper: "In the Palestinian Territories ... you need someone who knows the lay of the land—to dodge Israeli checkpoints and army patrols, if nothing else—and if you don't speak Arabic, you need the help of someone who does." Dicey work like "dodging army patrols" has a way of forging strong ties. Adams' piece, for instance, soon turns into a paean to his loyal Palestinian fixer "Nuha."

"[Nuha] dislikes the term fixer," Adams writes, "perhaps because it carries a slight flavour of corruption. . . . [The] former English teacher and press officer to the Palestinian politician Hanan Ashrawi . . . prefers 'media assistant', which is what it says on her press card, or simply 'translator.'"

When the Israelis began knocking down Yasser Arafat's Mukata (Arabic for "headquarters") in September 2002, Nuha was the first person—before even his editor, apparently—to attempt to get Adams to leave the Jerusalem swimming pool where he was spending "an unreasonably hot afternoon."

"The cell phone rang unanswered by the side of the pool," Adams explains. He felt bad about that, but was reassured to learn later that when Nuha failed to rouse him, she quickly got a call from "a Swiss television unit that wanted her to accompany them" to the Mukata. Adams applauds her selflessness:

> It is typical of Nuha that she would have been ready to bolt out and head to the scene of the action, at some risk to herself, even before she had found a paying client (or, as in this case, before a paying client found her).
>
> "Does that woman ever sleep?" another reporter asked me the other day as she arrived to meet me one morning at the American Colony Hotel—the media's favourite Jerusalem haunt—greeting the staff individually and waving to tables of journalists and diplomats breakfasting in the courtyard.

Adams explains that one of Nuha's many sidelines has been teaching Arabic and it was "one of her students, Neil MacDonald, CBC [Canadian Broadcasting Corporation] television's correspondent here, who suggested she try her hand as a fixer. It was Neil, too, who first suggested I work with her and I am enormously grateful that he did.

"Since then, we have had many adventures together," Adams writes:

We have driven between Israeli and Palestinian lines in taxicabs, protected only by the letters "TV" taped on the hood and windows.... Once, I did see her lose her nerve—though only for a moment. Last April, we were trying to get into Jenin refugee camp, the scene of fierce fighting a few days earlier. The Israelis had lifted the curfew for a few hours so Palestinians were moving in and out of the camp and we tried to join the flow. Perhaps the flak jackets gave us away. Pointing their machine guns, an Israeli army patrol shouted for us to halt. I kept on going but Nuha raised her hand and yelled shrilly in fear—and I stopped in my tracks.

The Israelis told us to get out of the area. Two minutes later, with the patrol out of sight, Nuha waved down a Palestinian man and his family in a pick-up truck. She lay under a tarpaulin in the rear box and I squished down in the cab, which also contained the driver and two of his daughters. Why they risked their safety for us, I do not know, but we successfully raced into Jenin camp, right past the patrol that had stopped us moments earlier.

Though they may occasionally have to scrunch down in the back of pickup trucks under tarpaulins, Palestinian fixers are, in general, a very white-collar, highly educated group. Media management is taken very seriously on the Palestinian side of the Green Line. Many fixers hone their skills at the Media Institute of Bir Zeit University in Ramallah—where the Hamas chapter recently won a majority of student council seats on a platform of having killed more Jews than the other groups running.* Others have attended a training program sponsored by an NGO called Palestinian Academic Society for the Study of International Affairs (PASSIA), which is funded by

---

*"At a debate, the Hamas candidate said to the Fatah candidate: 'Hamas activists in this university killed 135 Zionists. How many did Fatah activists from Bir Zeit kill?' ... The Fatah candidate refused to answer, suggesting his rival 'look at the paper, go to the archives and see for yourself. Al-Aqsa Martyrs' Brigades have not stopped fighting the occupation.' ... As part of their campaign for student government, students with Fatah set up models of Jewish settlements and then blew them up with fireworks. The display was meant to emphasize the group's focus on attacking settlers and their communities.... Students affiliated with Hamas countered by blowing up models of Israeli buses, a tribute to the dozens of suicide bombings its members have carried out in the past three years, killing hundreds of Israelis. fighting the occupation." (From a story by Khaled Abu Toameh, *Jerusalem Post*.)

U.S. Aid for International Development. One of the program text-books, *Media and Communication Skills,* sets a political tone on page nine when it declares that the "first challenge to Palestinian society arose with the Balfour Declaration of 1917, which called for the estab-lishment of a national home for the Jews in Palestine, a clear viola-tion of the rights of the Palestinian people." But for the most part, the rest of the book consists of rather banal practical tips ("pictures count" and "human drama is extremely important") for the lobby-ist or activist who wants to "sell" stories to news media.

The problem, as Israeli press spokesmen see it, is that the small army of Palestinian fixers often subtly control what reporters see, whom they meet, and even the very words they hear: In March 2002, *Ha'aretz* reporter Vered Levy-Barzilai detailed the difficul-ties that newly arrived Fox News reporter Jennifer Griffin had one day when she went out with an interpreter/fixer named Nidal Rafa, who, as the *Ha'aretz* reporter wrote, is "considered a top profes-sional." She is "a graduate of Bir Zeit University in the West Bank and possesses clear political awareness.... She is young, opinion-ated and assertive ... and, to put it mildly, she pretty well manage[d] the event" of Griffin's day in the field.

The *Ha'aretz* reporter wrote that at one point Griffin turned to ask her specifically if there was anything she could "tell her about the Wadi Ara region, as background." Levy-Barzilai, the *Ha'aretz* reporter, hadn't even opened her mouth before Rafa "interjected herself, in Eng-lish, with an obvious edge to her voice [to say] 'I will give you the background. This whole area was expropriated by Israel from the Arabs. Everything here belonged to the Arabs. There are Jewish settlements ... above: villas, beautiful homes. And all of it on our land.' "

In the course of Griffin's day in the field, Rafa "decide[d] what to translate and what to leave untranslated." At one point she even shot an Arab interviewee "a piercing look" and told Griffin, "He already answered that. Go on to the next question." She changed Griffin's original itinerary, and so it was she, according to Levy-Barzi-lai, "who finally decided what their news channel would broadcast...."

The language barrier creates even more problematic depend-encies. Many of the bureaus hire Palestinian editors to facilitate sto-ries (make introductions and such) and to translate materials from Arabic. But in exchange, in at least one major wire service, according to a journalist who works there and has asked not to be identified, any news involving Palestinians is then at "the mercy" of those Palestinian editors. The bureau's Palestinian editors are treated as experts on anything concerning the territories and expected to vet copy concerning the PA and happenings in the territories—which they do with a decidedly political bent.

The wire service reporter explained that Palestinians with the English-language skills necessary to work for an Anglo wire service tend to have come from wealthy families who, more often than not, are part of, or have benefited from, Yasser Arafat's "ruling cabal." They have probably spent most of their lives elsewhere—most wealthy Palestinians send their children abroad to go to school—and probably know the territories as a filmy abstraction more than a real place. However, like rich diaspora everywhere they are full of guilt; they have listened to PLO rhetoric most of their lives, and when they attain powerful positions in media they see it as their cultural duty to enforce political correctness PLO style.

The reporter, who would only meet with me far away from the wire service offices, gave me an example of how this PLO vetting plays out on the ground: One day, while in Ramallah reporting activity in local government, the reporter witnessed a spat between Yasser Arafat and a local leader. The local leader got so mad that he actually whacked Arafat hard enough to knock the *keffiyeh* off his head. This is equivalent to a local landowner knocking the crown off a king. The episode could have indicated many things, like a slide in Arafat's power or the birth of a new warring faction in the perpetual civil war in the territories. In any case, the reporter certainly thought the *keffiyeh* incident was newsworthy. He returned to his workplace and tapped the piece out on his keyboard. As a last vetting before it was put "on the wire," one of the senior Palestinian editors was called over to check the story. "She looked at the part about the spat, said 'That's a lie' and marched away; that was that," the reporter says. The story was "spiked" because the editor didn't want to humiliate "the Rais."

Foreign reporters I met generally scoffed when I asked them whether they thought their dependence on a pro with a political agenda could affect their copy. Not at all, they would answer. This is a purely practical matter, they would say. We must employ Palestinians as escorts in the territories because we must have translators and the Israeli government forbids Israelis from going into the territories. Actually, this turned out to be a misreading of the rules. It is simply not true that an Israeli cannot cross a checkpoint. On a daily basis these foreign reporters must have seen Israeli citizens (albeit with press cards) pass into the territories. *Jerusalem Post* reporter Matthew Gutman, a Jewish citizen of Israel, often goes into places like Bir Zeit University in the heart of Hamas territory. The unspoken fact was that people hired Palestinian guides for the Palestinian territories—even though there are Israelis who could be hired to translate from Arabic—because, unofficially, a Palestinian fixer was a kind of tithe to the community. It was understood that Palestinian fixers had special connections to, say, Hamas chieftains, though nobody questioned too much how far these connections extended or what one must do to keep them in good order.

■ ■ ■

I EXPERIENCED THE POLITICALLY-CONNECTED-FIXER phenomenon many times at press conferences, trials and other places where journalists herd. One day, for instance, I was milling with other journalists outside a Tel Aviv courtroom where the captured Tanzim leader Marwan Barghouti was in hearings to set dates for his upcoming murder trial. (Barghouti was accused by Israel of indirect and direct part in murders of twenty-two people, many of them civilians.) In the fall of 2002, there was a well-funded "Free Barghouti" movement with a network of highly sophisticated websites and other fundraising venues. All summer the territories (and Europe, for that matter) had been full of "Free Barghouti" agitation. Barghouti was "Israel's Nelson Mandela," organizers said, and he would make the court proceedings a trial of "the Israeli occupier." All summer long his posse had worked to make the Israel/South Africa convergence. There were periodic announcements that Nelson Mandela himself was going to show his solidarity by coming to Tel Aviv, and Barghouti's wife, Fadwa, was dispatched to Johannesburg for the UN's World Summit for Sustainable Development, where she told chanting, singing crowds at one rally that "Marwan is not in favor of killing civilians, but he is in favor of legitimate resistance."

When pretrial hearings started in September, it was clear that Barghouti's people had "globalized" his plight quite successfully.

The first day of hearings felt like the opening of Studio 54, as a sea of reporters surged around the two female Israeli government press aides who held clipboards with the names of the people allowed to sit in the small courtroom. They shoved each other to get within earshot, then waved press cards and yelled things like "Hey, remember me? TV 2 Norway!" Apparently most of them hadn't heard that only a small pool of reporters—chosen by the local Foreign Press Association chapter—would be allowed in. Eventually the crowd fell back and watched as the chosen few—a team of international observers come to monitor for Israeli infractions of international law, pool reporters, Barghouti's relatives—filed in.

The foyer had come to resemble an international cocktail party (as reporters and cameramen weren't about to leave this hot spot) when PLO legal advisor Diana Buttu, an attractive, soft-spoken Canadian educated at Stanford, and Michael Tarazi, a hyper-articulate American, arrived and circulated through the crowd, dispensing hellos, hugs, and copies of a thick manifesto that Barghouti had written, which charged Israel with "ethnic genocide," among other war crimes. Israeli press spokesman Daniel Seaman had invited relatives of suicide bomb victims to the hearing as well. Some stood silently outside the courthouse with photos of the dead held up for cameras, but a few also circulated through the crowd of press.

As the afternoon wore on, cameramen began to droop and producers were looking at their watches. Then there was a commotion in the foyer. Dozens of boom mikes craned in its direction like the necks of inquisitive giraffes, and men carrying video cameras charged toward the source of the noise. By the time I got to the scene of the commotion, a tight scrum of reporters pressing tape recorders forward had formed around a large Arab man in a business suit, who was mopping his sweat-drenched forehead and yelling, "This is the occupation. This is how it works!!"

Between gasps for breath, as reporters scribbled, he explained that he was Khader Shkirat,* one of Barghouti's lawyers, and that he had just been ejected from the courtroom. He said he had tried

---

*Shkirat may have been emotional in those months because the accountants Ernst & Young had just completed the first phase of an investigation of LAW, an NGO he founded and directed. Shkirat formed LAW ("Land and Water") with other Palestinian lawyers to

to move toward Barghouti to see if he was okay as the prisoner was led in but had been set upon by an Israeli soldier, who beat him up and threw him into the hall. There was no hallway between the courtroom and the foyer, so it was unclear where this beating would have taken place since Shkirat appeared to have come hurtling directly out the courtroom doors. But nobody asked him to explain. "I was just so worried about Marwan's life," he panted. "He could be assassinated by the criminals, by the settlers, by the fanatical people in the courtroom."

There was a radically different account available. According to a *Jerusalem Post* reporter who had been in the courtroom, Shkirat had been moving around the courtroom trying to distribute literature. He had refused to sit down when the judge asked, then he had refused to leave, so the court police had muscled him out the door.

Somewhere during this commotion, which was conducted partly in Arabic (seemingly for the benefit of camera crews for Al-Jazeera and Al-Arabia) and partly in English (for everybody else), a man sidled up to me. "Do you need a translation?" he asked. When I asked him if he had any connection with the large Barghouti entourage, he turned red, but finally admitted that yes, he was "connected to the Barghouti team." I'm sure I couldn't have afforded him anyway.

"defend Palestinian rights in accordance with international human rights law." It was funded by about thirty European and American entities, including the Ford Foundation, and had received about $10 million in donations from 1997 to 2002, when donors had begun to worry about the disposition of funds and hired Ernst & Young to go over the books. Ernst & Young eventually reported that nearly 40 percent of the $9.6 million given by foreign donors was "misappropriated" and that the organization used "fictitious financial reporting" to cover up the diversion of approximately $2.3 million into private bank accounts belonging to Shkirat and other principals. Another $4 million could not be accounted for.

NINE

OUTSIDE THE PRESS VAN: TRAVELS WITH FARAJ

"**R**EAL" FIXERS WERE EXPENSIVE because they were trained pros. It was obvious with the kind of shekels I was able to shell out (equal to about $10 an hour) that I would have to recruit a complete neophyte—who also happened to look imposing, know his way around the West Bank, have access to a vehicle, and speak English, Hebrew and Arabic. Amazingly enough, I was able to find all of this in my own backyard, so to speak, in the person of Faraj Hassan,* twenty-five, hotel cleaner and part-time night-school student.

Faraj had stood out among the cleaners and repairmen of the hotel maintenance staff. His eye contact was direct and openly friendly—which is unusual for an Arab man of what I presumed to be his class. It was what I think of as a Westernized gaze, the gaze of a man used to interacting with women as equals.

He was tall and slim, with a mop of jet-black hair and what another friend who knew him had described as "puppy-dog eyes"— like an olive-skinned Paul McCartney. His mother was born in the Arab town of Tulkarem on the West Bank. When he was still quite young, the family moved to East Jerusalem and he became an Israeli citizen and possessor of the all-important Israeli identity card. The eldest of five children, Faraj was about nine when his mother, overwhelmed with child care, farmed him out to his grandfather in Ramallah, where he grew up and went to high school. After graduating, he moved back in with his family in East Jerusalem and got a job cleaning rooms at the Lev Yerushalayim. Hanging around the desk and the guests, he learned English, perfected his Hebrew and

---

*Faraj Hassan is a pseudonym.

began to take night classes at the Hebrew University toward a degree in business.

In his late teens, because of his good looks, forthright manner and fluency in three languages, Faraj had been picked to be part of a traveling peace mission, a group of about twelve youths, half of them Jews and half Arabs, who were flown around Europe to appear at public events, make speeches, and suggest by their presence together on a stage that "peace is possible." When I asked Faraj if he had liked being a spokesman for peace, he grinned slyly and said he enjoyed it very much because the group was "half men, half women, all the same age, together all the time in hotels for two weeks."

He came back to Jerusalem determined to get working papers and to work in another country. Almost any reasonably prosperous country would do, but preferably Britain, Germany or the United States. All but Venezuela turned him down. (In a post-9/11 climate, no one was eager to grant entry to a twenty-five-year-old Arab man, he explained.) And so to Venezuela he went. There he found work in another hotel. He learned Spanish quickly, but still wasn't happy. He felt that he wasn't getting anywhere, and that there wasn't much to get *to* in Venezuela anyway. He came back to Israel and to work at the Lev, and began taking night classes again at Hebrew University. When an eighteen-year-old Russian girl joined the hotel's maintenance staff he fell in love with her, shared an apartment with her for a time and added "a little Russian" to his growing repertoire of languages before the rootless, troubled girl disappeared.

When I met him he was acutely restless, in a hurry to finish his bachelor's degree and begin the life he envisioned for himself. Though fairly vague about what this life would look like, he was adamant that it would include "a car and a nice house."

On the morning we were to begin our first trip, I walked out into the street behind the Lev and found Faraj standing next to the beat-up white van he had rented from a friend for these ventures. Despite the new coat of paint, it still had its double row of seats in the back and still looked very much like the West Bank taxi it had been. It was perfect for touring. It had a high, open cab, rather like a delivery truck, so as we crawled down streets crowded with pedestrians and merchants, we were at their eye level. The stick shift allowed good traction in more medieval sections of towns where the street narrowed down to flock-of-goats width.

Our first major expedition was to Ramallah, the headquarters of Yasser Arafat's government since 1998. After leaving central Jerusalem behind, we barreled along windy roads across a beautiful biblical landscape of valleys and plains and hills terraced with rows of white stones. As we drove, Faraj pointed out clusters of buildings, saying "this is an Israeli town" or "this is an Arab town." From a distance they all looked the same—little white sprinkles on the landscape, except that in some groupings the sprinkles were clustered around the spire of a mosque. We passed many three- and four-story villa-like homes with balconies and arched doors and a lot of stalled construction: scaffoldings, piles of bricks, half-built structures of white stone. Faraj would point authoritatively and say that this particular pile of concrete slabs was an unfinished Arab house, while that pile was Israeli. I was mystified at his ability to say which was which, but eventually I learned that the homes of settlers are clustered together, while wealthy Arabs feel confident enough in their surroundings to build freestanding villas at some distance from the nearest town.

Soon we began encountering roadblocks. Many were just concrete barricades blocking one lane, forcing drivers to slow down so the IDF soldier standing in the road could take a longer look at vehicles and drivers. But soon we were at Qualandia, the major checkpoint one must pass through to get in or out of Ramallah. As checkpoints go, it is much bigger than the checkpoints around other West Bank towns—which consist of a guard shack and several soldiers. We joined a long line of waiting cars and trucks all idling and spewing black, smelly exhaust into the air. Pedestrians had their own lane and it was full of men, women, teens, the odd goat or donkey going both directions in a purposeful way. As we sat listening to Faraj's cassette tapes (he liked Avril Lavigne and Jordanian pop), I looked out the window and watched for any cuffing, shoving or swearing by the soldiers as they processed the drivers and pedestrians. I ended up spending a good deal of time waiting in line at checkpoints and did not see any that day or any day. Actually, at Qualandia there often seemed to be some joking between guards and Palestinian truck drivers returning to Ramallah after a day of

work in Jerusalem delivering produce or olive oil. The Israeli soldiers working Qualandia—mostly very young-looking men and
women—seemed in fairly high spirits, which, I came to know, was
a sign that things operated fairly smoothly there. We did once see
an Arab man of about twenty-five follow an Israeli soldier into a
guard shack, where Faraj said he would probably be searched. But
the Israeli wasn't touching or pointing his gun at the man.

One day while we waited, idling unevenly and belching exhaust
along with the rest, Faraj marveled that things were so pacific. "This
used to be a very dangerous place, with bullets flying everywhere,"
he said. "It was easy to get shot."

"What changed?" I asked.

"Those people are all in jail now," Faraj said. That did not change
his feeling, however, that life to him now felt like "a big jail" because
of these checkpoints and the constant waiting.

I had worried about whether I should wear a headscarf to look
more like an Arab, but we attracted little attention; children did not
crowd to our side; people did not sidle up with "news tips"—as they
often do around vehicles marked as "Press" or vans carting the tall
spire of a TV antenna. Most of the time, Palestinian pedestrians saw
the taxi-like van, tried to hail us for cab service, and then looked
annoyed when we rattled past them. But we didn't always speed
past. Faraj had a soft spot for old women and anyone trying to hitchhike on deserted stretches of road, so a fair number of people got a
free lift in our "cab."

Because we were heading away from Jerusalem, the IDF soldiers were not so concerned about intercepting explosives, so on that
first day we passed through Qualandia in about twenty minutes
after being given a quick once-over by a soldier who peered into the
van and scrutinized our ID cards. After you passed through the
industrial zone that follows the checkpoint, the street became a
broad, primarily residential boulevard with modern apartment buildings on each side set back at some distance from the street. One clue
that you'd finally entered Ramallah proper was the vaguely Big
Brotherish billboard suspended over the street, featuring the face
of a waving, smiling Yasser Arafat with the caption "I am with you
always." The sight of the grinning president seemed to put Faraj in

a bad mood because he began a rant, the substance of which I would hear many times:

"Since he came here, he has broken everything. There used to be three groups here: rich, middle, and poor and not working. Now there is just one—a poor class. It is like living under the Mafia. They take all the money that's sent here and keep it. What happened to all the money that has been sent here?" he demanded rhetorically. "They send us billions." (He was referring to a recent "supplemental" transfer from the EU that had been mentioned in the newspapers.) "What happened to it?! He take it! And he give it to his friends. And if you complain about it they kill you, so everybody keeps quiet."

Having to "keep quiet" while in his own hometown was a persistent theme in Faraj's conversation. So many people—of his age group especially—had secret lives and fought in the shadow war in one way or another. Faraj had recently tried to reestablish contact with two friends from high school, only to hear that they had joined Hamas and were dead. But he was chilled by the thought that if they had lived he could easily have run afoul of them in some way and been subject to Hamas's brutal rules. On the other hand, there was also the possibility that someone he knew could go the other way and become an undercover informant for Israel—which, he figured, could probably get a guy in trouble some way or another too. The gist was, "You never know who you are talking to and you have to watch what you say. Always there is fear."

"It is like living in a jail," he said once again—although this time he was talking about impositions on Palestinians by other Palestinians.

It was a shame that Ramallah had begun to feel "like a jail" to people such as Faraj, because until fairly recently (many say the decline started in 1998 when Arafat moved his headquarters there and accelerated during the intifada), the city had been an especially cosmopolitan watering hole, with restaurants, jazz clubs and nightclubs filled, as one Israeli journalist put it, with "girls in miniskirts dancing to disco music." Israelis went there for a night out and danced and drank side by side with Palestinians and foreign tourists. Road signs, street signs, signs on shops were still in both Arabic and

English, a reminder of the once-flourishing tourist trade. I remembered Ramallah as a relatively diverse and vital city.

There had been countless pieces by journalists reporting from Ramallah about the devastation of the Palestinian economy after the beginning of the second intifada. A CNN reporter delivered a typical report for the fall of 2002 when he talked about Palestinians "confined" in Ramallah and "forced by Israel to live in extreme poverty." PLO legal advisor Diana Buttu had been going to college campuses that year telling audiences that "Malnutrition in [sic] Palestinian children ... is at the same rate as in sub-Saharan Africa." So I had expected to see that Ramallah had become a wasteland since I'd last been there, a Calcutta with legless people lying on the sidewalks, or something like the shantytowns outside Rio de Janeiro. Certainly we passed many storefronts that were shuttered or boarded over. On the other hand, in furniture showrooms, hair salons and car repair shops and in the open-air fruit market, bustling life was in progress.

We were heading for Arafat's Mukata, which had recently been the center of international attention when the IDF leveled most of it with a convoy of bulldozers. Tactically and morally, from an IDF standpoint, the demolition was long overdue. Several months before—during Operation Defensive Shield—it had found caches of weapons like RPGs there and documents signed by Arafat, his lieutenants like Marwan Barghouti, and others, authorizing payments to terror militias. It had become abundantly clear that the PA was using its official offices as a staging ground for terror attacks. When Arafat began harboring twenty men wanted by the IDF for the assassination of a minister of the Israeli government in the Mukata—telling the IDF, in effect, "If you want them you'll have to take me too"—the IDF decided that more drastic measures were needed.

All these wartime considerations seem to have become irrelevant in the face of pictures of the huge bulldozers crushing buildings, and debate within Israel turned vociferously to the topic of whether taking down Arafat's huge complex had been a good idea. Arafat was seventy-two years old, one Israeli pundit had pointed out; his hands quivered from Parkinson's disease; he was increasingly seen as doddering; but the "siege of the Mukata," as it was called in the press, had put him "back where he loves to be, at center stage." And it was true: reporters like Barbara Plett of the BBC had a field day with "the siege of the Mukata." It almost compared in drama to "the siege of Jenin."

"This is where Israel wants the Palestinian leader, totally isolated," Plett reported.

> From his lonely office building Mr. Arafat can see only the ruins of what was his presidential headquarters. Officially Israel still blames him for not doing enough to stop the suicide bombers but unofficially some Israeli voices say Arafat no longer controls the militias. This is something Palestinian political leaders have admitted for a long time; they say it is impossible in an atmosphere of military occupation. Meanwhile the Israeli noose is already tightening again on the Palestinian people. They watched last night's assault on the compound while under strict curfew.

Reporters had seemed unwilling to give the IDF any credit for anything in this operation. Whether it had been wrong or right, the Mukata demolition was, at least, surgical, because the IDF was adamant about demonstrating that its quarrel was with President Arafat and his regime and not with ordinary, noncombatant civilians; but even this precision was turned into an excuse for contemptuous coverage. One afternoon, for instance, a CNN camera had followed a bulldozer as it backed and filled, attempting to knock down one of Arafat's buildings while at the same time avoiding a water main that supplied the whole town. Ben Wedeman, CNN's Cairo bureau chief, who had been flown in to cover the Mukata affair, stood by watching with a disgusted look on his face: "I want to point something out to you," he said to his viewers. "They've just knocked down the entire compound but this bulldozer is trying to avoid this water pipe. Some people might call that ironic, I call it stupid."

And indeed the IDF's D-9 Caterpillar bulldozers had done a lot of knocking down. We drove past a couple of city blocks of shattered white concrete piled nearly as high as two-story buildings, until we came to a parking lot, overseen by a lone PA policeman armed with a rifle in a one-man guard shack. He slouched out and glanced at us. Faraj had a few words with him and he let us pass with a bored nod. On the other hand, I thought that I probably could have worn a chimpanzee suit and he wouldn't have looked twice. If this was this man's regular duty, he'd seen it all by now.

Despite his "isolation," Arafat had never stopped receiving a steady stream of visitors in this period of his "imprisonment" by Israel. Foreign dignitaries like Arun Gandhi (son of Mahatma), French foreign minister Dominique de Villepin, Egyptian president Hosni Mubarak, to name a few, had made the pilgrimage. An Italian choir had stopped in for lunch and serenaded the Rais with songs of the Italian antifascism movement. A group of International Solidarity Movement youths had staged a "die-in"—with much choreographing by an Arafat aide—for international cameras by lying down in the street in front of what one called "a heavily armed Israeli APC" (armored personnel carrier). Afterward they were invited in to have pizza with Arafat himself. Aid workers came regularly to check his condition and of course there were always the throngs of journalists around "the lonely office building."

After passing the guard shack, we came upon a dusty clearing. Having heard enumerable news stories in which Arafat was described as living and working out of a "devastated," "ruined" or "shell-pocked" office, I was surprised to see a tidy brick building of several stories that resembled a nineteenth-century schoolhouse. It was the only building that the IDF had left standing, but its actual appearance did not fit neatly into the standard news narrative. A speaking platform with a lectern had been set up in front for the president's personal appearances and around that was a scattering of Arab men in business suits talking into cell phones and a few more uniformed PA security men with rifles slung over their shoulders. Hovering around the entrance of this incongruously Western structure, craning their necks at any hint of movement within, were about fifteen middle-aged Europeans. They wore various kinds of floppy sun hats, voluminous khaki shorts, sandals with ankle socks, baggy white T-shirts inscribed with the words "Friends of Palestine," and earnest expressions on their faces. One woman explained to me that they were waiting because they had been told they might be allowed to go inside and talk with "him." In the periphery of my vision, I could see her discreetly taking stock of my Arab escort and my garb, a floaty yellow skirt with black flowers on it, Italian clogs, a lilac T-shirt and a green sun hat. Apparently deciding I looked harmless, she ventured a tremulous smile of solidarity.

About twenty yards across the clearing, men were hard at work pouring concrete and hanging great sheets of green glass. The frame of a new building was going up. They were nearly finished with the ground floor and it looked like it would be a grand atrium space with two-story arched windows. Was this to be Arafat's new residence? At the time, nobody seemed to know. (I learned later from an Arab journalist that when it was completed it became a "conference center" where Arafat received his guests—just "the big groups.") Perhaps the modern building with the green-tinted glass atrium is another one of those parts of the picture that doesn't fit the traditional frame for the Israeli versus Palestinian story because I have never seen it in any photograph or video pan of the area. As recently as August 2004, not long before his death, the Associated Press was still reporting that "Yasser Arafat turned 75 yesterday, but there were no birthday parties or parades. . . . [He] spent the day as usual—hunkered down behind sand-bags in the shell-pocked compound where he lives and works."

As soon as we were away from the headquarters and out of the earshot of PA security men, Faraj said with disgust, "He will not be here long. Everyone is sick of him; he is so old. He should give one of the younger ones a chance."

Driving south again down Ramallah's main drag, we pulled up next to the West Bank equivalent of a hamburger stand—a falafel restaurant with a great greasy chunk of pressed mystery meat (usually it is lamb or chicken) turning on a spit. Places like this line the streets in Israel and the territories but we chose this particular greasy spoon because Faraj knew the proprietor from high school. He appeared to be somewhat older than Faraj, about thirty, with a belly beginning to strain against his polyester slacks, and, as we were the only customers in the place, he flew to our sides when we sat down at one of the little Formica tables. He nodded absently when Faraj told him I was a writer working on a book, but when he added, "She lives in New York," the man focused on me intently and then, as if he had been holding this question inside for months, asked: "Did . . . You . . . See . . . Those . . . Towers . . . Fall . . . Down?" There was silence in the restaurant as his cook left the grill to hear the answer as well.

"Yeah," I answered, "but just about the same way you did, on TV. It happened about five miles from me."

The disappointment, the sound of dropping faces was almost audible. It would happen over and over again. When West Bank Palestinians found out that I was from New York, their eyes would gleam and then they would ask what Faraj and I began to call "The Question." The fallen faces, the looks of disappointment were so intense when I told them I hadn't been at the Twin Towers that Faraj and I discussed at one point whether I should make up a story about seeing the planes hit just to keep people happy.

"I always wanted to visit America," the falafel restaurant owner called over his shoulder as he headed for the curb to take an order from a drive-up customer, "but I don't want to go to someplace where towers fall down like that, no way!" The cook nodded emphatically.

After he was done, he scuttled back to our table with a second urgent, apparently saved-up question: "Is the United States going to attack Iraq?"

"Yes," I answered.

"When?" he demanded.

Enjoying my new status as an oracle, I squinted and made a show of ruminating for a few seconds before I told him what I actually believed back in October 2002: "In a couple of months."

"Why are they doing this?" he asked in a wounded tone. We were moving into dangerous waters but I felt safe with my fixer at my side and the van at the ready. I have always found that "sources" seem to be able to smell the difference between honesty and prevarication, that they prefer an honest answer even if they don't agree with it, and that they will not reveal much of themselves unless you sincerely reveal a part of yourself. So I said what I thought: "As part of a larger war on terrorism, they think they have to. Saddam jerked us around throughout the arms inspection process, remember? He'd tell us 'Come back tomorrow; I'm not ready today'; he was playing games and we let him."

The proprietor looked blank, but seemed to sympathize with my distaste for the dishonor of being "jerked around"—however Faraj chose to translate that.

"Besides," I continued, "there's Bin Laden and what he did to our country. It will be helpful to show our strength again; to regain respect."

The man's face had clouded again.

"The towers falling down," Faraj prodded.

"Oh, the towers!" exclaimed the proprietor, who now looked at us with a bit of smugness. "But everyone knows it was the Israelis who caused it! Four thousand Jews stayed home from work that day. How did they know? Tell me: How ... did ... they ... know!?"

At this, both Faraj and I said in unison that we'd seen Bin Laden take credit for it.

"He said it on television," Faraj repeated in a patient voice.

"If it was on television then it was faked," the proprietor said matter-of-factly. "They can fake all kinds of things, you know."

What was curious and encouraging to me—and I felt this way over and over again in other encounters with other people—was that although I challenged, even scoffed at his beliefs, the man did not turn away sullenly. He did not call his local militia. Instead, he drew up a chair and put more little dishes of this and that on the table and waved away our protests about the cost.

"Look," he said, "you do me a favor. I am hungry for this talk." After serving a drive-up customer, he hustled back to the table, repeating "I am hungry for talk like this."

I am not naïve enough to think I would have had the same experience with a member of Hamas, a member of the Palestinian security forces, or even a more educated and sophisticated West Banker, but this conversation with this Palestinian civilian became an emblem for me of the optimistic thinking that drove early discussions about the "Road Map for Peace" in 2003, and is still the basis of hope for the many Israelis and Palestinians who long for peace. There is a solid—although it is hard to know how large—strata of generally apolitical Palestinians who are tired of "keeping quiet," as Faraj put it, who hunger for open talk, and basically just want to continue with their lives by running businesses, making money, buying cars and eating nice meals—just like the rest of us. Polls have reported various discouraging things: that a majority of Palestinian people support suicide bombings, that they will not accept any peace agreement that doesn't include a right of return, et cetera. But I don't think polls can be terribly reliable in a culture where people fear representatives of government and even their neighbors.

Still, can someone (like the food stand owner—and his views were not uncommon) who believes that the Jews took down the World Trade Center live in peace next to Israelis and Jews? Actually, yes. It often seemed to me that Arabs I met in the territories could ascribe sinister supernatural powers to Israelis, Jews and Americans in the abstract—that the IDF distributed chewing gum to make men horny and belts to make them impotent, for example—but then get along with individual Jews, Americans or Israelis quite well. And power is generally revered in the Middle East, so fear of another is always accompanied with grudging respect. Anyway, most people think with their stomachs. Men like this small business owner have fond memories of the years after the Oslo Accords and before the second intifada, when 90 percent of Palestinian exports were sold to Israelis, when about 20 percent of the Palestinian work force went to work every day in Israel at wages about 90 percent higher than those available on the West Bank, and when the Palestinian economy was growing at about 5 percent of GNP a year.

Some Israeli leaders believed that curfews and such, brought down on towns by the terrorist militiamen, would have the welcome side effect of making ordinary Palestinian townspeople rise up against the terrorists in their midst. But this theory seemed to be based on the assumption that the less educated, less worldly townspeople would actually understand the causal relationship between IDF presence in towns and terror militias, i.e. that the latter brought on the former. The theory, in other words, did not seem to take into account the PA's thorough control of news media and of public education. In late 2002, when I was there, media censorship on the West Bank was so complete that it destroyed the cause-and-effect part of the equation. I found that if I mentioned the connection between the sudden presence of curfew troops and a suicide bombing carried out a week before by a terrorist from that town (as was almost always the pattern), working-class people looked at me blankly. All they heard, in the hypobaric chamber in which they lived, was what the PA wanted them to hear, so if the Israelis patrolled towns, searched and sometimes demolished houses, it was simply because, as the food stand proprietor put it, "Israel hates the Palestinian people."

The proprietor soon had a new, seemingly "saved-up" question for the Westerner who had landed in his restaurant: "Why do the Americans hate the Palestinians?" he demanded.

"Our government doesn't hate the Palestinians," I said. "They support an independent state next to Israel. They send money to the Palestinians, millions a year. Why do you think they hate the Palestinians?"

"Because they do not kill Arafat," he stated matter-of-factly. "They don't like Saddam; they go get Saddam. So why not Arafat?"

Given that news accounts had recently been full of heads of state and such calling Arafat "the personification of the ideals of the Palestinian people," I groped for words for a few seconds, and then started in carefully: "I think ... the Americans believe ... that Arafat is your guy; that you elected him; that he speaks for you ..."

"He is a crook, he is a thief," the proprietor interjected.

"I guess," I ventured, "they haven't gotten that yet."

At our parting we were near embracing. He pressed a pen with the name of his restaurant on me. I took his address and promised to send him a present when I got back to America. "But what can I send you that won't cost more in duty to pick up than it's actually worth?" I asked him. We all pondered this. It was, in fact, a real brain teaser, maybe the knottiest question we had attempted to solve all day.

I had a number of exchanges like this one in the weeks that followed. Each time I said something I feared would be felt as challenging, our disagreement over mere *facts* was batted away as an obstacle in the way of *this thing* they were hungry for but couldn't quite articulate. The thing seemed to be freedom, a freedom that included mental challenge, new ideas and frank talk. Media suppression, dictatorship and the constant repetition of PA-produced slogans and propaganda in their public life had combined to make life on the West Bank cramped, arid and stale.

■ ■ ■

THOUGH I MAY HAVE LURCHED into political incorrectness occasionally with people I met on the street, Faraj was simply too important to risk alienating, so I tried to avoid talking with him about "the conflict." But sometimes we couldn't help drifting toward that dangerous ground. One day, for instance, one of Faraj's dark soliloquies contained a reference to the "Jews who keep coming and coming and moving onto our land." (He talked this way about "the Jews" though I had reminded him repeatedly that I was half Jewish—another sign that for many Arabs, *the Jews* are an abstract concept that they separate from individual Jews.)

"They believe it's their land too," I said.

"But the Jews have only been here since . . . oh, in the thirties," he said.

"Nonsense, they've been around since biblical times, since as long as you, at least."

Faraj kept shaking his head, no, not true. His small smile indicated that he seemed to think he had me on this one.

"Two words," I said. "Jesus Christ . . . you know, *King of the Jews?* Jesus of *Nazareth,* born in *Bethlehem,* took his last walk with the cross through the *Old City.*"

"That is *very* interesting," Faraj said. Color rushed to his face, and he was quiet for a few minutes, nodding his head as he drove.

After one of those discussions, he told me in a rush that he loved these talks, that simply by talking about such things, "new worlds opened" for him. And of course he was opening a world for me too.

On another day, I asked him to take me to Ramallah's richest section and its poorest. Mostly what I had seen in Ramallah were signs of middle-class life: freestanding houses with yards; apartment buildings with cars in driveways; a gray-haired man wearing eyeglasses, a sports shirt and pressed tan slacks, leaving a neat bungalow, closing the front gate that surrounded his front yard and walking toward a clean, late-model car parked on the street.

The section that Faraj called the poorest also seemed to be one of the more ancient sections of the city—because as people acquired money they moved out into more modern houses or had them built. (Construction was a surging part of the Palestinian economy before the second intifada.) In the old section, the buildings were made of ancient Crusader-era stone. The streets were cobbled and so narrow in places that the van barely squeezed through. Chickens strolled in the street; laundry hung from windows; occasionally a dirty child with bare feet wandered out to stare at us; and women and men tended to be in traditional dress. The only clearly modern thing was the satellite dishes on most rooftops. It was, in other words, very much like many neighborhoods in Mexico, in the poorer sections of Jerusalem, in so many places around the world. It wasn't Shaker Heights, but it wasn't, say, the shantytowns outside Rio de Janeiro either. (Actually, the most primitive living conditions I saw in the region were in a shantytown in downtown Tel Aviv, composed mostly of illegal or temporary workers who had come to take jobs that had been held by Palestinians before the second intifada.) I began to wonder if a lot of reporters who had described Ramallah as crushingly poor were parachuters who had simply not seen much of the world outside American suburbs.

Although Arafat and the second intifada had brought the free market to a near standstill, there was little evidence that anyone was starving or lacking acute medical care in Ramallah. The cascade of NGOs like Oxfam, UNRWA, UNESCO, UNICEF and the Red Cross, and even the Israeli government, had seen to that. In the years since the beginning of the second intifada, foreign aid to the Palestinians from the European Union and NGOs—which has always been very high relative to other areas of the world—had doubled, according to the International Monetary Fund (IMF), making the region "the recipient of the biggest per capita transfers in the history of foreign aid." Arafat diverted much of the aid from governments, but there was also the flood of aid from churches, individuals and groups that was not "channeled through the Palestinian Authority," as the IMF put it, and low-income Palestinians received that more fully.

We drove north again on the boulevard until we were nearly out of the city, then turned west and followed a winding road up a gentle ridge. At the crest of the ridge, we were buffeted by a fresh wind and suddenly were able to see the great bowl of the valley stretching away below into the haze on the horizon. Dotted along the crest of the ridge and connected by a freshly blacktopped road were a string of about fifteen opulent houses, spaced evenly on this spectacular piece of acreage. McMansions, I guess you could call them. There was something clonelike about them. All the houses were about five stories, made of the same basic materials and

apparently at the same time. The only difference was the crazy mixture of architectural styles, as if the architects had offered residents-
to-be a menu of possible features—"check if you want: 1. a balcony;
2. a solarium; 3. decorative columns. . . ." One house mixed the
Romanesque with a dash of *Gone with the Wind* Southern planta-
tion: a high, locked iron gate guarded a stately circular drive and a
portico of white Roman-style columns. Another house was more in
the style of Richard Neutra: angular and modern with its own mul-
tiple-car garage and adjoining tennis court. Yet another imitated a
Spanish villa, with red tiling on the peaked roof and rococo detailing on the façade.

"This is what Arafat built for his friends," said Faraj grimly.
"It wasn't here before he was here. Then it comes."

The McMansions of Ramallah, I thought, what a great story
for television. You had your visuals: the out-of-control ostentation
contrasted with the chickens-in-the-street in the poorest section of
the city. And you had your investigative angle. In a city where malnutrition among children was said to be as common as in sub-Saharan Africa, as a PLO spokeswoman often put it, in a region that
Arafat continually told foreign donors was on the point of collapse,
why had houses like this been built so recently?

I got out of the van and began to wander, stopping sometimes
to take pictures. Nobody seemed to be home. No traffic moved on
the street and the only car parked in front of a house was a "vin-
tage" (circa 1960s) Volkswagen Beetle with European plates. I walked
over to look at it more closely and then looked up at the dark windows of the house behind it—and suddenly wanted to be back in
the van.

"If I hung around here and took more pictures, could I get . . .
like . . . shot at?" I asked Faraj.

"No, what would probably happen would be that someone
from the security forces would drive up and say that he 'couldn't
guarantee your safety' while you were in Ramallah. Maybe he would
take your camera."

I decided that I wasn't so keen to snoop around anymore.
Though it may have been self-induced and a bit hysterical, I had
felt a prickle on my neck, as if somebody in one of the houses were
watching me. Perhaps other reporters had felt this prickle because

I have never seen the McMansions of Ramallah so much as mentioned in any news story, feature, or even description of the city.

A little less than a year after my visit, in September 2003, the International Monetary Fund published a 131-page report that suggested, in a very indirect way, how the McMansions might have been financed. "Very indirect" is key here. The report, which is about the state of the PA's finances after three years of the intifada, spends a politically correct amount of time stressing the onerousness of closures and curfews by Israel, but nearly hidden in a forest of bureaucratic jargon there is some crucial information.

According to the report, the IMF had "been offering technical assistance and advice in the financial area" to the Palestinian Authority since its inception at the Oslo Accords. And indeed, before the second intifada, in the years "1994 to 1999, the economy grew at a remarkable rate and was able to generate jobs and increase standards of living for its population," which was growing at about 4.2 percent yearly, one of the highest rates of population growth in the world. By 2000, just before Yasser Arafat started the second intifada, tax revenue in the West Bank and Gaza had risen to 18 percent of GDP, putting "revenue performance in the West Bank and Gaza above all other countries in the southern Mediterranean with the exception of Israel and Morocco."

There was a problem, however: "from the onset of the Oslo peace process and the empowerment of the PA, revenues did not automatically accrue to the PA but to a private bank account controlled by Yasser Arafat.... Petroleum excises, for example, were transferred to a special account in an Israeli bank controlled by Yasser Arafat and his finance minister Mohammed Rachid."

There were other problems, the IMF report said, involving "weaknesses [that] ... developed in tax administration, revenue management and expenditure control." In 1999, for instance, Arafat was paying out 55 percent of the government budget in salaries; in 2002, the figure was 70 percent, with most of this going to his "security services." By 2002, the IMF estimated that Arafat had about 86,000 security service employees, but it was impossible to know what they were paid because Arafat paid them in cash out of his own personal bank account, rather than by issuing checks. (It was not a "check-based economy," the understanding officials of the European Union explained.) The PA was never without "large foreign transfers," but "the Ministry of Finance [the department set up to control the PA budget] continued to face a tight liquidity position because of the diversion of excise revenue to accounts outside its control."

In 2003, the IMF held a press conference in Dubai to announce the release of the study and to announce that the PA was beginning a new era of reform. IMF official Karim Nashashibi announced that, in the new spirit of "transparent financial record-keeping," the new minister of finance, Salaam Fayad, was in the process of convincing security forces to sign up for their own bank accounts so that the government could pay them through direct deposit. (Nashashibi didn't mention that 33,000 members of the security service had yet to complete the paperwork for direct deposit.) Above all, Nashashibi stressed, it would now be clear how the PA spent its money.

In fact, at the new PA website, "You can all obtain the details of expenditures and revenues, which is quite extraordinary in this region," Nashashibi told reporters. "For instance, for the first time," he said, detailing the kind of data that could be found on the website, "we have a table which covers the period from '95 to 2000, outlining the diversion of revenue from the budget to a special bank account controlled by President Arafat. We estimated that amount to be around US$900 million over a period of five years. So, I mean, this is the type of things that we were able to do in this new kind of atmosphere of openness."

When it was time for questions, one of the reporters (who is not identified) wanted to back up a bit. "You mentioned, more or less in passing, that 900 million dollars had been diverted to a private bank account. Do you think this was a misuse of funds?"

"No," replied Nashashibi, "this money was basically, as I said, in a special account.... Most of it has been used to invest in Palestinian assets, both internally and abroad.... The tally of this current level of asset is around US$700 million in terms of at today's market prices, which probably in '99 were US$900 million.... So I would say that the large majority of this money has been invested in assets that today are still within the public domain."

"That's the large majority," the reporter said, "but what happened to the rest?"

"Well, I think that there will be accounting for the rest at some point, but we're taking it all a step at a time," Mr. Nashashibi answered.

Within a minute or so, the reporters had moved on to other topics.

In the winter of 2004, more disclosure about where the aid money went began to trickle out. French banks and an antilaundering organization got curious about monthly transfers of one million euros from a Swiss bank to two French bank accounts. These, it turned out, belonged to Arafat's wife, Suha, who had been living in Paris since the start of the second intifada. Further investigations revealed that Mrs. Arafat had been receiving $100,000 a month from her husband. She did not deny the transfers. "What is strange in the fact that he should send money to his wife abroad," she asked reporters, "especially since I am working for the Palestinian cause and interests?"

In her work for the Palestinian cause, Mrs. Arafat sometimes did interviews. In one for an Arab magazine, for instance, she reinforced the duty of parents to embrace their children's choice of martyrdom by saying that there would be "no greater honor" for her than to have a martyred son. "Would you expect me and my children to be less patriotic and more eager to live than my countrymen and their father and leader who is seeking martyrdom?" she asked the magazine interviewer. The hitch is that Mrs. Arafat has a daughter, not a son. In a different interview, Mrs. Arafat was asked if her daughter had been born in Gaza. "No, medical conditions there are terrible," she replied.

Maybe that explained why there was no one home in Ramallah's McMansion subdivision the day I wandered around it. Maybe the residents were at second homes in Paris.

■ ■ ■

OF COURSE I CONSIDERED IT MY reportorial duty to go to Jenin. There were only a few problems with that. Number one was the way my indispensable driver and guide looked sick every time I mentioned the town. His mother certainly didn't want him to go to Jenin. One day we had set forth and were just outside Jerusalem heading for the north/south artery that connects Ramallah to Nablus and Jenin when his mobile rang.

"It was my mother," he said when he got off. "She wanted to know where we are going."

"Did you tell her Jenin?"

"Are you kidding?" he said.

The *New York Times'* James Bennet had called Jenin the "seat of the Palestinian resistance" in a piece about Operation Defensive Shield, but for many ordinary Palestinians, Jenin was a sort of Dodge City, a lawless place you tried to avoid.

And in fact we never did get to Jenin—not because of Faraj's forceful mother, but because there is only one main road to it and inevitably something happened to shut down traffic, usually just outside of Nablus, the terror militia haven that lies before Jenin on this central artery. We could have gotten to Jenin by taking side roads and bypassing checkpoints, but, though Faraj's van looked like a typical West Bank cab in all other ways, it had Israeli plates and he was afraid that fedayeen might think we were settlers and shoot at us.

It wasn't too important. There was always plenty to see on that north/south corridor. One day we joined the queue of vehicles at the checkpoint outside Nablus only to find out that it wasn't moving. It turned out that the IDF soldiers at the checkpoint had just found an explosive device of some sort in one of the Israel-bound trucks and they had taken it away to do a controlled detonation. Since they didn't have enough personnel to check vehicles and detonate bombs at the same time, traffic was stopped entirely and people had begun to get out of their cars, hobnob, complain, and stretch their legs. As I strolled around, I passed about ten Arab men clustered around a bearded man who was shaking his fist and orating with such fury that the veins in his face and neck popped out. "This is it," I thought, "a genuine home-grown expression of rage from an occupied people."

I dispatched Faraj to listen in and he returned with a bemused look. "This one guy, the big guy with the beard, he is really mad at the two girls at the head of the line," he said. We had all noticed the two young Arab women who were sitting at the head of the stalled checkpoint line in their shiny, late-model car. Alone (that is, without male escorts) and with brazenly uncovered heads, they were hard to miss. One of the girls, who wore tight jeans and whose glossy

black hair flowed down her back, had gotten out of the car and saun-
tered over to the Israeli soldiers to ask them something, then swayed
back to the driver's seat.

"It is disgusting," the man was raging to the rapt crowd. "It is
outrageous; their hair, their tight pants are bad enough, but that
they got out of the car dressed like that, showed themselves . . . That
girls dare to do those kinds of things today is a sign of how badly
things have gone downhill. Now if we had a real Muslim in charge
. . ." (Instead of the secular Palestinian Liberation Organization,
Fatah, and Yasser Arafat, he meant.)

On another day we again sat idling at the checkpoint outside
Nablus while one of the soldiers went into the guard shack with my
passport—the usual procedure. They were automatically suspicious
of, and a bit hostile toward, journalists, and after watching the demo-
nization on the European cable networks I did not blame them. As
an Israeli citizen (without a press card), Faraj wasn't allowed to go
into the West Bank because the IDF would be obligated to rescue
him if he got into trouble. On the other hand, he was an Arab and
therefore, they reasoned, less likely to get into trouble. It was a
quandary.

Usually the young soldiers had to bring an older soldier to
come squint at us and our papers. Then they usually bent the rules
and let Faraj pass. The process actually seemed fairly subjective. Not
just for me, an "Anglo," but for Palestinians as well. In fact, what
made the border guards' jobs difficult was that who went, who stayed,
who got searched, who was waved through seemed often to be a
series of judgment calls. Sometimes trucks were searched thoroughly; sometimes they were waved through; sometimes there was
joking between IDF soldiers and the Arab drivers; sometimes there
was arguing, and Arabs came back cursing. Things were taken on a
case-by-case basis and seemed open to negotiation. The young IDF
soldiers seemed to be relying on instinct more than anything else.
The standard procedure, in addition to looking at papers, was to have
a conversation that seemed mostly an excuse to make deep, searching eye contact: They may have asked "Where are you going? Where
are you from? Why are you going there?" But I always sensed that
the real data they were interested in lay deep in one's eyes. I had
noticed that when I made open, forthright eye contact I was waved

through, but if I was, say, overcaffeinated and jumpy I was held longer. My instinct was right. One day a soldier told me, "They are watching you while you talk with them—if you get nervous, you sweat, you seem to be hiding something."

Checkpoints are a favorite image for reporters. Once again, the raw dynamics of the conflict seemed to be summarized by the sight of Israeli soldiers with guns reviewing the papers or checking the belongings of Palestinian civilians. And Israeli and Palestinian alike hated the checkpoints, but all in all, it was a far more human process than portrayed in the news media.

Waiting while they went away with my passport on another day, at a different checkpoint, I talked with the guards.

"So you are a writer; what are you writing?" said the young red-haired IDF soldier whose job it was to stand near the head of the line with a rifle ready.

"A book about Israel," I said, trying to be as noncommittal as possible.

"You got to say something good about us," he said, "'cause everybody says shit things."

"We want you to see checkpoints from our side," piped up another.

"And what would I see?" I asked. "What is your job like?"

"It sucks," said the freckle-faced redhead, who looked twenty-five but turned out to be in his early thirties, "because you have to decide who goes and who doesn't. Senior officers complain if you let someone through, if you hold someone up, the rules seem to change every day. Meanwhile, you know, bullets come sometimes."

Just earlier that week, he told me, their commander, a man only a few years older than they, had been shot to death as he walked from one guard shack to the other.

"What are the journalists like to deal with?" I asked him.

"They like to come and film here because in the valley there is a big army base, and in the hills," he pointed, "an Arab village. So: big base, little village. They like that shot; they get down on the ground to make the contrast bigger. And when the cameraman comes on they [the locals] act up and make a mess. . . . Sometimes TV trucks park and wait for hours until there is yelling and arguing so they can film it. . . . I guess they have a lot of money to spend so much time waiting,"

In fact, waiting for trouble to break out seems to have been standard operating procedure among network cameramen. An Israeli soldier stationed at the Qualandia checkpoint outside Ramallah wrote that:

> [news] cameramen would often show up and wait for hours for something to take pictures of. 99% of the time there was nothing to photograph so the reporter would wait and wait. . . . I remember once we helped a really old guy get out of the checkpoint when he walked in the wrong direction, he didn't really understand us so we just stood in his way so he would understand that this was the wrong path and turn around. Anyways this AP photographer was just snapping away when this happened. There were tons of incidents like this. . . . 99% of the physical work I did at that checkpoint involved preventing Arab on Arab violence.

One day at the main checkpoint before Nablus, the commander on duty ruled that if I wanted to go into the town I would have to leave Faraj behind. Faraj did not like the idea of a woman alone in this terror militia redoubt, so he and I began the now familiar process of nagging, cajoling, smiling, inviting full searches of our vehicle—anything to demonstrate our innocence and work out a deal. "Okay," the exasperated soldier on duty finally said, "I'll let you go, but you better be out before sundown or you'll be stuck there." Nablus was, at that time, under overnight curfew, which meant that people came and went during the day, but were under orders to stay in their homes at night. He also pointed out that there would be a change of shifts and we would have to deal with a new cast of soldiers who wouldn't be familiar with us and the terms of our arrangement.

As it was now late afternoon, we had just enough time to drive on the main boulevards—Faraj was afraid to take the van down side streets—and to have tea and cake in a café. Nablus was more deserted, or seemed so, than any town I had been in so far. On the other hand, many of the residents were very wealthy, Faraj said, as he pointed out the villas built on the sides of the steep hill around the main square. They must have come to the center of town sometimes, for there was a Vichy cosmetics outlet and a watch shop selling fancy European brands.

We began the drive out just as the sun was setting and just as IDF tanks roared past us in the other direction into the town to enforce the curfew. By the time we got to the checkpoint, a long line of outgoing vehicles had formed and we found ourselves at the end of it, and surrounded now by darkness, the very complete darkness of the desert, broken only by the glow of the guard shack ahead, an occasional car headlight, or the sudden flare of a match lighting a cigarette. Waiting in line at a checkpoint was different at night. Time seemed to pass more slowly and the darkness on each side of the road was a constant seduction; it felt like it would be warmly enveloping, like a black velvet cloak. As the minutes ticked by, I imagined wrenching the steering wheel, plunging into that enveloping darkness, into the freedom of the empty desert, and speeding past the checkpoint so we could get home.

And often people succumbed to this temptation. Sometimes drivers (just ordinary people going home or taxi drivers) used the cloaking darkness to make end runs around checkpoints. The problem was that there were others who also used the darkness—to make kamikaze-style attacks on the IDF checkpoints. When the soldiers standing at these tiny promontories of light heard car noises in the night, they didn't know if it was just a taxicab with a carload full of people trying to sprint past them, or if a vehicle full of armed men was going to come hurtling out of the darkness and plow into their shack. Either way they were supposed to stop the vehicle. Sometimes soldiers waited too long to confront the vehicle and were killed; sometimes they acted a few seconds too quickly and civilians who were just trying to get home got killed.

As we sat in the darkness trying to plot our next move, we heard wailing nearby. We hopped down from the cab to look and found a knot of people, primarily women and gray-bearded men, standing around a woman of about twenty-four who was sobbing. She did not live in Nablus, she said, but the soldiers would not let her pass through the checkpoint and leave the town because she could not produce an identity card. (If she did not have an identity card, they could not tell if she was on a "wanted" list, and their job was to intercept people on their list.)

Now she was trapped in Nablus with no place to stay for the night, she sniffled. Seeing me jump down from the cab, the little

group seemed to perk up a little bit. They looked at me with hopeful faces. Could I go to the soldiers and talk to them about the girl?
As usual they seemed to think that Westerners had near-magical
powers. I hated having the hopes of this little group pinned on me,
but what the hell, I thought, at least I could get Faraj to stop staring at me with his great, accusing, These-Are-My-People-You-West-
ern-Imperialist puppy-dog eyes.

A young soldier stood in the center of the road illuminated
only by one spotlight attached to the guard shack a few yards away.
He seemed very alone in the middle of the blackness, in this small
pool of light, and as I got closer I could see that his brow was beaded
with sweat, even though it was a chilly night. To his left, a few feet
away, a little group of Arabs in civilian garb stood, staring expec-
tantly at him like he was the center of their existence. There did not
seem to be a lot of people manning this checkpoint. I did what one
does around a skittish horse—move slowly, stay within the field of
direct vision, make no ambiguous or sudden gestures. When I was
finally sure I had his attention, I started in: "Look, there's this girl . . ."

"I know about the girl," he snapped. "She's already been up here.
What am I supposed to do? You see all these people?" he gestured to
the little group. "None have identity cards. So why do I let her go?
Because she's a woman? Because she's crying? She can cry all night."

Anyway, he said, the girl and a friend had already tried to give
him an obviously faked doctor's note in place of an identity card
and that made him mad.

"Why don't you just give her a quick search, make sure she's
not carrying anything and let her go?" I ventured. "We will take
her in our van after you've searched it."

"Yeah, except that I am not allowed to search a woman. If I
touch her there is scandal," he said. Often the IDF puts female soldiers at checkpoints expressly for this purpose, but they didn't have
one at this time. He did say that because of our "deal" with the previous guard, we could drive past the other waiting cars and he would
let us through.

I came back and reported the bad news about the girl; we briefly
considered trying to hide her in the back of the truck until I told
Faraj I wasn't going to risk getting thrown out of Israel for her. The

little group watched this intense discussion between us, but there seemed to be no hard feelings when the verdict was reached.

"Why do you wait around outside? You can go, you are lucky," one woman said, waving her hand at us.

Journalists continually complain of rudeness and harassment by IDF soldiers; I never found any, or at least I found it was easy enough to avoid if you respected that they were doing an extremely difficult job, didn't assume you were entitled to special treatment, and showed appreciation if you got it.

It's possible, however, that I never felt the full fury of the IDF's hatred for foreign press because I never quite managed the squared-away professional journalist look. I think I flew beneath the professional-journalist radar. My presence didn't arouse the same mix of fear and resentment. I think that they probably saw my purple T-shirts and floppy sun hats and dismissed me as one of a perennial but harmless fixture of the Mideast landscape, the female Arabist. One finds her in the margins of the histories and in obscure memoirs in the deepest depths of the largest library stacks: the slightly loopy foreign adventuress who has always come to "paint" or to "write poetry" and always has a handsome young Arab companion to drive her around.

There is a profusion of human types beetling around the West Bank and all kinds of shifting allegiances and classifications besides Occupier versus Occupied. The man railing at the Nablus checkpoint, for instance, was a Palestinian but he was also a *man*, furious at the perfidy of women (one of the great subtexts of the Arab Middle East), and a Muslim angry at the secularists of the Palestinian Authority.

Even between the Israelis and the Palestinians at checkpoints, allegiances could shift and could take different forms. In one heartwarming incident, for example, gender trumped "the conflict." We were at the checkpoint before Bethlehem. Faraj had walked to the front of the line to ask the soldiers standing guard if we could jump the line and had come back with a bashful look.

"What were you all talking about?" I asked, having noticed more banter than usual between him and the young soldiers.

"I can't tell you," he said, turning red. "It is very bad."

"You can tell me!" I badgered.

"Okay," he finally said with a devilish smile. "They asked me, 'Is she rich?' I told them, 'Beyond your wildest dreams'"

The IDF boys had given him a thumbs-up.

TEN

HIS OWN PRIVATE JIHAD

WHEN I WASN'T DRIVING AROUND with Faraj looking at the
material that journalists had come here to cover, I was looking at the other side of the narrative: the folks in the Israeli
government charged with dealing with the stuff those journalists wrote. One day in early September while visiting the Ministry of Foreign Affairs, I mentioned to an official there that I planned
to spend some time with Danny Seaman, the director of the Government Press Office. The MFA official waved his hand dismissively:
"If you really want to know what's going on [with Israel's *hasbara*
effort]," he sniffed, "you need to talk to someone who's in the foreign ministry; this is the brains of the operation. Danny Seaman . . .
He just takes care of . . . logistics."

There was also apparently something a little *comme il faut*
about Seaman. Lowering his voice, the official told me that all previous GPO directors had been appointed by the prime minister; they
came from political inner circles or had had high positions in the
military—they were of a certain class, he seemed to imply. Seaman,
he said, was the first to work his way up the civil service ranks. "That
is causing some people some problems," he said darkly.

Seaman's outré status seemed to be signaled by his physical
distance from everybody else—on a quiet block of Hillel Street several miles away from the foreign ministry. In the 1970s, when newspaper work actually demanded writers who worked in close proximity
to their offices, the Beit Agron International Press Center (home to
bureaus of the *New York Times,* the *Los Angeles Times, Le Monde*
and many other print outlets) felt like a nerve center. These days,
with newspapermen tethered to work by phones, faxes and email,

the print media headquarters has come to seem like a backwater on an out-of-the-way block.

And, once again, anyone looking for what the *New York Times* had called "Israel's vast public relations apparatus" would be disappointed. The Government Press Office itself occupies only one floor of the Beit Agron. After you clatter up several flights of spare industrial stairs—passing rabbity, depressed-looking creatures who are probably the bureau chiefs of the aforementioned newspapers in residence—you come to an uncarpeted corridor, which looks a bit like your old junior high school. In the gloaming of an underlit hallway you can make out a water cooler, a shelf with the day's press releases on it, bulletin boards on the wall covered with memos on government letterhead and "Apartment for Rent" notices.

Danny Seaman, who was in his early forties, could be seen in a suit and tie sometimes, but the rest of his small staff were mostly women and they wore platform sandals, jeans, tank tops and the shrunken, Britney Spears style midriff-baring T-shirts that were in fashion that summer. Like any other executive, Seaman could ask a visitor if they would like something to drink—"Coffee? Water? A Coke?"—but if the visitor accepted, his silver-haired secretary, Noa, who sat just outside at a typing stand made of wood laminate, would have to go to the pantry down the hall and tiptoe back with brackish coffee or water in a Styrofoam cup. There was no lobby to speak of. Visitors waiting to see Seaman tended to be confused: did they sit at the picnic-table thing near his secretary, or outside in the hall on the metal folding chair? They usually ended up hovering awkwardly in the doorway, jumping to one side if an employee elbowed past.

Seaman could usually be found at a desk piled high with paper, a land line receiver glued to one ear and his cell phone to the other. Handling several calls involved shouting back and forth to Noa over the perpetual low murmur emitted by his office television. Suspended from the ceiling with one of those hospital-style braces, it was usually tuned to one of the 24/7 cable news channels (Fox News, BBC, or Israel's Channel 1), and Seaman would click at it fitfully as he talked on the phone.

A former IDF paratrooper and a graduate of Hunter College in Manhattan, Seaman was the proverbial man on a mission in the fall of 2002, and he seemed to light the dim halls with his energy when he stormed out of the building bound for one appointment or another. When I had met him two years earlier he had been a lower-level functionary, always standing at the back of press conferences watching with an inscrutable expression on his face. With his slightly hooded Asiatic eyes, his spiky black crew cut, his controlled, outwardly placid face, and his straight, military-style posture he could have been a palace guard. When I had asked him a few questions one day in 2000 about the foreign media's coverage of Israel, he was polite but careful. There were many long, painful silences in our conversation as he seemed to be weighing whether to elaborate. I sensed that he was an extremely bright man who knew where the bodies were buried but was bound by "his station" or office politics or political correctness to keep his opinions to himself.

"I am not that man anymore," he told me two year later, when I talked with him in the fall of 2002. Several months before, he had had an epiphany, an experience that "flipped a switch" in his mind and changed the way he thought about his job.

It happened early in the evening of June 19, 2002. Seaman had still been at his desk, pawing at the daily tsunami of paper he was required to digest. It had been another busy day. The press was still asking for details about a suicide bombing the day before, the second in two days, and the twenty-eighth since the beginning of the year. A man had boarded a city bus heading for central Jerusalem from the town of Gilo. Per his training, the *shaheed* had waited a couple of stops until he'd situated himself in the center of the bus, where the blast would kill the most people, and then pulled his rip cord. Nails had been packed into the explosive material, so nineteen people—mostly mothers with children and teenagers going to or from school—were killed immediately and seventy were left with injuries ranging from a gash to loss of a limb or an eye or a presentable face.

Given the recent pace of things, Seaman told me he had not felt particularly surprised that evening when the police headquarters beeper attached to his waist went off to announce reports of a *new* bus bombing, this one in French Hill, an old, long-settled neighborhood in north Jerusalem that straddles the Green Line and is thus on contested territory.

He made a point of getting to these sites as fast as he could. It was important that someone be on the scene to get the facts straight and speak to reporters looking for a reaction from the Israeli government. The government didn't have precise rules about who would talk to the press in these situations. When news broke, reporters would put anyone who could claim any affiliation with the government on camera, so "official" spokesman duties often fell to whoever got there first. Abstractedly, Seaman gathered his car keys, jacket and cell phone and drove north from his office in the Beit Agron to Jerusalem's central bus depot. The depot was a frequent bomb target, so Seaman had no trouble finding it.

As he approached on the road, he could see the concrete bay of the bus stop below him and the little clots of reporters and TV crews already coalescing on the scene. They were always there so fast—like moths drawn to light.

He had gotten out and begun to walk around, trying to get a sense of what had happened. As he passed by, a reporter doing a stand-up boomed, "We are at the scene of an alleged bombing" in a stentorian tone, as if imparting highly privileged information. Seaman understood the ground rules. One did not say there had been "a bombing" until one was absolutely sure *it had been* a bombing. (Maybe there had been a gas tank explosion, for instance.) Still, on that day, the word "alleged" irritated him. Why was it that reporters were overwhelmed by professional skepticism only on the Israeli side of the Green Line? The top of the Egged bus had been peeled back like the lid of a sardine tin and the inside was coated with the kind of black sludge produced when plastic and human flesh roast together inside a metal container. "What's *alleged* about this?" Seaman had said to himself. "It's bomb damage; what else could it be?"

Strewn around the concrete lot were personal belongings, body parts, and a number of black, larvae-like shapes—people who had died at the scene and had been hastily covered with what looked like black plastic trash bags. He continued to wander among the book bags and shoes and legs and arms that hadn't been collected yet, until he found himself arrested by one object in particular: a crumpled baby carriage lying on its side with a wrapped body draped across it. "Where's the baby?" Seaman murmured to the policeman standing nearby, without taking his eyes off this strange tableau. The wounded infant had been taken to a hospital, the policeman said, and they just "didn't know yet" how it would fare. He added that a seven-year-old girl in this group had been sitting with the baby but she had died on the way to the hospital.

The ever-present Jerusalem wind had been tugging at the black plastic covering and had finally succeeded in dragging away most of the plastic sheet to expose the corpse that was draped over the carriage. The clothes had somehow been burned or blown off, leaving her nude, so Seaman could now see that this had been a woman. The face, which was "grotesque, horribly distorted" by the blast, held no clue to her identity, but the protective posture suggested that this had been the children's mother.

Long before this, Seaman told me, he had learned to detach his emotions. He'd been in combat in Israel's war in Lebanon and he'd been to many terror attack sites over the years. He "never had bad dreams." And he didn't ordinarily linger, but sometimes intense fires (fires that explode in a contained space and burn very hot, accelerated by engine oil and plastic) seem to freeze life at the moment of death, and he felt compelled to look at the moment that had been frozen in time here.

"It was clear from the way she lay on the carriage that her last thought had been to protect the child. She couldn't protect the child on her lap but she may have saved the baby with her body."

A sort of newsreel began to unwind in his mind of images from the Holocaust—grainy pictures of parents trying, usually futilely, to shield their children. For the first time in his experience, he told me, this wasn't "just a body" to him.

"These are *my people*," he found himself thinking. "This is *us*."

Following quickly upon that was the thought, "But we are *not supposed to be seeing scenes like this in the state of Israel*. The state of Israel was built so we wouldn't see scenes like this *ever* again."

It was like a switch was flicked in his mind, he said. He had never really thought of the second intifada as a war directed against his people; it was never represented in the press as a war, only as a series of incidents. Even IDF generals referred to it as "a low-intensity conflict."

"But it is happening again," he thought. "Just as in the Holocaust or the Six Day War, we are fighting for our survival. This is not some PR campaign we are in; it's a war being conducted and one of the battlefields is the media because they believe they can create doubt among Israelis, among supporters and eventually affect us on the ground."

Seaman said he decided right then that he would "not play games with reporters who don't take this as seriously as we do." He was charged with two tasks: He was supposed to assist the foreign press as it endeavored to cover his country, but also to assist the government of Israel in remaining the government of Israel. It was not always clear how far he was obligated to go. Was he obligated to assist a reporter who seemed to have come to the country on a mission to undermine the government of Israel? One thing was clear to him and that was that the Israeli government's new concern with "how things would look" was causing it to back down from self-defense—in the arena of public opinion and even on the battlefield—and this was "costing the lives of Israelis and endangering the state."

His colleagues in the other press divisions operated on a theory he summarized as: "If we're nice to [the news media], maybe they'll be nice to us." This wasn't working and it was time to get tough. "Everybody would like us to be those uncomplaining, accommodating people who were in the concentration camps again but we are never going to be in that situation again! If they don't like it, tough luck!"

He stopped for a moment when he realized how loud his voice had gotten as he told the story of his sea change at French Hill. "This may sound overly dramatic," he said a little sheepishly, "but it *was* dramatic."

■ ■ ■

THE "DESIRE TO BE LIKED," as Seaman put it, on the part of the younger, more dovish MFA staffers was only encouraging "all those people who just show up here with their cameras."

"It's politically incorrect to say this," he told me that afternoon in his office, "but one of our big problems is that there are too many reporters here, and they came here as opposed to, say, Somalia because we make things so comfortable for them. Israel is a nice place, a Western democracy. We're very open. We try to help them. There's a lot of news, but the country's a manageable size. That means that even though there are no new angles, everybody's trying to find one. Everyone comes here to get their career going, to get their Pulitzer. It's like there's nothing else going on in the world." A few weeks before, he noted angrily, a boat had gone down in a storm off the coast of Gambia and over three hundred people had died, but it "hadn't gotten two sentences."

"One of my major purposes is to reduce the number of journalists coming here, to make it a less attractive place to come," he said in a matter-of-fact way, as if he didn't care how the statement would sound.

Seaman's new "if they don't like it, tough luck" program had several dimensions. Number one was his personal "shit list." He would still give newly arrived Mideast correspondents the benefit of the doubt. He would set them up with contacts, arrange briefings, take their calls. But he would also watch their coverage carefully and if he began to see what he called "unprofessional behavior"—a lack of balance, for instance, or failure to check a source's relation to the story—he would stop making an extra effort for them.

"I don't expect them to be pro-Israel all the time. I don't care about sympathy to the Palestinians or background about the poverty and the lack of education there," he said to me on another afternoon. "What I care about is the 'one-armed Palestinian resistance fighter' who gets the big sentimental write-up because the IDF destroyed his house—except that the story never says he lost his arm when a bomb he was making in that house to kill Jews exploded on him."

Three of the first to make it on to Seaman's shit list were Suzanne Goldenberg of the *Guardian,* Lee Hockstader of the *Washington Post*—whose florid dispatches often read like they'd been ghostwritten by the PA's house organ *Al-Hayat al-Jadeeda*—and Gillian Findlay of ABC News, who seemed incapable of even uttering the word "Israel" in her on-air reports without scowling to telegraph her disapproval. "I simply boycotted them," he said. "I didn't revoke their press cards. I can't do that and wouldn't, but I stopped working with them and when the *Washington Post* saw that a smaller newspaper, such as the *Baltimore Sun,* was getting exclusive material, they understood that they had a problem. The editorial boards got the message and replaced their people." (All three outlets vehemently deny that Seaman had anything to do with the eventual reassignment of the three correspondents, each of whom had put in long tours in the area at the time they were transferred.)

His second move involved actually enforcing regulations that had been on the GPO books for years. One of them, for example, stipulated that cameramen had to have permits to work in Israel. Foreign television producers had long been in the habit of arriving in the country and immediately putting together a pick-up crew with imported Cypriots, Jordanians, Greeks and Palestinians, who would work "off the books" and for lower wages than Israelis. As the intifada-linked recession deepened, Israeli cameramen had grown increasingly angry about being undercut by nonresidents, so they formed a union and began to put pressure on Seaman to protect their livelihoods. Seaman figured that his new policy would have a three-for-one benefit. He'd get the unions off his back, bring work to some recession-battered Israelis, and draw a new "no more Mr. Nice Guy" line in the sand. Under his plan, appeals to the work-permit rule would be allowed and exceptions granted in some cases, but while he was in charge, television producers who wanted to hire a nonresident "would have to prove it's not coming at the expense of an Israeli here."

Seaman had only his little corner of the world to work with and he had decided he would do what he could in it with the bit of power he had. And there was plenty of slack to take up in all these "logistical" matters.

One of the reasons that reporters flocked to Israel was that nearly anyone who wanted a press card could get one. Cards were allotted to "working members of the press," but the interpretation of "working press" was quite flexible. All one generally had to do was produce a note on media outlet stationery, with the signature of someone who sounded official, saying something vague about one doing "some reporting" for them. Under these definitions, in the first seven months of 2002 alone, the GPO issued 3,500 three-month press cards and renewed about 1,000 longstanding credentials for longer periods. Most applicants got their cards within fifteen minutes of turning in a two-page form.

A press card is not essential to reporting from Israel or the territories. No one will stop you from, say, interviewing people on the street or calling officials in their offices. No one will stop you (except around, for instance, a nuclear installation) from filming or writing about what you see. But government-issued press cards ease the way at checkpoints, and they allow access to Israeli government press conferences and Knesset sessions, at which one can sit a few feet away from people like the prime minister. The cards also bring perks. Once one's name is on the list of accredited press in the area, a constant stream of invitations arrives by email—to soirées at the grand house of the Israeli president, to cocktails parties with Jerusalem's mayor, to lectures, briefings, and conferences with leading intellectuals. There are even offers of free Christmas trees at Christmas time.

The problem that Seaman faced was that with the proliferation of websites and cable TV channels offering news, more and more people calling themselves reporters were coming into the country citing their right to "access." Some of these people were quite serious about reporting the news to their niche readerships, but some only reported part-time and seemed to have used the press card mainly as cover to do other things. Increasingly, for example, members of far-left organizations like the International Solidarity Movement—an organization dedicated to stopping IDF operations in the Palestinian territories—had come in with a letter detailing an assignment from a local newspaper or something and then spent the rest of their time acting as human shields in front of Palestinian structures targeted for destruction, which entailed "playing cat and mouse" (as a *Ma'ariv* reporter once described the ISM modus operandi) with IDF tanks and D-9 armored bulldozers. The GPO couldn't block these people from entry; that was not the GPO's jurisdiction. But Seaman's view was that his division shouldn't have to facilitate their activism either.

In a perfect world, one could count on the media outlets themselves to weed out people who were more activist than committed reporter. Reporters at reputable outlets are told continually (via code-of-conduct booklets and such) that they are not allowed to

;e in public political activity. The *New York Times,* for instance,
butes ethical guidelines informing their staffers and stringers
that they must not do anything that "might raise questions about
political neutrality." They are told, for example, that they "may not
campaign, demonstrate for or endorse candidates, ballot causes or
efforts to enact legislation."

Apparently the *Times* doesn't enforce this regulation in the
Middle East. Several men who claim to have worked as stringers
for the *Times* also advertise their services on amin.org, a website
shared by a number of Arab journalists and photographers. One
Palestinian journalist says on his résumé that he worked for the
Times and then lists "political activist" as another occupation a few
lines down. Khaled Zighari, a Palestinian photographer who works
for Reuters and CBS, has a link on amin.org to his personal website. It features a controversial "One Palestine" picture of the region
and provides a link to a cartoonist who presents cartoons of Ariel
Sharon eating Palestinian babies. In May 2001, a correspondent for
the BBC, Fayad Abu Shamala, told a crowd at a Hamas rally in Gaza
that "journalists and media organizations [are] waging the campaign shoulder-to-shoulder together with the Palestinian people."
When the Israeli government showed proof of this to the BBC, the
latter issued a statement saying: "Fayad's remarks were made in a
private capacity. His reports have always matched the best standards
of balance required by the BBC."

Seaman decided that if the outlets weren't ensuring that the
people who came to him applying for press cards met the usual
description of a working journalist, the GPO would have to do the
sorting—with a more specific definition of "working press." The
GPO's old, long-ignored rule had defined "working press," in part,
as "people who derived the bulk of their income from journalism."
So thereafter, Seaman would require that applicants prove full-time
journalism status by presenting evidence of "a body of work" and
prove "bulk of their income" with actual contracts that stipulated
fees and deadlines.

In May 2002, an Italian journalist named Patrizia Viglino
assumed a starring role in the investigation of a suicide bombing—
and demonstrated why credentialing policies needed attention.
Viglino was given a GPO press card on the basis of a letter from the

editor of an entertainment and celebrity news website who said she would be working on stories for them in Israel. I searched "Patrizia Viglino" on Google and did not come up with any entertainment stories, but I did come up with a large oeuvre of polemics by Viglino about, for example, Israel's "pogroms of Palestinians." Invariably these were posted on fervently anti-Israel websites with names like *italiapalestina.it* and *informationguerilla.org*, which carry a little of what might be called news but mainly exhortations to demonstrate against Israel at upcoming political actions they list. Writing for or being reprinted on virulently anti-Israel websites is not a crime. (GPO rules do not discriminate on the basis of ideology. Israel accredits reporters for Al-Jazeera and networks from Egypt, Jordan, Dubai and Abu Dhabi.) But activist websites don't pay very much, and if the new rules had been in place, Viglino would probably not have been able to show that she derived the bulk of her income from journalism, which in turn might have prevented a terrible tragedy.

Viglino's work appears on websites affiliated with the International Solidarity Movement, and it may have been her ISM contacts who put her in touch with a British citizen named Asif Hanif who had claimed ISM affiliation when he entered Israel. One day in May 2002, Viglino brought Hanif and a friend named Omar Khan Sharif over the border from Gaza to Israel. The two young British nationals matched terrorist profiles in several ways and they might have been stopped for more probing questioning when they were stopped at the Erez crossing; instead, they passed through with relative ease because they were with a "journalist." Viglino dropped the two off in Tel Aviv, where Hanif detonated himself with a suicide belt in the entrance to a café on Tel Aviv's boardwalk, killing two people and wounding sixty others.

As part of the "We Aim to Please!" routine, GPO officials had also, before Seaman's epiphany, traditionally spent a significant amount of time replacing press cards that had been lost and stolen. The procedure to get a duplicate was not onerous and the fee was trivial. Seaman raised the fee up to the pain threshold, about $100, and stipulated that journos would have to go to Jerusalem's Kafkaesque central police headquarters to file a request for a duplicate.

In 2001, after the bombing of a Tel Aviv discothèque, the state had strengthened the "general closure" of its border with the West

Bank and Gaza, which meant dramatic cuts in the number of work permits granted to Palestinians who wanted to work in Israel. Seaman decided that security concerns merited applying the same standards to Palestinian journalists who wanted press credentials, so at the beginning of 2002 he declined to issue or renew press accreditation for all but a few Palestinian reporters and photographers. This did not mean they could not enter Israel—entry was an IDF decision; it did mean that Palestinians would not have an Israeli government-issued press card as a justification for entry. Exceptions would be made for reporters who needed to do humanitarian work and in other special cases. Reporters and cameramen could still work with Jerusalemites via telephones, faxes and the internet, but the GPO would no longer facilitate their entry into and work within Israel.

The new hassles about fees and having to prove that one was part of the working press were bad enough, but restrictions on their Palestinian stringers seem to have been the final straw for foreign press chiefs. One by one they began to make pilgrimages to Seaman's office to protest. Some threatened that they were ready to "just pull out and move their operations to Ramallah." Seaman shrugged and said "go right ahead." He knew there wasn't a chance they'd leave comfortable digs in Jerusalem. Next, some came back with a new tack that Seaman summed up as: "But if we don't have our stringers, we can't cover the story!" Seaman's reaction had been "OK, and ... ?"—by which he meant, "Do you think there's maybe a story in the fact you have to hire protection to attempt to work as a reporter over there?" A third reaction was what Seaman called "veiled threats " about "negative coverage" if he didn't relent. And indeed, negative coverage—specifically, stories about Seaman that cast him as a draconian censor—began to appear.

Rather than try to calm the flames, Seaman did a pugnacious, provocative interview with *Kol Ha'ir*, an Israeli weekly, in October 2002. The young Israeli reporter sat back in awe at his luck as Seaman made news by blithely throwing down gauntlet after gauntlet at the foreign press corps:

> The offices of the foreign networks in Jerusalem are compelled to hire Palestinian directors and producers. Those people determine

what is broadcast. The journalists will certainly deny that, but that is reality. . . . Three senior producers were coordinated with Marwan Barghouti. Barghouti used to call them and inform them about what was about to happen. They always received early warning about gunfire on Gilo. Then they shot for TV only the Israeli response fire on Beit Jala. Those producers advised Barghouti how to get the Palestinian message across better.

As the young reporter was shakily collecting his gear to go back to the office, I wondered if I had just witnessed Seaman self-destruct. Probably not, I reasoned. *Kol Ha'ir* does not publish an English version, so the comments would not get very far. I forgot how much the journalistic community is interested in coverage of itself. Within days, someone had translated the interview into English and it was circling the globe through email. Within days, responses from the local foreign press began to land at Beit Agron. The *Guardian* actually devoted part of its editorial page to this relatively intramural issue. Under the title "Seaman Lets It Slip" (with a subhead reading "Israel's bully has nothing to boast about"), the *Guardian* charged that "The Alastair Campbell of Israel . . . has at least been candid about his futile attempts to bully and penalize foreign reporters and news organizations, but he has done his organization and his government no favours at all."

Seaman seemed to enjoy this kind of sparring. He promptly dispatched a letter thanking *Guardian* editor Alan Rusbridger for the off-target but flattering comparison to Tony Blair's onetime right-hand man and said he would "withdraw any statements about [your coverage] when your newspaper withdraws the biased, sometimes malicious, and often incorrect reports which were filed by [reporter Suzanne Goldenberg] during her unpleasant stay in Israel."

It was just the beginning of a long and ongoing low-intensity conflict that lasts to this day. Over the next two years, this relatively low-level civil servant was to morph, at least in the minds of the foreign press, into an all-powerful Darth Vader sort of figure. Seaman is "hated," "polarizing," "the right-wing colonel," and "the representation of everything that is evil in Israel," in the words of various reporters. When Al-Jazeera.net posted a piece titled "Israel Muzzles Palestinian Journalists," Seaman was listed as the prime muzzler. In an internal memo obtained by *Ha'aretz*, the BBC's Middle

East bureau chief Andrew Steele called Seaman's denial of press cards "part of a long war of attrition between the Prime Minister's Bureau and the foreign media." Steele wrote to his higher-ups in London: "It is difficult to find appropriate ways of retaliation without losing our journalistic objectivity, [but at least we can] deprive the prime minister's spokesmen of their platform. Until we resolve this, I would appreciate it if any guest bookers would approach Foreign Ministry officials only and not [those] who work for Sharon."

Seaman also received letters of reprimand from his own government. Liberal members of Knesset filed a report claiming that the GPO was hostile to the foreign press, and Seaman was called before the Knesset several times to defend his policies. Meanwhile, outlets began to bring lawsuits on behalf of their Palestinian stringers.

Seaman began to spend a lot of his time in court. He lost some cases and won others. After he refused to renew press credentials for Palestinian cameraman Khaled Zighari (the photographer who links his website to baby-eating cartoons), one of Zighari's many employers in the foreign press, CBS, took the issue to court. They lost. They appealed. The issue finally went to the Israeli Supreme Court, where Seaman submitted classified Shin Bet material that he said "proved [Zighari] had personal connections with a terrorist organization beyond his work as a journalist, and [that] his position in the media was used by the terrorist organization for their purposes." The Supreme Court upheld the previous courts, but apparently CBS wasn't terribly disturbed by the classified Shin Bet material because, aided by heavier use of fax, phone and internet, Zighari continued to work for the network from a base in the West Bank. (CBS would not respond to my questions about the case.)

In 2003, Seaman faced the Supreme Court again. This time, various media outlets (including Al-Jazeera and Reuters) banded together with various aid groups to argue for the right to give Israeli press accreditation to residents of the Palestinian territories. This time, the court decided that Seaman's policy, as an across-the-board policy pertaining to a particular class, was contrary to the spirit of a free press. Denying a GPO card to a resident of the territories "makes it significantly harder for them to be journalists."

"The card gives them access to information from the branches of government, which is essential for their professional work," the court said. "Making it harder for them to obtain this information causes injury to freedom of expression and access to information."

■ ■ ■

LIKE THE SPECULATION ABOUT HOW Palestinian journalist Khaled Abu Toameh survives to report another day, there is always speculation in the journalistic community about when (not if) Danny Seaman will be fired. (Not all of this is unfriendly speculation. Some reporters call Seaman a hero—though they won't say it for attribution.) He came very close once more in 2003 when he decided to begin submitting applications for press cards to the Shin Bet for a security vetting. He argued that the White House press corps is vetted by the CIA. The Shin Bet proposal was quickly rejected by the Israeli government, apologies for "this crazy idea" were made, and higher-ups told *Ha'aretz* and the *Jerusalem Post* that his replacement was imminent.

In any case, when 2005 began, Seaman was still at his desk, still "the acting director" (which means he has to reapply for his job every year), still using his precarious perch to fight for what he believes, and even arguing in his characteristic speed-talking style that he had won a "partial victory." "Things have gotten better," he insisted to me.

If bias is a collection of small things coming together like mosaic tiles to form one big picture, taking down bias is a matter of small victories. One of the victories that Seaman was claiming for 2004 was that because of his "refusal to work with them," the influential journalism trade association Reporters Without Borders had stopped including Prime Minister Sharon on its annual list of "Predators of Democracy."

"It takes a while," Seaman told me. "They put up a huge struggle; they deny a lot of what we were saying, but slowly they come around. They won't announce it; they won't admit to it; but in those offices where we were very tough, it worked. When we attack them on the issues of professionalism and honesty and on upholding the principles of journalism, they go screaming and kicking but they give in."

ELEVEN

FROM OBSERVERS TO PARTICIPANTS

One day, historians examining this period of crisis will have to consider the circular process by which the media were transformed from observers to participants. From covering the story to playing a major part in it, to stimulating and sometimes agitating the environment for their own media purposes.

—Hanoch Marmari, editor-in-chief (retired) of the newspaper *Ha'aretz*, in a lecture to the World Editors Forum in Bruges, Belgium, May 2002

D ANNY SEAMAN IS RIGHT. There have been many small victories since 2000. Everyone who monitors media coverage agrees that major media in the United States cover the Palestinian/Israeli conflict with more balance and accuracy than they did in the first years of this latest "intifada." Since bias and distortion are expressed by patterns of subtle details (the wording of headlines, the use of prejudicing adjectives, the balance of "pro" and "con" experts, and the like), one has to look to the details to see the progress. In a *New York Times* article about possible successors to Yasser Arafat, for instance, Steve Erlanger, the paper's new Jerusalem bureau chief, wrote that the next leader of the Palestinian Authority would have to begin "restoring a semblance of fairness, security and stability to the institutions that profess to represent Palestinians. . . ." This single sentence is a world away from, say, James Bennet's April 2002 description of the Jenin refugee camp, a place where ordinary Palestinians are actually loath to visit, as "a fortress of Palestinian resistance that has crumbled before overwhelming Israeli force." (A more accurate description of the camp would have been something more specific, like "a fortress of Hamas and other militia activity," avoiding the implication that the terror militias represent and speak for all "Palestinians.") Similarly, a February 2004 headline reading "Palestinian Bomber Kills 8 and Wounds 50 in Jerusalem" is a vast improvement over previous *New York Times* headlines such as "Car Bomb Kills 2 Israelis and Threatens Truce Effort."

Changes in a top tier paper like the *New York Times* are important—not just because *Times* content now is distributed globally through a subscription wire like the Associated Press and Reuters, but because smaller regional papers take it as a kind of spiritual leader. Journalism has been a nervous, conformist industry for some time and is more so than ever because of increased competition. Most of life is really just high school writ large—and the news industry is more high school than most. Insecure editors and publishers look to a paper like the *Times* to tell them what is important in the news of the day and even what to think about that news. An appearance of sympathy to Israel is considered as uncool as it was when I was growing up in politically charged Ann Arbor, Michigan, but if "popular kids" like the *New York Times* send those subtle signals to the rest of the tribe (the placement of photos, the wording of captions, etc.), change could ripple through the industry. Failing that, there is always the power of the pocketbook. CNN (the Atlanta-based version, at least) now does studiously balanced coverage of the conflict, mostly because it has been given a ratings black eye by the more conservative—and thus assumed to be more pro-Israel—Fox News. Still, this new mood has not touched, may never touch, some major U.S. and global outlets, as the following recent episodes show:

In May 2004, a 34-year-old Israeli woman named Tali Hatuel was driving with her four daughters, ages two to eleven, near the Gaza Strip settlement where they lived when they were ambushed by Palestinian gunmen. When Israeli police found the car it was awash in blood. Hatuel and her little girls—including the two-year-old, who was still strapped into her car-seat—had each been shot in the head at point-blank range. Hatuel, who was eight months pregnant, had also been shot twice in the belly. Soon afterward, Islamic Jihad and Fatah called the Associated Press to take joint credit for the "victory."

Islamic Jihad and Fatah were firmly within modern PLO doc-
trine in their use of this word. The PLO considers any settler, of any
age, a combatant and thus a legitimate target for "armed resistance."
The organization retains a stable of highly educated, cosmopolitan
men and women who travel the world meeting with editorial boards
and journalism trade organizations to educate them on the importance of distinguishing between settlers and ordinary people, and
to urge them to use terms like "settler-baby" and "female settler"
so readers understand context. As Stanford-educated PLO spokeswoman Diana Buttu explained to an earnestly listening audience of
Columbia University journalism students in April, 2004, she "didn't
condone" the killing of children, but "settlers are not chosen ran-
domly . . . this is a legitimate form of resistance."

Perhaps Julie McCarthy of National Public Radio's Jerusalem
bureau had met at some time with the personable Ms. Buttu, because
in the radio reporter's piece, the pregnant woman and her four children are not even deemed important enough to be "the lead." Instead,
the killings are brought in almost as an aside, and then with the
implication that mother and children had provoked their own deaths
with their "continued presence in Gaza":

> The settlers rallied support saying Israel was withdrawing under fire.
> But there was ample evidence yesterday to show that their contin-
> ued presence in Gaza is provoking bloodshed. Israeli troops shot dead
> two Palestinian gunmen after the men ambushed a mother and her
> four small daughters outside the Gaza settlement of Gush Katif. The
> family was shot and killed on their way to the Israeli city of Ashkelon
> where they intended to campaign against Ariel Sharon and his plan
> to uproot them from Gaza.

In April 2005, Reuters ran a headline that set a new standard in
moral relativism: "Palestinian, Israeli Killed at West Bank Roadblock."
This was to headline a story in which—as Reuters' own lead put it—
"A Palestinian driver ran over and killed an Israeli at an army checkpoint in the West Bank on Monday before soldiers shot him dead in
the latest violence to strain a de facto cease-fire, witnesses said."

Other examples of recent press bias are more subtle. In August
2003, the late actor Christopher Reeve, who was then chairman of

an international foundation that funds spinal cord research, accepted an invitation to tour Israeli rehabilitation wards and see the results of its promising research on nerve regeneration. The Israeli Ministry of Foreign Affairs' press division acted quite star struck and fired off perhaps a few too many breathless press releases announcing photo ops and details of the movie star's upcoming visit. Perhaps Jon Maceda of NBC thought the MFA's excited tone was a bit gauche; perhaps he sensed what Danny Seaman called the new Israeli desire "to be liked." For instead of ignoring the story entirely—as most outlets did—Maceda bizarrely turned it into an opportunity to make gratuitous editorial comments about Middle East policy, as if to punish Israeli officials for trying to make themselves look good:

> Christopher Reeve, praying at Jerusalem's Wailing Wall. It's a public relations bonanza for Israel, struggling to improve its image.... Many celebrities have balked at [invitations to visit], often to protest Israel's military occupation. But Reeve, of "Superman" fame, says it was paralysis, not politics, that brought him here.... The Israeli government, which helped sponsor Reeve's $100,000 five-day trip, was careful to show [him] Israelis and Palestinians healing together in a rehab center, not confronting each other at West Bank checkpoints.

The last sentence is a textbook specimen of gratuitous editorializing—as well as being patronizing to Reeve. Of course the Israeli government "was careful" to show him "Israelis and Palestinians healing together ... not confronting each other" at a checkpoint. Reeve came to Israel to look at hospitals, not checkpoints. Presumably he had specified what he wanted to see on his visit as the representative of a medical research foundation.

The irony is that when the Israeli press apparatus does what their critics have always said they should do, be proactive, tell "their story," the press takes a kind of perverse revenge. Nearly every government on the planet employs a staff to generate good PR (and on slow news days, producers are often only too happy to work with these staffs), but I do not think I had ever before seen an attempt at PR used as the "nut" of a news story. Why should it be newsworthy if Israel attempts to make itself look good? The implication in Maceda's piece is that it is shameless enough to be newsworthy if Israel—of all places—attempts to point at what is good in its society.

This tendency has been most blatant in European coverage, in which reporters continue to parrot PA/PLO spinmeisters as credulously, and to disdain the word of Israel's spokesmen as contemptuously, as they did in 2000. In the spring of 2004, for example, the new proactive Israeli press staff promoted a story that, by all reasonable standards, should have helped to "tell Israel's story." There had been a rash of attempted suicide bombings by Palestinian children under the age of sixteen. (Demoralized after a string of successful targeted killings of key leaders, the terror militias had begun to have trouble recruiting adult and teenage men, and so had turned to children, even mentally deficient ones, to carry bombs.) News stories are often played up, downplayed, or even ignored entirely depending on whether they have come with pictures—and this child bomber story came with pictures galore.

There was no prearrangement with the Israeli government. It just happened that—as is often the case—an AP cameraman had been waiting in a checkpoint line when IDF soldiers noticed that a twelve-year-old boy, apparently traveling alone, looked bulkier than normal in the chest area. A quick pat-down revealed a suicide bomber's vest under his sweater. Getting these things off without detonating them is tricky. All passage through the checkpoint stopped. Onlookers crouched behind the concrete barriers that line the sides of the road near checkpoints. The boy stood alone in the middle of the road while an IDF soldier sent a spiderlike, remote-controlled robot to him to snip the cords that bound the vest to his body with scissors held at the end of one of its tentacle-like arms. When the robot failed, dropping its scissors, the boy began to panic and wrestle with the vest, but after a few heart-stopping seconds, he freed himself and flung his little arms in the air in triumph. In the photos taken by the AP cameraman, the boy's exuberant relief is palpable, and stills from this incredible sequence began to appear on front pages in the United States. In the European press, however, the story was mostly ignored. One foreign reporter explained to an Israeli colleague at the newspaper Ma'ariv that he had not reported the "boy bomber" story because he had "the unpleasant feeling that the Israelis were trying to exploit this poor child's story for public relations. It would have been different if he had actually been hurt by the bomb."

One foreign outlet, the BBC, did give the incident a lot of coverage, but characteristically it saw a dark conspiracy in Israel's behavior. The piece by BBC reporter Orla Guerin (which can still be found in Real Player format on the Web) is about sadistic, possibly dishonest, certainly cynical IDF soldiers and their attempt to use a frightened little boy . . . to hide other dark deeds . . . as an opportunity to act macho . . . actually, it is not clear why they have seized the little boy, but clearly something sinister is afoot. Guerin, it was clear from her voice and her grimacing face, was suspicious of virtually everything the IDF had to say about the incident—particularly its claim that the boy knew what he was doing, as if the IDF had further "victimized the victim" with this suggestion. "The boy's relatives say that he is developmentally disabled but the Israeli army insists he was a willing and able human bomb," she said in a voice dripping with skepticism. (Many months later, when the boy did a long interview with a number of outlets, it turned out that these two conditions didn't rule each other out. He was mentally disabled, according to his relatives, and he was also willing to kill himself because he had been told that martyrdom was "better than being a singer or a footballer. It's better than everything.") "The only time we have seen the boy he has been under tight Israeli army control," Guerin added with grim significance, as if trying to imply that it was somehow unnatural that army soldiers would take an unclaimed little boy who had attempted to turn himself into a human bomb into custody for a few hours or that they then might want to keep him around for a debrief. Then, Guerin said, he had been "produced" by the army and "paraded in front of reporters . . . [who] then forced him to pose for pictures." (But what reporters had gotten wind of the incident from the AP and then been told by the IDF that the little boy was not available for pictures?) "This," she concluded darkly, "is the picture the Israeli army would like you to see—a little boy allegedly ready to kill himself."

The obvious lesson of the story is that groups like the Al-Aqsa Martyrs Brigade (the group that eventually took credit) are willing to exploit children in the cruelest way, but the BBC reporter performed a strange act of logical gymnastics, turning the Israelis into the cruel exploiters, or at least putting their "exploitation"—such as it was—in the forefront of her coverage.

The BBC's conspiracy chasing might have been easier to shrug off—except it was only the tip of the iceberg of seething, jeering, openly anti-Israel reporting that has been coming out of Europe. In January 2003, for instance, on Britain's Holocaust Memorial Day, the *Independent* published a political cartoon depicting a gigantic, Gulliver-sized Prime Minister Ariel Sharon kneeling atop a pile of ruined houses and holding the headless body of a Palestinian child to eager, blood-covered lips. He is naked, except for a state fair sort of prize ribbon with the legend "Vote Likud," which covers his crotch. "What's the matter?" the caption bubble reads. "You've never seen a politician kiss babies before?"

It's hard to imagine the oldest, most hateful myth about any other minority group being resurrected in mainstream media as was, in this case, the ancient "blood libel" of Jews stealing and eating gentile babies. Nevertheless, this cartoon was voted "Cartoon of the Year" for 2003 by Britain's Political Cartoon Society.

Looking at the virulent, vituperative tone of European coverage, and particularly at how openly jeering it grows when Israel tries to defend itself in the media war, it is hard to imagine that any Israeli public relations staff with any amount of resources at its disposal could have an impact in Europe. Douglas Davis, European correspondent for the *Jerusalem Post*, for example, now refuses to appear as a talking head on the BBC because, he says, "the volume and intensity of unchallenged [anti-Israel] diatribe" on that state-supported network have "transcended mere criticism of Israel" and have "become the principal agent for re-infecting British society with the virus of anti-Semitism." Perhaps Benjamin Netanyahu has found the best way to think about this: "We have lost Europe."

■ ■ ■

BUT THERE IS, IN FACT, A POSITIVE SIDE. The media war did rouse Israel's *hasbara* apparatus. It is doing a better job than in 2000. The Ministry of Foreign Affairs has brought in new superstar media spokesmen, razor-sharp people like Mark Regev and Daniel Taub who speak English impeccably. The GPO now supplies the foreign press with a surfeit of background information, and—though not as often as it would like, of course—this backgrounding finds its way into stories.

The MFA has also become extremely proactive about getting "good pictures" into the hands of always picture-hungry TV news producers. In late January 2004, for instance, when a suicide bomber detonated amid men, women and children on their way to work and school, on a bus in Jerusalem's quiet German Colony district, Ilan Sztulman of the MFA was on the scene within minutes with a video camera. What one sees in the first ten minutes of a bus bombing is very different from what even hardened war correspondents see because they must wait for paramedics and police to open the area. As a government official Sztulman was able to capture the far more searing sight that rescue workers see. Within an hour or so, this heartbreaking footage was on the MFA website and had been broadcast to the entire GPO press list for the convenience of any TV producers who cared to use it in their news reports that night. As it happened, the footage was too graphic for primetime news broadcasts, but Sztulman says that even if it wasn't used, posting it on the Web brought "a perspective on the conflict that people did not know."

Other steps include, of course, the now famous tightening of GPO press credentialing policies. The Israeli government has taken an extraordinary amount of heat for this (the BBC's Orla Guerin, for instance, compared the new policy to press restrictions in Zimbabwe), but the tightening has reduced the power of those Palestinian stringers who put activism before honest journalism. Many of the old guard are still there, but, as Israeli radio host Danny Zaken puts it, "Their word is no longer accepted on hearsay alone."

The one weak link is still the IDF, which needs to find spokespeople who can explain military exigencies to a foreign press corps that is generally hostile to militaries in general and ignorant of how and why they function. Still, even the fortress-like IDF has accepted that it must communicate with the civilian press. As Miri Eisen (now semi-retired while she completes a doctorate for Haifa University and raises two children), puts it, "Once upon a time, nobody [in the IDF] cared about the media and now at least they take it into consideration, even if in the end they decide against changing an operational decision. We have become incredibly open compared to what we were."

The central problem for the IDF is—and will always be—that, Eisen explains, "We are a small military, a small army, with the

entire world focused on us. There is a question of how many jour-
nalists you can have running around in your army at a given time.
We can never give everybody the answers to all their questions."
Since they must choose whom to spend precious resources on, the
IDF often decides to give the tour or interview to reporters in the
Israeli press or the bigger outlets of the foreign press like the *New
York Times*. Inevitably, this means that smaller outlets such as the
"Minneapolis Saint Paul Herald"—as Eisen puts it, making up a
newspaper name by way of example—will say, " 'Why didn't we get
it?' For them, their readership is huge, but at the end of the day
[giving everybody special attention is] not going to work."

Given that Israel doesn't have the resources to counter every
story in every "Minneapolis Saint Paul Herald," the other positive
outgrowth of the media war has been the mustering of civilians outside of Israel in defense of Israel. This volunteer brigade—which is
made up of people from a spectrum of religions and from nearly
every country you can imagine—uses a variety of tactics. Boycotts
of papers like the *New York Times* and the *Los Angeles Times* have
been started and many privately funded public relations drives have
been launched. The organization Israel21C, which promotes the
Israeli high-tech sector, is one. Another is the Eagles' Wings Ministry, which sends Christian youths to Israel for training to serve
as "emissaries" on behalf of Israel in the United States and to fight
anti-Israel sentiments on American campuses.

Some of the work is based in brick-and-mortar, but the great
facilitator of organization and action has been, of course, the internet and what Terry Teachout recently called "the break-up of the
big-media monopoly" that is occurring in the blogosphere. It is
driven by political blogs like littlegreenfootballs.com, Instapundit.com
and Strategypage.com, which deconstruct mainstream media coverage of everything—including Israel—on a daily basis.

For over a decade, CAMERA (Committee for Accurate Middle East Reporting of America) was the lone Web-based voice calling for more fair and accurate coverage of Israel. In 2000, and after
the beginning of Israel's first real media war, CAMERA was joined
by the brasher, flashier-looking HonestReporting.com, which is managed by a veteran of the Israeli Air Force. After 2000, the number
of on-line media monitors grew exponentially. (There are an equally

uncountable number of websites attempting to combat what they
see as pro-Israel bias in the news media.) There is now a media-
monitoring website focusing on any newspaper or media franchise
or geographical region you can imagine. One website, for example,
covers nothing but the *Los Angeles Times'* reporting of the conflict.
Eyeonthepost.org focuses on the *Washington Post.* Tampa-
bayprimer.org follows Florida media; and so on. As for "the alpha-
bets," there is a site that takes on the Canadian Broadcasting
Corporation (CBC in those parts) and the Australian Broadcasting
Corporation (Australia's ABC). And the BBC has its own subgenre:
sites like biased-bbc.blogspot.com that do nothing but track its
coverage.

The excellent watch.windsofchange.net monitors French media
like *Le Monde* and Agence France-Presse and translates key articles for its English-speaking users. The Association of Jewish Journalists of the French Press is an inspiring example of gutsy journalists
bucking the tide in France. This year HonestReporting.com expanded,
adding versions in Spanish, Italian and Russian, as well as new affiliates based in Brazil, Canada and Australia. Palestinian Media Watch
(pmw.org.il) is an excellent translator and archivist of Palestinian
media. The Middle East Media Research Institute (MEMRI.org)
does the same for all Arab-language media.

What these websites do—besides dispute, educate, and drag
out important documents like the PLO Charter from the neglected
historical record—is mobilize great displays of cyber activism. Some-
day media outlets will build electronic moats around themselves to
block out unwanted phone, fax and email; but for now, deluges of
phone, fax and email are the weapon of choice. HonestReporting.com,
for example, crows that in 2002 its readers bombarded CNN
executives with up to six thousand emails a day, eventually forcing
"major editorial changes . . . which greatly shifted public perception
of the Arab-Israel conflict in general, and the role of Palestinian suicide bombers in particular." (They exaggerate a bit. CNN took meetings with Israeli press division staffers because they had been
softened up by a ratings drubbing in their contest with Fox News,
but deluges of complaints from citizens helped.)

What the blogs are doing—besides correcting the record on
Israel—is bringing about a fundamental, much-needed change in

thinking about "the news." In April 2005, for example, after over a year of bombardment by citizens' monitors like CAMERA on its Israel coverage and public embarrassments like the Jayson Blair fabrication episode, the *New York Times* appointed a "public editor" to handle the volume of reader mail and write columns explaining the newspaper's side of the story to the restive public. The new public editor, Daniel Okrent, made what I think is a historic admission:

> It eventually comes to this: Journalism itself is inadequate.... Like recorded music, which is only a facsimile of music, journalism is a substitute, a stand-in. It's what we call on when we can't know something firsthand. It's not reality, but a version of reality, and both daily deadlines and limited space make even the best journalism a reductionist version of reality.

But exactly. If the *New York Times* put this disclaimer on its front page, it wouldn't be in the trouble it's in today. People are abandoning papers like the *Times* not so much because it has reported things that turned out to be untrue or even because its overwhelmingly liberal reporters and editors leak their political opinions into news and feature stories whenever possible. (Everyone makes mistakes and an "unbiased" newspaper is an impossibility.) No, the mainstream media's biggest mistake was the imperious quality it developed in the years after the breaking of the "Watergate" story, which made journalism a glamour profession and spawned new postgraduate schools of journalism that had to justify their existences by making journalism look like brain surgery. In other words, instead of letting their tone reflect who they are—human beings with preferences, and holes in their body of knowledge, and prejudices—editors and producers promoted the idea that "trained journalists" were a special caste of people who had renounced the petty passions of the masses and could then somehow render impartial judgments.

But as Rupert Murdoch put it recently in a speech to the American Society of Newspaper Editors, people "don't want to rely on a godlike figure from above to tell them what's important . . . and they certainly don't want news presented as gospel." And the major media simply have not been able to sustain the illusion of godlike impartiality and omniscience in the age of the internet.

We know (largely because the blogs gleefully circulated this
tidbit among Americans who probably would have missed it) that
on the day the dying Yasser Arafat was transferred from Ramallah
to a hospital in France, BBC reporter Barbara Plett "started to cry
. . . as the helicopter carrying the frail old man rose above his ruined
compound," and that she then penned a breathless hagiography
about this "symbol of Palestinian unity, steadfastness, and resistance" who had "languished in the twilight of world indifference to
his plight."

Again, largely because of the blogosphere, we know that the
New York Times reporter (and former Jerusalem bureau chief) Chris
Hedges, who is not supposed to act in ways that "might raise ques-
tions about political neutrality," told a commencement audience at
an Illinois college in May 2003 that by invading Iraq, the United
States became:

> part now of a dubious troika in the war against terror with Vladimir
> Putin and Ariel Sharon, two leaders who do not shrink in Palestine
> or Chechnya from carrying out gratuitous and senseless acts of vio-
> lence. . . . The real injustices, the Israeli occupation of Palestinian land,
> the brutal and corrupt dictatorships we fund in the Middle East, will
> mean that we will not rid the extremists who hate us with bombs.
> Indeed we will swell their ranks. Once you master people by force
> you depend on force for control. . . .

We know that the natural tendency of journalism and terrorism to collude may be reaching its nadir in Iraq, where cameramen
for the Associated Press and Reuters, by amazing coincidence, keep
finding themselves on the spot when insurgents achieve some of
their greatest car-jacking and kidnapping "successes." We know that
CNN was able to maintain a bureau in Baghdad (right down the
hall from offices of Saddam Hussein's Ministry of Information)
when everyone else was sent packing because there were understandings about what it would broadcast, and we know that Eason
Jordan, the retired CNN of CEO, was such a consummate, level-
headed journalist that he was willing, based on shaky hearsay, to
tell an international audience that U.S. soldiers in Iraq may have
targeted and killed working reporters in the field—presumably to
silence them.

We know, in other words, that reporters and editors and producers aren't priests of neutrality, that they frequently stray from their professed journalistic standards. In the past year we have been reminded over and over again that their dispatches are, as Phil Scheffler put it, "constructions" or human creations—nothing more and nothing less, informed by all the things that inform human creations: petty vendettas, ambitions, craven desires to be with the cool kids, secret shames, blind spots—and sometimes even diligence and brilliance. We know that journalism is an industry like any other (and these days an increasingly desperate industry), which means that the news product of one company or another should be vetted as skeptically as we vet, say, the claims of air conditioner makers.

Most of all, the democratic, irreverent spirit of the blogs has reminded news consumers to keep our own "amateur" counsel, to ask for proof, to subject those proofs to hard tests, to stay smart, and to stay vigilant. This will certainly bring about better coverage of Israel—and everything else.

ACKNOWLEDGMENTS

I want to thank everybody at Encounter Books, especially my editor, Peter Collier, and associate editor Carol Staswick. Thanks also to the staff at the Lev Yerushalayim Hotel in Jerusalem, and to everybody—named and unnamed—who talked to me for this book.

INDEX

ABC News, 36, 249–50; on al-
Dura episode, 50; on Gilo, 120;
in Ramallah, 168; on Ramallah
lynching, 86–87
Abdullah, King of Jordan, 79
Abu Gharib, 4
Adams, Paul, 207–9
Adler, Renata, 103
Age, The (Australia), 51
Agence France-Presse (AFP), 2,
148–49, 201; on al-Dura, 51–52,
64; monitoring of, 268; on
Ramallah lynching, 91
Ajami, Fouad, 205
Ajaz, Saib, 70
Akawi, Omar, 158–59
American-Arab Anti-Discrimina-
tion Committee, 41
American Colony Hotel, 101–5,
118–19, 124, 208; amenities,
102–3; anti-Zionism at, 104–5;
fixers at, 105, 109; history, 102
American Society of Newspaper
Editors, 269
amin.org, 252
Amir, Yigal, 136, 137
Amnesty International, 105, 163,
187; on Jenin, 174, 175
Amr, Nabil, 200
Anderson, Chris, 145–49

Anderson, Scott, 103–4, 105, 168,
171–72
Anglican Church School
(Jerusalem), 204–5
Annan, Kofi, 88
Anti-Defamation League, 189–90
anti-Semitism, 189–90, 265
Al-Aqsa Martyrs Brigade, 81, 161,
200, 209*n*; and child martyrs,
264
Al-Aqsa Mosque riots, 9, 15,
32–37, 45
Arab Liberation Front, 80
Al-Arabia, 214
Arabic-language media, 272–74;
on Al-Aqsa riots, 33–37; *see
also Al-Hayat al-Jadeeda*; Al-
Jazeera; Palestinian journalists
Arafat, Suha, 233
Arafat, Yasser, 28, 35, 119, 144,
200, 217; on Al-Aqsa riots, 32,
35, 36–37; on al-Dura, 39, 64,
80; foreign fans of, 222–23, 227,
270; on "Jeningrad," 165; and
Karine A, 158, 159–60; media
crackdown, 43, 134, 227; media
manipulator, 2–3, 151, 201–3;
media protection of, 211; as
"mystery," 30–31; Palestinian
critics of, 200, 205–6, 219, 223,

227, 235; pocketing of foreign aid, 187, 219, 229, 230, 231–33; Ramallah headquarters, 192, 208, 217, 218–22; rejects Barak offer, 14–15, 33, 141; terror support, 220; *see also* Fatah; Palestinian Authority

ARD (German TV network), 65, 72, 73; *Three Bullets* broadcast, 78–79

Ashrawi, Hanan, 21–23, 69, 139, 208

Associated Press (AP), 2, 260; al-Dura episode, 49, 52–54, 64, 69–70; child suicide bomber photo, 263–64; influence of, 52–53; in Iraq, 270; Temple Mount photo, 17–18; threats to, 117, 132–33, 152–53, 201

Association of Jewish Journalists of the French Press, 268

Atlantic, The, 50

Atta, Nasser, 89–90, 91, 93

Attari, Bashir, 202

Australia: Channel 9 TV, 89, 174

Australian Broadcasting Corporation, 268

Avrahami, Yosef, 85–90

Awadallay, Adel, 158

Ayalon, Moshe, 52

Al-Ayam, 203

Bakri, Muhammed, 175–76

Balfour Declaration, 210

Baltimore Sun, 250

Banfield, Ashleigh, 168

Barak, Ehud, 58, 61, 132, 143; GPO downsizing, 141, 150; peace talks, 14–15, 141

Barghouti, Fadwa, 212

Barghouti, Marwan, 119, 126–27, 220, 255; on Al-Aqsa riots, 34–35; murder trial, 212–14

BBC (British Broadcasting Corporation), 2, 78, 184–87, 252, 266, 270; anti-Americanism, 184–85; anti-Semitism, 265; on child suicide bomber, 264; double standard, 78, 190; on al-Dura, 50–51, 57, 58, 60, 67; "Gotcha" style, 196; on *Karine A,* 159; monitoring of, 268; on Ramallah lynching, 87–88, 93; on Seaman, 255–56; on "siege" of Mukata, 221

Bedein, David, 151

Beit Agron International Press Center, 243–44

Beit Jalla, 120–24, 255

Bellow, Saul, 140

Ben-Ami, Shlomo, 34

Ben-Gurion, David, 140

Bennet, James, 171, 234, 259

Bethlehem, 96, 109–11, 163, 187, 240

biased-bbc.blogspot.com, 268

bin Laden, Osama, 41, 225

Binah, Baruch, 115–16, 191–92

Bir Zeit University, 212; Media Institute, 209

Bird, Eugene, 4

Bishara, Azni, 21

Blair, Jayson, 18, 269

Boucher, Richard, 159

Britain: in Mandate period, 26–27, 28; public opinion, 3–4, 5; Political Cartoon Society, 265; *see also* BBC, *Guardian; Independent*

Brokaw, Tom, 36, 37

Burns, Eric, 1
Burns, John, 127
Bush, George W., 4, 137
Buttu, Diana, 213, 220, 261

CAMERA (Committee for Accurate Middle East Reporting of America), 30, 267, 269
Camp David negotiations, 33, 141
Campbell, Alastair, 255
Canadian Broadcasting Corporation (CBC), 4, 24–25, 208, 268
Carleton, Richard, 89
CBS News, 7, 126, 252; on al-Dura, 41, 49–50, 59, 62, 64; on Ramallah lynching, 90; suit against Seaman, 256
CBS 60 Minutes, 68–69
cease-fire (Sharm el-Sheikh), 100–1, 119, 123–25, 132, 138, 158
censorship: by Israeli government, 115–16, 134–35; by PA, 132, 134, 152–53, 192, 199, 200–4; by Palestinian editors, 210–11; self-censorship, 30–32, 202–3; see also intimidation
Chazen, Naomi, 21
checkpoints, 181, 186, 187, 234–41, 262; child bomber disarmed, 263; and press cards, 251; Qualandia, 114, 217–18, 237
Chicago Tribune, 30
children: as martyrs/soldiers, 77–78, 112, 126–29, 263–64; as targets, 260–61; see also al-Dura, Mohammed
Christian Arabs, 120, 123–24
Christian Science Monitor, 24, 115, 150

Clinton, Bill, 9, 115, 132, 137; on al-Dura, 79; peace talks, 14
CNN, 8, 21n; change of tone, 260, 268; on al-Dura, 43; ignores PA incitement, 129; in Iraq, 270; on Jenin, 171, 172; and Karine A, 156, 159; on Mukata demolition, 221; and Rahme, 43, 81; on Ramallah lynching, 88; in Serbia, 2; trust in, 8, 24, 25
CNN-World, 184
Cold War, 28
"collaborators" (Palestinian), 76–77, 113–14, 200–1, 203, 206
Columbia Journalism Review, 96
Committee to Protect Journalists, 150
Conyers, John, 20
Council for the National Interest, 4
Cristiano, Riccardo, 91–93, 116, 117
curfews, 186–87, 221, 226, 237
"cycle of violence," 86, 88–90, 126

Daily Telegraph (London), 3, 91
Dajani, Mohammed, 171
David vs. Goliath theme, 15, 19, 20, 25, 28
Davis, Douglas, 3, 265
Dayan, Moshe, 28
"Days of Rage," 87
Dearden, Chris, 109–12
Death in Gaza, 77n
Diary of a Small War (Kelly), 131
Diker, Dan, 37
Doriel, Josef, 63
Dreifus, Claudia, 101
Dugger, Celia, 122
al-Dura, Amal, 67–68, 80
al-Dura, Jamal, 40, 42, 47–48, 50–51, 60, 61, 66–68; as

celebrity, 79–80; as "collabora-
tor," 76–77
al-Dura, Mohammed (shooting
of), 22, 39, 42, 47, 83; AP on,
52–55, 64; ballistics, 70, 71;
conspiracy theories, 74–78; and
Daniel Pearl, 42; eyewitnesses,
40, 46–47; government
response, 56–60; and Hamas,
77–78; IDF comments on, 49,
51, 52; IDF investigation,
59–65, 71–72, 135–36; memo-
rials to, 42; on *Nightline,*
22–23; PA response, 55–56,
66, 76, 80, 82–83; Schapira
documentary, 45*n,* 48–49,
65–74; "second-day" photo
op, 66–67; as *shaheed* (martyr),
68, 70, 74, 79, 80, 81–83;
videotape (France 2), 39–41,
46–51, 53–55, 62–63, 66,
71–73, 75

Eagles' Wings Ministry, 267
Earth Summit, 185
Eiland, Gloria, 57, 58
Eisen, Miri, 58, 59, 73, 78, 195,
266–67; on *Karine A,* 160; on
Operation Defensive Shield,
167
El Bureish, 47, 54–55, 81
Enderlin, Charles, 43, 48–49; and
Schapira investigation, 71–73
Erekat, Saeb, 21–23, 50, 139, 171
Erlanger, Steve, 259
Ernst & Young, 213–14*n*
Europe, 6; aid to PA, 219, 229,
231–232; anti-Semitism in,
189–90, 265; biases, 147, 149,
188–90, 235, 263–65; public

opinion, 3–5, 6; *see also* Agence
France-Press; ARD, BBC;
Guardian; Reuters; RTI
Eyeonthoport.org, 268

Fallows, James, 7, 50
Fatah, 33, 35, 78, 115, 119, 149,
163, 164, 204, 209*n;* and *Karine
A,* 158, 159; media intimidation,
149, 203; terrorism, 161, 200,
260–61; *see also* Al-Aqsa Martyrs Brigade
Fighel, Yoni, 177
Findlay, Gillian, 36, 50, 86, 249–50
Fisk, Robert, 57
"fixers" (translators), 207–14;
author's, 215–19, 223–25, 230,
233–35, 237–41; backgrounds/
training, 209–10, 211; connections, 212, 214; expense, 215;
vetting by, 211
Fletcher, Martin, 82
Ford Foundation, 214*n*
Foreign Press Association, 106,
133, 134, 149, 188, 213
Fox News, 96, 107, 158, 165, 210,
260, 268
Foxman, Abraham, 189–90
France 2 television, 41, 43, 48–50,
53–54, 55, 62, 66, 70, 71–72, 75
French press, 25, 172, 175, 268; *see
also* Agence France-Presse

Gandhi, Arun, 222
Gantz, Benny (Brig. Gen.), 68–69
Garrels, Arrne, 60
Gaza Strip, 9, 19, 115, 125, 233;
border closure, 253–54; Hamas
in, 252; Jewish settlers in, 4,
260–61; Netzarim Junction,

43–48, 59–60; photo anthology, 188–89

Gelernter, David, 88

Germany: ARD, 65, 72, 73, 78–79; public opinion, 4

Gibson, John, 165

Gilo, 120–25, 255; media neglect of, 120, 124–25

Gissin, Ra'aan, 152

Gold, Dore, 194

Goldenberg, Suzanne, 52, 57–58, 65, 96, 249–50, 255

Graves, Keith, 107

Green Line, 32, 101, 102, 105, 161, 183, 245, 246

Greenberg, Joel, 162

Griffin, Jennifer, 96, 210

Grossman, Tuvia, 17–18, 32

Guardian, The (U.K.), 96, 249–50; on al-Dura, 41, 52, 57, 65; on Seaman, 255

Guerin, Orla, 78, 93, 264, 266

Gulf War (first): media coverage, 1, 9–10; Shai on, 130–31

Gutman, Matthew, 116, 212

Ha'aretz, 96, 131, 143, 150–51, 168–70, 255, 259; Bakri interview, 176; on al-Dura, 62, 63, 136; on *Karine A*, 155; on Palestinian fixers, 210; on Shai, 130

Haganah, 26–27

Halabaya, Ahmad Abu, 128

Halevi, Jossi Klein, 183

Halliburton, 5

Hamas, 119, 161, 163, 179, 187, 204, 212, 219, 252; on Al-Aqsa riots, 32, 34, 43; and child martyrs, 77–78; "Days of Rage," 87; and al-Duras, 76, 77–78; intimi-

dation of journalists, 201; in Jenin, 176, 259; in student government (Bir Zeit), 209

Hammer, Josh, 149

Hanif, Asif, 253

Hanna, Mike, 88

hasbara, 138, 168; budget for, 140, 141; discomfort with, 139–40; mixed messages, 143; new approach, 177–78, 192–95; and victimhood, 194–95

Hatuel, Tali, 260

Hatzofeh, 143

Hawkins, David, 64

Al-Hayat al-Jadeeda, 33, 34, 249; as Arafat mouthpiece, 203; Cristiano letter, 91–92; on al-Dura, 56; threat to AP, 117

headline writing, 30

Hebrew University, 73, 109, 216

Hebron, 163

Hedges, Chris, 270

Herzog, Yitzhak, 57

Hezbollah, 131, 136

Hockstader, Lee, 31, 50, 249–50

Holocaust refugees, 11–12

HonestReporting.com, 267, 268

Human Rights Watch, 105

Hume, Brit, 107

Hussein, Saddam, 2, 79, 227; and al-Dura, 80; and Gulf War, 130; martyr payments, 80, 129, 224

Ibish, Hussein, 41

Ignatieff, Michael, 2

imams (preaching), 33, 35, 36, 126, 127–28

Immanuel, Jon, 157–58

"incitement," 125–29, 138; and Al-Aqsa, 33–35; media

indifference, 126–29; Protest
Days, 45–46, 67–68; in schools,
187; *see also* imams
Independent, The (UK), 107,
173–74; anti-Semitism in, 265
Instapundit.com, 267
International Monetary Fund,
185, 229, 231–32
International Solidarity Movement, 222, 251, 253
internet, 1, 7, 19, 253, 266; alternative views, 267–70, 271
intifada (first), 20–21, 97, 104,
124–25
intimidation of journalists: by
Palestinians, 89–93, 91, 109–18,
147–49, 152, 201–4; by Israel,
134–35, 149–50, 169–71; *see
also* censorship
Iran, 6
Iraq, 4–5, 224, 270; embedded
journalists, 176–77; *see also*
Hussein, Saddam
Islamic Jihad, 260–61
Israel Channel 2, 57
Israel21C, 267
Israeli Air Force, 60, 86
Israeli Broadcasting Authority,
130, 152; Arabic-language station, 177
Israeli Defense Force (IDF), 75–76,
146, 154; checkpoints, 181, 187,
217–18, 234–41; conflict with
MFA, 142, 156, 195–97; demonizing of, 15, 16–17, 26, 146,
148; and al-Dura case, 40–41,
44–52, 55–65, 67, 71–73,
135–36; at Gilo, 122–24; informality, 26; in Jenin, 163–67;
joint policing, 35, 44, 45; jour-

nalistic neglect of, 125; on
Karine A, 154–58; media
restrictions, 130, 167–70; new
media approach, 266–67; Operation Defensive Shield, 163–77;
as "people's military" (ubiquity), 15–16, 181–82; photographing of, 111; press staff,
106, 108, 141–42, 154, 266–67;
refuseniks, 181; reservist lynching, 85–93; women in, 125
Israeli Government Press Office
(GPO), 73–74, 97, 98, 108, 129,
132, 133, 141–43; backgrounding, 265; cameraman permits,
250; on Cristiano letter, 93;
downsizing, 150–51; facilities,
244; on Martin intimidation,
114–15; press cards (credentialing), 93, 98, 115, 135, 249–57,
266; Seaman at, 243–44; *see also*
Seaman, Daniel
Israeli Ministry of Foreign Affairs,
92, 168; conflict with IDF, 142,
156, 195–97; on GPO, 243; on
Karine A, 156; press division,
108, 141–42, 156; press strategy,
105–6, 151, 192–97, 266; on
Reeve visit, 262; security at,
191–92; Shai press conference,
129–38; superstar spokesmen,
265
Israeli Navy, 153–54, 156
Israeli Prime Minister's Office,
106, 108, 141, 142
Israeli Supreme Court, 256–57
Isrotel Jerusalem Tower, 98–100;
closure of, 184; PA press at, 151;
press center, 105–9, 118

Al-Jazeera, 175, 177, 214, 253; on
    Seaman, 255, 256
Jenin, 75–76, 233–34; Amnesty
    International report, 174, 175;
    "massacre" allegations, 171–75;
    mischaracterization of, 259–60;
    and Operation Defensive
    Shield, 163–67, 171–77, 195;
    terror militias in, 163, 176,
    259–60; UN report, 174n, 175
Jenin, Jenin (film), 175–76
Jennings, Peter, 101; on Ramallah
    lynching, 86–87
Jerusalem: architecture, 180;
    demographics, 180–81, 182; East
    Jerusalem, 127, 199–200, 215;
    journalists in, 95–105, 248–49;
    news bureaus in, 5–6, 43, 243;
    press center, 105–9; recession,
    179–80; security measures in,
    182–84
Jerusalem Capital Studios, 43, 72,
    116, 193
Jerusalem Hilton, 105
Jerusalem Post, 16, 32, 63, 116,
    130, 180, 186, 209n, 212, 214;
    on Cristiano affair, 92, 93; on
    media war, 143; Toameh report-
    ing, 199–202, 204, 205
Jordan, Eason, 270

Kaplan, Rick, 20
Karine A, 153–60
Kashmir, 6
Katz, Noam, 108
Keller-Lind, Helene, 138, 147
Kelly, Michael, 130–31, 159
Khobar Towers, 153
King, Laura, 54–55
Knesset, 96, 251, 256

Knight-Ridder, 48, 51
Kogan, Deborah Copaken, 96–97,
    99, 103, 104, 110
Kol Ha'ir, 254–55
Koppel, Ted, 19–23; on al-Dura &
    Ramallah, 89–90, 91, 93
Kosovo, 2
Kyoto Protocol, 185

Laub, Karin, 53–54
League of Nations Mandate
    (Palestine), 12
Lebanon: Hezbollah in, 136;
    refugee camps in, 187
Leibovich-Dar, Sara, 168–170
Lev Yerushalayim, 184, 215
Levy-Barzilai, Vered, 210
Lewis, Bernard, 205
Lewis, Dana, 169
Life magazine, 28–29
Likud party, 21, 265
littlegreenfootballs.com, 267
Livingstone, Ken, 4
Long, Dorit, 89–90
Lord, Amnon, 3
Los Angeles Times, 267, 268
Ludden, Jennifer, 19, 124
Luterman, Andy, 150–51
Lyden, Jacki, 48

Ma'ariv, 251, 263
MacDonald, Neil, 4–5, 208
Maceda, Jon, 262
Majalat al-Dirasat al-
    Filastiniyya, 36
Al-Manar, 177
Mandela, Nelson, 14, 212
Marco, Michael J., 156
Marmari, Hanoch, 259
Martin, Jean Pierre, 113

martyrdom (*shadaha*), 68–69, 101;
    children, 77–78, 112, 263–64; al-
    Dura, 68, 70, 74, 79, 80, 81–83;
    payments for, 80, 129, 224;
    promotion of, 82–83, 126–27,
    233; *see also* suicide bombers
Marxism, 23–24, 87
McAllister, Matthew, 80
McCarthy, Julie, 261
McFarquhar, Larissa, 5*n*
McLuhan, Marshall, 2
McNally, Steve, 96
Meir, Gideon, 156, 197
Meir, Golda, 28
Mekel, Arye, 120, 145–49, 192–93,
    194
Mentana, Enrico, 93
Meretz party, 21
Michalopoulos, Deirdre, 168
Middle East Media Research Insti-
    tute (MEMRI.org), 268
Mignotto, Anna, 93
Miller, Keith, 169
Milosevic, Slobodan, 2
Mofaz, Shaul, 154, 155, 157
Monakhov, Yola, 95
Monde, Le, 268
Moore, Michael, 5
moral equivalence, 86–87, 96,
    161–62, 261
Morris, Nomi, 48, 51
Moskona-Lerman, Billie, 81
Mossad, 78, 87
MSNBC, 168
Mubarak, Hosni, 222
Mukata, 192, 208; leveling of,
    220–22
Murdoch, Rupert, 107, 269
Mus, Conny, 133–35
Musharraf, Pervez, 41

Nablus, 120, 152, 163, 187, 234,
    237–38; checkpoint, 235, 237,
    238–40
Nashashibi, Karim, 232–33
Nasser, Gammal Abdel, 28
National Press Club, 81
National Public Radio (NPR), 19,
    96, 124, 261; on Arafat, 31; on
    al-Dura, 48, 60, 81
Nazis, 28; comparisons to, 4, 26,
    131
NBC News, 204, 262; on al-Dura,
    49–50; in Ramallah, 169
Netanyahu, Benjamin, 97, 140,
    162–63, 265
Network of Arab-American
    Alumni and Professionals, 81
Netzarim Junction, 43–48, 53,
    59–60, 68
New Statesman, 188
New York Times, 25, 27, 31, 63,
    101, 104, 127, 234; boycotts of,
    267; change of tone, 259–60; on
    al-Dura, 41, 49, 50, 58; influence
    of, 260; on Israeli PR apparatus,
    191, 194, 244; on Jenin, 171;
    neutrality guidelines, 252, 270;
    "public editor" for, 269; on
    Temple Mount riots, 9, 17–19,
    36; on terror attacks, 161–62;
    trust in, 25
New York Times Magazine, 103–4,
    145, 168
Newsday, 80
Newsweek, 80, 149
Nightline, 19–23
*Nightline: History in the Making
    and the Making of History*
    (Koppel), 19–20
Nirenstein, Fiamma, 139

Nofal, Mamduh, 36–37
non-governmental organizations
(NGOs), 102, 104–5, 186, 229
North Korea, 6
Nourezitz, Vadim, 85–93
Nouvel Observateur, Le, 171, 175
Noveck, Jocelyn, 117–18
NPR. *See* National Public Radio

Observer, The, 149–50
Okrent, Daniel, 269
Olmert, Ehud, 21
Operation Defensive Shield,
163–77, 192, 220–22; coverage
of, 165–66, 169–74; and pack
journalism, 170; press restrictions, 167–70; results of, 176–78
Orme, William, 41, 127–28
Orwell, George, 200
Oslo Accords, 140, 203, 226, 231;
joint policing, 44; PA violation
of, 153–54; weakness of, 206
Overseas Press Club of America,
145

Palestine Media Center, 101
Palestinian Broadcasting Corporation, 39, 199, 203
Palestinian Academic Society for
the Study of International
Affairs (PASSIA), 209–10
Palestinian Authority, 2, 32, 34,
43; "boys with stones" image,
19; cease-fire agreement, 119,
158, 132, 138; censorship, 199,
134, 152–53, 192, 199, 201–4,
226; on al-Dura, 55–56, 66–67,
75–76; economy, 185–87, 226,
229, 231–33; exploitation of
children, 68–69, 74, 127–29;

foreign aid to, 185, 187, 219,
229, 231–33; and Hamas, 119;
and IDF reservist lynching,
85–93; incitement to violence,
127–29, 138, 187; intelligence
services, 114–15; joint patrols,
35, 44, 45; and *Karine A*,
153–55, 157–60; news "produc-
tions," 75–76; Protest Days,
45–46, 67–68; security forces,
44, 46–47, 50, 85, 93, 222, 225;
spokesmen, 21, 23–24, 131, 139,
171; summary executions, 76,
113–14, 201–2; unified message,
21–23; *see also* Arafat, Yasser;
Al-Hayat al-Jadeeda
Palestinian journalists, 171, 201;
activists, 109, 252, 255; cameramen, 113–14, 134, 250; docility,
202–3, 206; editors, 210–12,
254–55; film crews, 44;
stringers, 45; *see also* Rahme,
Talal Abu; Toameh, Khaled Abu
Palestinian Journalists' Union
(Syndicate), 92, 199; threat to
AP, 117, 132–33
Palestinian Liberation Organization (PLO), 21, 151; "days of
rage," 87; Marxism, 87; media
agents, 261; on "settlers," 261
Palestinian Media Watch, 39, 268
Palestinian Ministry of Education,
82
Palestinian Ministry of Informa-
tion, 42, 152, 199; on al-Dura,
55, 76; martyr recruitment, 82
Palestinian National Council, 35
Palestinian Preventive Security
Organization, 34
Palestinian TV, 201

Pearl, Daniel, 42
Peled, Jonathan, 106–7, 141, 193, 194
Peres, Shimon, 140
Perry, Dan, 152
Peters, Ralph, 1
Philadelphia City Paper, 104
Physicians for Human Rights, 163
Pinnes, Ofir, 62
Plett, Barbara, 221, 270
Political Cartoon Society (Britain), 265
Powell, Colin, 160
Psalm in Jenin, A, 166
public opinion: British, 3–4, 5; German, 4; U.S., 5, 23–26; Palestinian, 13–14, 223–27

al-Qazzaaz, Yussef, 199
Quadafi, Moamar, 79
Qualandia checkpoint, 114, 217–18, 237
Qalqilya, 35, 45, 163
Al-Quds, 203
Qur'an, 33
Qurei, Ahmad, 35, 204

Rabin, Yitzhak, 80, 136, 140
Raboo, Yasser Abed, 152–53
Rachid, Mohammed, 231
Rafa, Nidal, 210
Rahme, Talal Abu, 43–45, 47–49, 53, 66, 75; awards, 71, 81; and Schapira investigation, 70–71
RAI (Italy), 91, 93; on Cristiano affair, 116, 117
Rajoub, Jibril, 34
Ramallah, 95, 96, 217–33; Arafat headquarters, 192, 208, 220–21; cosmopolitan past, 219–20; deterioration, 219–20; foreign

aid, 229, 231–33; and Operation Defensive Shield, 163, 167, 169, 220–22; Palestine Media Center, 101; poverty in, 219, 220; wealth in, 229–31
Ramallah lynching, 85–93, 114, 201, 228–31; conspiracy theories, 87–88; and "cycle of violence," 86, 88–90; vs. "al-Dura," 88–90; IAF retaliation, 86; imams' incitement, 127–28; intimidation of journalists, 91–93, 117; photographic record, 90–91, 117
Rather, Dan, 101
Raynal, Clement Weill, 51–52
Reckless Disregard (Adler), 103
Red Cross, 102, 105
Reeve, Christopher, 261–62
Reeves, Phil, 173–74
Regev, Mark, 265
Regev, Miri, 154
Reid, Richard, 153
Reporters Without Borders, 257
Reuters, 2, 201, 252, 256, 260; al-Dura episode, 49; in Iraq, 270; on *Karine A,* 157, 158, 159; moral relativism, 261; photo selection, 95
Roberts, Nigel, 185
Roth, Richard, 90, 126, 129
Roumeileh, Ata Abu, 164, 173
RTI (Italy), 92–93
Rudeineh, Nabil Abu, 49
Rumsfeld, Donald, 197
Rusbridger, Alan, 255
Rutland Herald, 24

Sabra & Shatilla, 171
al-Sadr, Moqtada, 2

Samia, Yom Tov, 57, 59–60, 64–65, 70, 75, 77

Saraf, Eyad, 77–78

Saudi Arabia, 6, 80

Schapira, Esther, 45n, 48–49, 65–74, 79; smearing of, 73; *Three Bullets . . .*, 67–68, 71, 73–74, 76

Scheffler, Phil, 7, 271

Schimmel, Bruce, 104

Schmeman, Serge, 31

Scott, Michel, 172

Seager, Mark, 91

Seaman, Daniel, 27–28, 97, 141, 150–51, 168, 259, 262; attacks on, 255–56; and Barghouti trial, 213; "boycotts" reporters, 249–50; cameraman permits, 250; criticism of MFA, 248; epiphany, 245–48; *Kol Ha'ir* interview, 254–55; outré status, 243–44; press card restrictions, 249.–57

security wall, 6

Seeds of Peace, 21

September 11 attacks, 41, 151, 194, 216; celebration of, 152; curiosity about, 223–24, 225; Jews blamed for, 225, 226

"settlements," 4, 124, 260–61

Sha'ath, Nabil, 49–50

Shah, Saira, 77n

shahada. See martyrdom

Shai, Nachman, 129–38, 143, 151; on al-Dura, 135–36, 138; in first Gulf War, 130–31

Shamala, Fayad Abu, 252

Shamir, Yitzhak, 130

Sharif, Omar Khan, 253

Sharm el-Sheikh cease-fire, 100–1, 119, 123–25, 132, 138

Sharm el-Sheikh Fact-Finding Committee, 115

Sharon, Ariel, 61, 204; access to, 192; demonizing of, 3, 4, 26, 31, 137, 252, 257, 265; Gaza withdrawal, 261; and *Karine A*, 157, 158; at Temple Mount, 9, 15, 32, 34–36

Shin Beit, 154, 158, 159; and press cards, 256, 257

Shipler, David, 26

Shkirat, Khader, 213–14

Al-Shuhada ("The Martyrs"), 33

Shutterbabe: Adventures in Love and War (Kogan), 97, 99

Siegenthaler, John, 50

Simon, Bob, 41, 59, 62, 68–69

Six Day War, 26, 28–30, 124

60 Minutes, 68–69

Sky News, 107, 184

Smith, Ben, 112

Sneh, Ephraim, 21–23, 144

Sontag, Deborah, 36, 58–59

Sony Corporation 71, 81

South Africa, 19–20, 23

Soviet Union, 28

Starr, Richard, 93

Steele, Andrew, 256

Stephens, Bret, 16, 186

Strategypage.com, 267

Subbiah, Renga, 110–12

suicide bombers, 160–62, 182, 183–84, 187, 209n, 213, 245–47, 253, 266; child, 263–64; and Jenin, 163; pride in, 25–26; public opinion on, 225; rewards to families, 80, 129, 224

Sztulman, Ilan, 168, 173, 266

Tailhook Convention, 3
Tamal, Moshe, 76–77
Tampabayprimer.org, 268
Tanzim militia, 119, 126, 153, 212;
    Barghouti trial, 212–14
Tarazi, Michael, 213
Taub, Daniel, 265
Teachout, Terry, 267
technology (media), 1–2, 7; *see
    also* internet
Temple Mount (Al-Aqsa), 9, 15,
    17–18, 32–37, 39, 126
Tennenbaum, Elhanan, 131
terror attacks, 160–62, 200–1, 253;
    see also suicide bombers
terror militias, 85, 119, 152, 220;
    in Beit Jalla, 123–24; breaking
    cease-fires, 186–87; "Days of
    Rage," 87; recruiting children,
    263–64; *see also* Al-Aqsa Mar-
    tyrs Brigade; Hamas
TF1 (France), 172
*Three Bullets and a Dead Child:
    Who Shot Mohammed al-
    Dura?* (Schapira), 67–68, 71,
    73–74, 76; ARD broadcast,
    78–79; reception of, 73–74
Time (magazine), 164, 165, 172, 173
Time.com, 51
Times, The (London),152
Toameh, Khaled Abu, 33, 199–206,
    257; criticism of Arafat, 205–6;
    education, 204–5; on Palestinian
    violence, 200–2
Toronto Globe and Mail, 207–8
translators. *See* fixers
Tulkarem, 163, 200, 204

UNICEF, 186
United Nations, 41, 107, 163; Con-
ference on Racism (Durban), 80;
    Jenin report, 174*n*; partition
    plan, 140; Relief Workers
    Agency (UNRWA), 164*n*
United States: anti-Zionism in, 10,
    14; change in media slant,
    27–30; ignorance about Israel,
    140; and Iraq war, 176–77; Jew-
    ish immigrants in, 10–11; Mexi-
    can border, 6; public opinion, 5,
    14, 23–26; "virtual wars," 2;
    White House press corps, 257
U.S. Aid for International Devel-
    opment, 210
U.S. State Department, 157, 159
USA Today, 205
USS *Cole*, 153
Utley, Garrick, 31

Van Creveld, Martin, 26–27
Viglino, Patrizia, 252–53
Villepin, Dominique de, 222
Virtual War: Kosovo and Beyond
    (Ignatieff), 2
Voice of Palestine radio, 86, 203

Washington Post, 159, 249–50; on
    al-Dura, 50; on Jenin, 171; mon-
    itoring of, 268
Watergate, 269
Wedeman, Ben, 221
Weekly Standard, 93, 122–23
West Bank, 9, 13–14, 24, 35, 45,
    115, 185–87, 204, 207, 215–41,
    261; *see also* Jenin; Ramallah
Western Wall, 35–36, 262
Whaley, Jim, 174
White, Theodore H., 26
Wilson, Simon, 190
windsofchange.net, 268

wire services. *See* Agence France-Presse; Associated Press

Ya'ari, Ehud, 44
Yaron, Ruth, 177–78
Yediot Aharonot, 67
Yom Kippur War, 13, 16

al-Zahar, Mahmoud, 179
Zaken, Danny, 152–53, 205, 266
Zanen, Ibrahim, 80
Zangen, David, 175–76
Zighari, Khaled, 252, 256
Zinni, Anthony, 154–55